THE REVOLUTION IN
HORSEMANSHIP

THE REVOLUTION IN
HORSEMANSHIP

AND WHAT IT MEANS TO MANKIND

Robert M. Miller, D.V.M.
and Rick Lamb

Foreword by Hugh Downs

THE LYONS PRESS
Guilford, Connecticut
An Imprint of The Globe Pequot Press

The Lyons Press is an imprint of The Globe Pequot Press.

10 9 8 7 6 5 4 3 2

Printed in the United States of America
Designed by Maggie Peterson

ISBN 1-59228-387-X

Library of Congress Cataloging-in-Publication data is available on file.

*This book is dedicated to the memory of Tom Dorrance,
the father of this revolution in horsemanship.*

CONTENTS

ACKNOWLEDGMENTS

I wanted to do a book titled *The Revolution in Horsemanship* for many years, but my diversified interests and pursuits, which include medical science, horsemanship, behavioral science, anthropology, history, skiing, writing, and cartooning, left me with no time to undertake such a formidable project.

So, I am very grateful to my co-author, Rick Lamb, with his media expertise, experience in the horse industries, and communication skills, for proposing in 2002 that we collaborate on this book.

Although we are from different backgrounds and separated age-wise by more than a generation, we are remarkably compatible and equally devoted to this revolution.

The opinions of my wife, Debby, who has been my life and love partner and who shares my passion for horsemanship, have been very helpful.

Lastly, I must express deep gratitude to the clinicians involved in this revolution. They proved that the concepts of horse training which I conceived of in my youth were valid. Without them, the revolution, with its far-reaching lesson of how living beings can communicate while spurning the use of coercion, would never have happened.

Robert M. Miller, D.V.M.
January 2004

While my partner in this project has several books under his belt, this is my first, and I would like to extend my sincere thanks to some of those who helped me, directly or indirectly, to complete it.

To Bob Miller for his friendship, generosity, and dedication to both the equine and science; to Hugh Downs for his kind foreword; to J. P. Giacomini, Cherry Hill, Fran Jurga, Dr. Michael Collier, Jane Crosen, and Steve Price for their invaluable comments on the manuscript; to the numerous photographers and artists credited herein for allowing us to use their works; to my longtime friends and employees at Lambchops Studios, Susan Bolin and Jim

Sherry, for keeping the business going while I played horsey; to the sponsors, affiliate stations, guests, and listeners of my radio shows for believing that what I have to say is worth hearing; to my children Ryan, Todd, and Blair, and my parents, Dick and Ann Lamb, for supporting everything I've ever attempted; to my mother-in-law, Laura Baines, for feeding the horses when I couldn't; and most of all to my wife and best friend, Diana, for giving me the confidence to try new things and joy in everyday life.

Rick Lamb
February 2004

FOREWORD

In the relationship between species on this planet it is very seldom that a widespread, sudden, and profound change occurs. Symbiotic relationships have come about, but these have developed over long periods of time.

Equus caballus and *Homo sapiens* have been partners for a sizable fraction of humanity's time on Earth. The dog-sized "dawn horse" of the Eocene was destined to become full-sized by the time the first true humans appeared; and the horse has been in mankind's life one way or another since before any history was written. In Homer's *Iliad*, Hector was a tamer of horses, an occupation that called for skill and nerve since a horse could be ten times the weight of the "tamer."

While in local enclaves there have surely been individuals from time to time who sought to be gentle with horses and not subject them to abuse, the revolution in horsemanship we are seeing today all over the globe is unique.

The spread of the idea that the new and more humane techniques for getting horses to cooperate with human masters result in better training and a more dependable partnership, makes us wonder why all those centuries went by with so many people believing that a horse's spirit must be "broken" before the horse can be safely ridden. There are several reasons for this, and this book details them clearly.

There is some coincidence in my knowing Rick Lamb for several years and Bob Miller for a half-century. I recorded many audio tracks at Rick's studio before I even knew of his interest in horses; and I stayed on a ranch where Bob Miller was a wrangler, before he became a Doctor of Veterinary Medicine.

If you have little interest in the world of horses and read this book, you will become interested. If you are already interested, you will be enthralled. One of the things that impressed me most is the authors' thesis that this revolution is doing wonders not only for the horse, but for the human: the self-understanding and the enhancement of cooperation among ourselves come out of the application of these new techniques.

Hugh Downs
June 2, 2004

PREFACE

It is the authors' hope that this book will provide both historical perspective and technical understanding of the phenomenon we have called the revolution in horsemanship. It is also our hope that this book will be a unifying force within the global equine community, which has become a bit factionalized and proprietary as public interest in this subject has increased.

The biggest fear an author faces in tackling a subject of this size is that he will miss something, either leave out someone or something that should have been included or get some fact wrong. It is entirely possible that some readers will take exception to our work on those or other grounds. If so, we encourage them to share their feelings with us.

Although it should go without saying, let us make very clear that there is no gender associated with the word horseman, just as there is no gender associated with the word mankind. Indeed, without the female of the human species, there would be no revolution in horsemanship for us to discuss.

Finally, we hope that all who read this book will appreciate its larger implication: that communication is possible between different individuals without the use of force. We understand that to be coercive is a natural and inborn trait within many species, including our own, but this revolution in horsemanship has again proven that, as a reasoning species, we can put that instinct aside, and immensely improve our ability to communicate.

PART I

CHAPTER 1

NATURAL
HORSEMANSHIP

IN THE FINAL DECADES of the twentieth century, a revolution began in America and spread through much of the world. It wasn't the usual sort of revolution. No shots were fired, no government was overthrown, and no geographical boundaries were changed. There were casualties, however. Ignorance and injustice, and behaviors born of them, died just as surely as if pierced through the heart with a broadsword. In their places arose new ways of thinking and acting informed by enlightenment and empowerment. When the dust settled, the revolution had dramatically improved relations between millions of people . . . and their horses.

For more than 6,000 years, man had tried to bridge the chasm that existed between his own species, the ultimate predator, and the horse, the ultimate prey animal. The reason was simple: Man needed the horse. He needed its power, its speed, its stamina. He needed the edge the horse gave him in his battle for survival and growth. But nature had programmed the horse to be anything but a servant to man, and in face of this challenge, man adopted his most familiar tool: brute force. It was crude, inefficient, and unworthy of his noble purpose, but force was the basis of horsemanship practiced by the common man for millennia.

The revolution in horsemanship that occurred at the end of the twentieth century had, at its heart, a simple theme: that horses can be controlled more effectively *without* the use of force.

This was not a new idea. Time and again throughout history, good horsemen had proven the efficacy of humane, psychological methods of handling horses. Some shared their techniques; others did not. Some became celebrities and gave command performances for royalty. Others were accused of trickery or something much worse. In the 1600s, God-fearing peasants in Arles, France, burned an itinerant Italian horse trainer and his trick horse, Mauroco, in the marketplace. To them, real horsemanship was so unnatural that it could only come from an alliance with the devil.

Whatever their contemporaries thought of them, these horsemen failed to effect permanent, widespread change in the way the average human related to horses. Instinctively, man always returned to what was natural for a predator, using muscle and violence to get what he needed from the horse. The revolution that broke this cycle did so at a time when, for most people, horses were no longer part of everyday life.

THE HORSE IN AMERICA

At the beginning of the twentieth century, Americans still needed a great deal from the horse. They relied upon it for transportation, for agriculture, for commerce, and for warfare. Nearly every man, woman, and child had some measure of experience with horses.

But times were changing. Steam engines were already well established, and the first horseless carriages, powered by internal-combustion engines, were venturing out on America's crude byways. By the time Henry Ford introduced the Model T in 1908, it was clear that the motor vehicle was the future and the horse was the past.

Over the next few decades, mechanization redefined man's long relationship with the horse. In just fifty years, America's equine population dropped by nearly 20 million. Horses all but disappeared from cities and towns. Modern methods of warfare rendered them nearly useless in battle, although up to 10 million horses and mules, from nineteen countries, are believed to have died in World War II. Even on the farm, horsepower took on a new meaning, as motor-driven equipment took over tasks traditionally done by equines. The horses that remained were kept mostly for plea-

Coauthor Rick Lamb in 1962. By this time, most horses in America were pets. *(Richard M. Lamb, Jr.)*

sure riding or as pets. For thousands of years a necessary life skill, horsemanship in the twentieth century became a recreational pastime, like skiing, fishing, or needlepoint.

It was a fortunate turn of events. The revolution in horsemanship might never have occurred without this quantum shift in the role of the horse. For no matter how much Americans put into their jobs, there is an extra bit of passion that we reserve for our hobbies. It was largely Americans pursuing a *hobby* interest in horses that gave impetus to a revolution in horse–human relations.

THE COMEBACK

The horse's comeback in America started in the mid-1970s, the "Me" decade. The war in Vietnam had ended and disco music was pumping from car radios. The nation's spirit was lightening up, and it was culturally acceptable to spend time and money—and many Americans now had expendable quantities of both—on the pursuit of what made you feel good. For a surprising number of people, that was horses.

It may have been a fantasy fed by years of television viewing, a desire to return to a pleasure of youth, an interest in getting closer to nature, or the simple magnetism of this magnificent beast. Whatever their reasons, people from all walks of life—in rural, suburban and urban areas alike—found themselves drawn to horses. Horse enthusiasts became horse owners, and horse owners longed to become real horsemen. To a greater or lesser degree, they all wanted to learn more and do better with their horses, and most importantly, this generation was willing to look at nontraditional approaches.

By the late 1970s, a new breed of horsemanship clinic had sprung up in the West to meet the increased demand for education. Old, nonviolent training philosophies were presented side-by-side with modern, creative horse-handling techniques. The common thread was a consideration for the horse's point of view. Students were encouraged to think as a horse would think and operate within the framework of what mattered to him. This new way struck a chord. Students liked what they saw and heard. It spoke to their hearts as well as their minds and they were excited by how well it worked.

Word spread. Followers became evangelists, students became teachers, and in a matter of a few years, this approach to horsemanship spread across America and jumped its borders to Canada, Australia, and New Zealand, to England, Europe, and the rest of the world. An industry took form, and by

The philosophical underpinnings of the revolution appeal to people of all ages and walks of life. Even veteran horsemen like legendary trainer Jack Brainard are joining with younger clinicians to help spread the word. *(Photos by Coco)*

the mid-1990s what began as a modest movement became, by anyone's standard, an international phenomenon.

Clearly, people were ready for this. But where did this old-but-new-again approach to horsemanship come from?

NATURAL HORSEMANSHIP

One place where mechanization had not completely replaced the horse was the Western cattle ranch. Although ranchers used trucks and tractors extensively, and experimented with jeeps, motorcycles, ATVs, and even helicopters, they found that no machine could match a good stock horse when it came to rounding up cattle or cutting a cow from a herd.

In California, there was an especially rich heritage of horsemanship that traced back through the *vaquero* and *Californio* to Mexico and mother Spain. Through the twentieth century, even as technology exploded around him, the California stockman continued to work cattle from a horse's back as his forebears did.

He considered the horse a partner, a thinking and feeling creature that was as psychologically delicate as it was physically strong. The challenge and joy he found in riding came not from dominating a larger species but from building a relationship and taking it to the highest levels of finesse. Whether he realized it or not, he was an important link to the great horsemen of the past.

These men had no intention of starting a revolution, of changing the world, or even of changing anyone else's mind. The stockmen had work to do, and being good horsemen made it easier. They loved their horses and, for the sake of the horse, were willing to share what they had learned with those who showed real interest.

Even as technology exploded around him, the California stockman continued to work cattle from a horse's back as his forebears did. *(Peter Campbell Collection)*

It was when their philosophies and methods fell into the hands of gifted teachers and entrepreneurs in the 1980s that the revolution in horsemanship began in earnest: It was then that clinics began introducing these techniques to the public, and systems of teaching that blended these techniques

In the mid-1980s, Californian Pat Parelli coined the term "natural horsemanship." *(Photos by Coco)*

seamlessly with those of the great nonviolent horsemen of the past began to emerge.

At the time, this way of working with horses had no particular name, but it was easily distinguished from others by its commitment to seeing the world through the horse's eyes, to using the nature of the horse rather than fighting it, and to communicating with the horse in ways he instinctively understood. Thus, one of its early students, a young rodeo cowboy–turned–horse trainer, with horse savvy and a gift of gab that would eventually take this approach to the far corners of the Earth, dubbed it "natural" horsemanship. The name stuck.

Purists may argue the accuracy of the term, claiming that nothing man does with a horse is truly natural for either of them. It matters not. Natural horsemanship is the name by which the system of principles and techniques that revolutionized horsemanship is best known around the world today.

AMERICAN VS. EUROPEAN

Of course, American cowboys didn't invent riding or horsemanship. In Europe, riding for hunting, military, and artistic purposes preceded the American cowboy by more than two millenia. These riding styles constitute what the public often calls "English" riding and are the basis for most international equestrian competition, including the Olympics.

Perhaps the revolution should have started there, but it didn't. What moved legions of average horse enthusiasts in the late twentieth century were not the teachings of the great dressage masters who had perfected control of a horse's body, but the examples set by a few quiet cowhands who had perfected communication with a horse's mind.

Because of where it started, natural horsemanship was perceived initially as a form of Western horsemanship. That perception is fading, and rightly so. Much of the work occurs on the ground, well before saddle, bridle, riding attire, and riding purpose have been chosen. Horsemen today often participate in more than one riding discipline, taking their natural horsemanship skills with them when they trade their cowboy hats for hunt caps, dressage derbies, or riding helmets. Olympic medalists and other world-class competitors in a variety of equestrian sports are now outspoken proponents of natural horsemanship and have integrated its philosophies and methods into their training programs.

The principles at the heart of the revolution transcend disciplines, breeds, and individuals. They are truly universal and are facilitating the open exchange of ideas and information among all horse enthusiasts.

BIG BUSINESS

Still, many of these principles have drifted in and out of popularity in the past. Why should we think they are here to stay this time?

Perhaps the most powerful reason has little to do with the substance of these principles and more to do with the degree to which they have rooted their way into the culture. Natural horsemanship is no longer an upstart movement; it is a large and lucrative industry. Too many people have a vested interest in its survival to let it die. Indeed, they have every reason to put their energies into making it thrive.

Every year, throughout America and in many foreign countries, hundreds of horse fairs and expos are staged, some reportedly drawing more than 100,000 horse enthusiasts in a single weekend. The majority of these events use natural horsemanship clinicians almost exclusively for their headliners. Arenas are packed for groundwork and riding demonstrations. Exhibit halls are crammed with vendors hawking the tools of the natural horseman. Books and videos on this form of training spill from brightly lit display racks.

Clinicians at the top of the heap attract fans the way rock musicians and professional athletes do. Hands rough and calloused from years of handling ropes and reins now cramp from signing autographs. A few years ago, some of these very people were working cowboys, one of the lowest-paying professions in America.

Now they have entourages. Semi-trailers jammed with products and horses precede them to their public appearances. Some travel in lavish motor homes; others fly everywhere they go. Their efforts generate untold

Hands rough and calloused from years of handling ropes and reins now cramp from signing autographs. *(Emily Kitching)*

millions of dollars in revenue each year from demonstrations, clinics, courses, books, videos, CDs, round pens, halters, lead ropes, bridles, bits, spurs, saddles, bareback pads, branded clothing, subscriptions, and corporate sponsorships. Several have strong international followings.

Many clinicians offer certification programs that prepare advanced students to teach their methods in a franchise type of arrangement. Certification is not easy, nor is it cheap—a student may pay tens of thousands of dollars to get the full package of training—but it offers the serious horseman hope for a career more emotionally and financially rewarding than many traditional ones, while further stoking the coffers of the parent organization.

Clinicians are the figureheads, superstars, and cheerleaders for the industry. They are out front selling the product, but the money machine behind them is bigger than most people can imagine. Behind the scenes, hundreds, perhaps thousands of companies churn out information and product for the horse-loving consumer. Some of this is simply to meet their horse-keeping needs and has little to do with training. But the entire horse industry thrives from the shot in the arm given it by natural horsemanship.

Hundreds of regional or national horse periodicals, ranging from newsprint freebies to four-color glossy magazines, are published in the United States alone. Even more exist in cyberspace. Nearly all of them devote some portion of their pages to natural horsemanship topics and advertising.

Colleges and universities across America offer equine science courses and even degree programs that expose students to the theories and techniques of natural horsemanship. The same is true in many other countries as well.

As an industry, natural horsemanship has a comfortable life of its own, a secure and sizable niche within the larger equine industry. It feeds the hopes and dreams of countless backyard horsemen, and an increasing number of serious competitors. All are more than happy to pay for the sustenance. The product is that good. Everybody wins.

Natural horsemanship is all about gentle persuasion. *(Photos by Coco)*

According to a study conducted in 1996 by the American Horse Council,

Synchronicity by Veryl Goodnight (2004). *(Veryl Goodnight)*

the horse industry in America directly produces goods and services valued at $25.3 billion per year, with a total impact each year on the American gross domestic product of $112 billion.

These numbers startled everyone when they were published in 1997. Who would have thought that the horse, long ago replaced at its original jobs by machines, would return as one of the country's most important sport and recreational interests? While these statistics reflect a contribution by the natural horsemanship movement, that movement was just beginning to hit its stride in the mid-1990s. One can only imagine its contribution to the industry today.

A century ago, people had horses in order to live; today many people live to have horses. Horses have gone from being a means to an end to the end itself for millions of people in America and throughout the world. Natural horsemanship can claim at least part of the credit for that.

THE CHANGE IN WESTERN ART

Nowhere can the change in the nature of the horse–human relationship be seen more vividly than in America's Western art.

The horse as a bucking, often-terrified adversary, depicted so beautifully in the works of Western masters such as Frederic Remington (1861–1909), Charles M. Russell (1864–1926), and Will James (1892–1942), has all but disappeared.

The Broncho Buster by Frederic Remington (1895). *(Courtesy Frederic Remington Art Museum, Ogdensburg, New York)*

The horse as a partner, only rarely portrayed in traditional Western art, is now a common theme. The cowboy sharing an apple with his horse (*Sharing an Apple* by Tom Ryan), the young couple with their children perched in front of them riding down a golden autumn lane (*Quality Time* by Tim Cox), the cowboy performing a piaff on his horse without saddle or bridle (*Synchronicity* by Veryl Goodnight), all define the new feeling of Western art.

Gone are images of snubbing posts, quirts, and sharp-roweled spurs, of horses with eyes wide, heads high, mouths gaping, and muscles straining, and of man forcing his will upon another creature. The new look of America's Western art is one of quiet competence, fellowship, good breeding, and good behavior on the part of horse and human, captured in the most beautiful of natural Western settings.

A NEW LANGUAGE

There are other sure signs of the way the revolution has taken hold.

Take the language of the horseman. Today we don't *break* a horse—we *start* a horse. Rather than *working* with a horse, a natural horseman will *play* with him, hoping in the process to unlock the horse's *play drive*. *Games* are often preferred over *exercises*. *Discomfort* has replaced *pain* as a way to motivate a horse to move. *Comfort zones* and *lesson plans* are discussed, and the *replacement concept* is used to substitute desired behaviors for undesired ones.

Joining up or *hooking on* is understood to mean that special moment when the horse accepts the human's leadership and bonds with him.

Sensitization, habituation, dominance hierarchy, conditioned response, and *alpha behavior*, terms once used almost exclusively by scientists and academics, are now part of the lexicon of the natural horseman, for the underlying concepts are key to effective communication with the horse.

Groundwork, the handling of a horse from the ground, is a study unto itself today. In the past, it was not known by such a name, and if practiced at all, usually received only cursory attention on the way to riding the horse. Today, groundwork begins at a horse's birth and is reinforced throughout its life. Most behavior problems, even those experienced while riding, are solved by groundwork.

Perhaps most important is *rewarding the try*. This is a modern version of the famous maxim of Captain Etienne Beudant (1863–1949), "Ask often, be happy with little, reward always." The natural horseman does not demand instant perfection from his horse; he asks only that the horse make an honest attempt and do a little better than last time, and when that happens, he provides an instant reward. With patience, persistence, and consistency in the asking, the horseman helps the horse find the correct answer.

The new language of the horseman reflects new ways of thinking and new patterns of behavior. Academics would call this a paradigm shift. Horses don't care about fancy labels, but you can be sure that they, too, know that something special has happened. You can see it

By unlocking your horse's play drive, you become recreation for him, just as he is recreation for you. *(Photos by Coco)*

when a good horseman approaches a nervous horse: there is a perceptible change in demeanor. The horse knows when the human understands, just as he knows when the human does not.

Granted, some of this language was originally coined for marketing purposes, to give the coiner's "product" a more defined image in the marketplace. Some among the public find this distasteful and seem to believe that only poor products need to be skillfully marketed. On the contrary, marketing only brings attention to a product, and poor products cannot stand the scrutiny. Indeed, the demand for education has resulted in vastly improved systems of communicating timeless principles of horse psychology and horse handling, enabling *ordinary* horsemen to achieve *extraordinary* results with their horses in greater numbers than history has ever known.

POPULAR AWARENESS

Those of us who love horses are understandably drawn in by the revolution in horsemanship. But it is the interest shown by the general public that is particularly telling.

In 1996, California natural horseman Monty Roberts caught their imagination with his autobiography, *The Man Who Listens to Horses*. Originally released in England and Australia, the book became an international bestseller, spending fifty-eight weeks on the New York Times bestseller list.

About the same time, Nicholas Evans's blockbuster novel, *The Horse Whisperer*, resurrected an early term for the natural horseman and

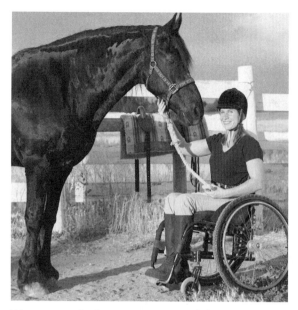

We now see the horse as an agent of change in the human condition. *(L. Hanselmann/NARHA)*

introduced the concepts to the fiction-reading world. Actor/director Robert Redford, with technical advice from natural horseman Buck Brannaman, brought the story to the silver screen, reaching millions more in the process.

In 2001, the core principles of the revolution rocketed again into public consciousness with another best-selling book, *Seabiscuit: An American Legend*, the true story of the 1930s racehorse who became a national obsession in Depression-era America. Written by equine journalist Laura Hillenbrand, the book had a message that came through loud and clear: humane, intelligent training is the path to great accomplishments with a horse. Both the book and the major motion picture that followed were commercial and critical successes.

Authors, filmmakers, and advertisers regularly tap into the ageless fascination we have with the kind of relationship that can exist between a horse and a human.

But horses do far more than help fuel the economy. They are increasingly being used to improve the lives of people who need it most. The revolution has allowed us to see horses in a whole new way, *as agents of change in the human condition.*

Walter Farley's timeless novels about the Black Stallion form the backbone of a progressive reading program that touches the lives of thousands of youngsters. The Black Stallion Literacy Project couples hands-on experiences with live horses and gift books—often the first book a child will own—to engage the imaginations of youngsters and instill in them the desire to read.

The North American Riding for the Handicapped Association and other similar organizations channel the healing power of the horse to strengthen and empower emotionally and physically disabled individuals of all ages.

America's justice system has recognized the uncanny way horses can change lives and has instituted mustang-gentling programs built upon the principles of natural horsemanship for prisoners, gang members, and other at-risk youth. The rehabilitative effect has exceeded all expectations, with recidivism among the participants reaching all-time lows.

Natural horsemanship clinicians are being invited into corporate boardrooms to teach the arts of gentle persuasion, benevolent leadership, and nonverbal communication to companies wishing to have better managers and happier, more productive employees.

The revolution in horsemanship coincides with an evolution in the role horses play in human life. Once quantitative, it has slowly and surely become *qualitative*. It is no longer about how many miles can be ridden or how many acres can be plowed. For many of us, the horse has become a reason and a vehicle for self-improvement. A relationship with nature's most magnificent beast, the horse, is the carrot on the stick that keeps us moving forward, striving to be better.

The qualitative ideals of communication, leadership, and justice, upon which the revolution is based, are the building blocks of an improved horse–human relationship. As we internalize them, they can't help but begin affecting the other parts of our lives, in our homes, offices, and classrooms.

Natural horsemanship is not only making better horses, it is making better people.

CHAPTER 2

THE HORSE IN NATURE
AND DOMESTICATION

Archaeological evidence has allowed us to paint a credible picture of how the Earth and its inhabitants developed. North, South, and Central America, or the New World, as it became known after its discovery by Europeans, once had no human population. Man originated in what we now know as Africa. North America, however, became the site of origin for many species, including the horse.

Originally a small, multi-toed, browsing creature that inhabited the swamps and rain forests, the horse evolved as its habitat slowly dried out to

The horse evolved to live on grasslands. *(Heidi Nyland)*

become grasslands, what we now variously call prairie, steppes, or veldt. One toe, ideal for running on turf, replaced the several digits on each foot. A flexible spine, so important for weaving quickly through forest undergrowth, gave way to a more rigid spine and limbs that were optimized for running fast in a straight line. The horse increased in size, and its anatomy, its cardiovascular system, its senses, and its behavior all became modified to help it survive in a habitat filled with hungry predators. It became the ultimate flight animal, able to survive because it could usually detect and outrun its enemies.

Its natural enemies, especially the large carnivores of the dog and cat families, were formidable. Climatic changes and predation took a toll on the horse, and sometime after the last ice age—researchers now say about 12,500 years ago—it became extinct in the land of its origin.

Fortunately, enough horses had already escaped the North American continent to ensure the survival of the species. With ocean levels lowered significantly by large continental glaciers, a land bridge existed where the Bering Strait now separates Alaska and Siberia. Hardy, mobile, and highly adaptable, horses were among the first of the hooved animals to make use of this bridge into Asia.

The horse thrived on the plains of Asia, even as it disappeared from the North American continent, and eventually it spread in all directions, into Europe, the Middle East, and Africa. Many thousands of years passed before adventurers from Spain reintroduced horses into the New World at the dawn of the sixteenth century.

The rapidly growing human populations in Eurasia welcomed the horse, and not only for its value as a food source. Cave paintings in what are now France and Spain clearly show that the horse was admired early on for its beauty and majesty as well. These sentiments ultimately resulted in man domesticating the horse, a twist of fate that probably saved the species in Europe

Although the horse originated in North America, it disappeared from the continent about 12,500 years ago. Spanish explorers reintroduced the horse to North America. They rode ancestors of this Lusitano stallion. *(J. P. Giacomini Collection)*

and Asia from what had happened to it in North America. The horse would not be here today if the deadliest of all predators—the planning, reasoning, tool-using human being—had not found another use for it.

Domestication of the horse was not purely an act of human will, however. Archaeological and animal behavior studies now suggest that domestication was a long, slow process of *mutual adaptation.* We evolved together.

The horse was well suited for domestication. It was not a picky eater. Nutritionally, it had become a generalist; it could survive and even flourish on a wide variety of food sources provided by nature, and later, by man. Its reproductive and socialization patterns were relatively simple and adapted well to life with humans. This was especially important, as domestication does not mean simply that an animal can be tamed but that it will reproduce reliably in captivity. Of the some 4,000 mammal species that have inhabited the Earth in the past 10,000 years, the horse is one of only a dozen that have been truly successful in domestication. Man can only take partial credit for that. The horse came to us with all the ingredients needed for our future partnership.

The horse probably served us first as a pack animal, helping us move our things from place to place. Then, after the wheel was invented about 5,000 years ago, we attached him to a cart and used him as a draft animal.

It has long been believed that riding came later, but new archaeological evidence has changed this belief. Teeth from a stallion that lived at least 6,000 years ago have been excavated from Dereivka in the Ukrainian steppes. These teeth show signs of wear that could only have come from a bit. The wheel had not yet been invented at that time, so this particular horse must have been ridden. Riding, at least for casual purposes, thus preceded driving.

We will never know who was the first human to ride a horse, but knowing wild horses and their reaction to anything they perceive as a threat, and also being familiar with the behavior of our own species, we can conjecture a believable scenario. The first human to ride a horse was probably a boy, mounting a foal he had befriended and bonded with. He was observed by his father and other mature males in his group, who promptly seized upon the possibilities. "If we were mounted on horses," someone undoubtedly said, "we could wreak havoc on the neighboring tribe!"

In any case, long before the saddle was invented and even longer before the stirrup was conceived of, Asian warriors, mounted on sturdy little horses, swept across the land, killing, pillaging, looting, raping, and enslaving. We *are* a predatory species.

It is difficult for us to realize today the profound effect that domestication of the horse had on early societies. Early man could travel no faster than he could run, and a rabbit can outrun an Olympic sprinter. We are not a fast species. Suddenly, we could move with the speed of a horse, and much farther than we ever could afoot. This dramatically enhanced our ability to hunt and procure food from our environment.

We are not especially strong as a species. But with horses, we could carry or pull great loads. The horse also made us more lethal in battle. The ancient Hittite empire owed much of its success in warfare to the use of chariots drawn by horses. A few centuries later, the Scythians proved the superiority of organized mounted troops, whose greater maneuverability made them even deadlier than charioteers.

Horses were so important to ancient man that they became a kind of currency, a measure of wealth. The Scythians, who believed that material life continued after death, buried horses with their dead. One of their wealthy went to his grave with 400 horses.

Dependence upon horses affected the Scythian culture in other ways. At a time when most of the civilized world dressed in scanty or flowing garments, they invented trousers to make riding more comfortable.

Civilization began when early nomads learned to assure their food supply by tilling the soil and by breeding food animals, rather than solely by hunting and gathering. The horse was valued, not only as a draft animal that could plow fields and pull heavy loads, but also because it facilitated the herding of other domestic species such as cattle, goats, and sheep.

Horses and other draft animals like oxen greatly increased the amount of acreage that could be farmed. It was agricultural technology that led to man's ability to live in villages and cities, rather than in primitive tribal units limited in size by the locally available game and plant foods. It was an important change to the only lifestyle man had known for thousands of years.

The horse had an effect upon man's progress unlike anything that had come before, or anything that would follow until the invention of the steam engine and the internal-combustion engine.

THE MYTH OF NATIVE HORSEMANSHIP

From the earliest of times, in all human cultures that have domesticated the horse, the horsemen of that culture have been glorified and glamorized. They have been given elevated status, and their prowess and skill have been exaggerated.

Domestic animals are held in variable esteem in various cultures. We, for example, have enormous respect for the dog, calling it "Man's Best Friend." Yet, in some cultures, the dog is despised, seen as a lowly creature, and in other cultures, valued primarily as food. The cow is deified in India, seen as chattel or a symbol of wealth in Africa, and as a lowly beast of burden elsewhere. The horse, however, is highly regarded nearly everywhere and has been throughout history.

Monarchs who may never have ridden are memorialized on statues astride noble stallions. The horse as a fetish has served as a god, has been portrayed as flying through the heavens, is used to sell beer, and transports and guards British royalty. It is the central hero figure of such cinematic successes as *Black Beauty*, *The Black Stallion*, *Pharlap*, and *Seabiscuit*. It is not surprising, therefore, that each culture glorifies its horsemen, often creating of them national symbols completely disproportionate with the actual importance of their roles in society, especially in modern times. Thus, the Argentine gaucho, the Mexican charro, the American cowboy, the Mongol nomad, the Bedouin, the Aussie stockman, and the British foxhunter are virtually emblematic of their cultures.

Each of these cultures has enormous pride in its respective breeds of horses, and in the horsemen who ride them, and each proclaims its horsemen and its horsemanship to be the finest in the world.

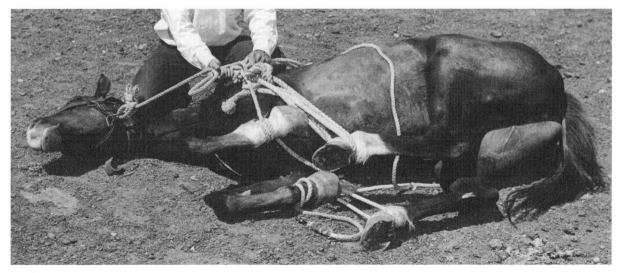

Coercion is typical of native horsemanship throughout the world because it comes naturally to humans. Psychological methods, which we must learn, are safer and more effective. *(Monty Roberts Collection)*

The truth is these horsemen are all crude. They may be great *riders*, but they are still crude horsemen relative to the horsemanship sweeping the world today. Let us explain.

Most of the techniques of horsemanship that have evolved in the world are techniques that are natural to *our* species. Human beings are predatory, tool-using primates. We have remarkable intelligence, but we're primates nonetheless, possessing 98 percent of the DNA borne by our nearest relative, the chimpanzee.

Like other primates, we establish our dominance hierarchy with what are known as "intimidation displays." In the great apes, this manifests itself as breast beating, hooting, shrieking, jumping up and down, and throwing things. Although we humans often do all of these, civilization has encouraged us to subdue these instincts and to be a bit subtler. Still, oaths, threatening gestures, vocal tirades, and other expressions of frustration and temper are common. Tantrums are not necessarily condoned, but they are certainly understood.

It must be appreciated that all of the above, which is natural behavior to the human species, elicits in the horse a desire to flee. That behavior does *not* convey the desire to follow and be close to us.

We are a reasoning species. If we say to anyone, other than a very small child, "If you don't do what I want, you will be punished for it," the threat is readily understood.

Horses cannot understand the concept of punishment. Yet we see at too many horse shows a disappointed competitor out behind the grandstand whipping a horse for its inadequate performance long ago. For a horse, three minutes is long ago.

Go to any tack shop and view the tools of punishment: bits that could have been designed by an Inquisition enforcer, spurs that are examples of the swordsmith's art. Do these tools work? Of course they do! Do they work optimally? Not when used to hurt the horse. Horses *can* be trained, and largely have been trained throughout history, with fear, pain, and intimidation. The revolution has shown us, however, that this is not the path to optimal performance.

One of the authors and his wife have had the privilege of observing and riding with native horsemen all over the world: gauchos in Argentina, chalans of Peru, charros of Mexico, Native Americans, and guardians of the French Camargue. They have thrilled to the sight of Bedouin horsemen racing alongside their rented automobile, robes flying, but then noticed the Arabian horses painfully gaping at the mouth and with noses held high in the air.

Native horsemanship is all a myth, not because these cultures are incapable of producing top horsemen. They are, and they have. It is a myth because it generalizes from the extraordinary few to the ordinary many. Certainly each culture has produced superb horsemen, but the *average* Mongolian rider, the *average* North American cowboy, the *average* vaquero, the *average* Cossack, no doubt the *average* native horseman anywhere, although a good *rider*, is most likely a crude *horseman*.

COLONIAL CALIFORNIA

Nowhere did native horsemanship attain a greater level of finesse than it did in colonial California. Influenced by the horsemen of North Africa, who occupied Spain for more than 700 years, and the work of the Italian and French riding masters, Spanish horsemanship became highly refined during the eighteenth century. Landed gentry brought this tradition to early California.

There, in the more than a century that preceded the advent of the internal-combustion engine, mankind's relationship with the horse reached its peak, and in colonial California, a vast grazing empire, the horse was king.

Western (American) horsemanship had three starts, all of Mexican/Spanish origin.

First, in the late 1700s, as California was colonized and a chain of missions was established there, vast herds of cattle roamed the open range, and the California horseman was born. This was possibly the most sophisticated native horsemanship the world had yet seen, but it was still coercive by the standards of today's revolution.

Then, in 1832, three Mexican *vaqueros* were imported into the Hawaiian Islands to teach the Polynesian natives how to rope and ride, in order to round up the thousands of wild cattle and horses that had been introduced into Hawaii and had proliferated into great herds. The *paniolos* (a mispronunciation of *españols*) of Hawaii learned well, and remain today rough and ready, skilled riders and ropers, but typically crude horsemen.

Lastly, after the Civil War, the great Texas trail herds were moved northward to the railroad terminals and the Texas cowboy was born, emulating in dress, language, and equipment the Mexican *vaquero*.

Although superior to other schools of colonial horsemanship, the California method still suffered from some crude techniques and lacked many of the elements being taught today, which are more correct from the standards

In colonial California, a vast grazing empire, the horse was king. *(Ernest Morris)*

of behavioral science. Some modern horsemen who have kept the vaquero tradition alive have improved it in subtle but important ways.

It is interesting to note that the men who precipitated this revolution in horsemanship were all cowboys, as were their students who took the message to the public. All were justifiably proud of their cowboy background and skills, but would also concede that traditional American cowboy horsemanship is crude, often unnecessarily harsh, and often scientifically incorrect. Many have expressed regret for the methods they used when they were young. Pat Parelli said in 1985, "If I teach these better methods for the rest of my life, it will never atone for the wrong things I did to horses when I was younger."

Native horsemanship is seldom characterized by deliberate, wanton cruelty. Methods that are inhumane and ineffective, when examined objectively, are often the products of traditions that have never been seriously questioned. People used these methods because they were taught to. They didn't know that there was a better way. Thankfully for the horse, the revolution in horsemanship is bringing that better way to light in more countries every year.

CHAPTER 3

THE REVOLUTION BEGINS

IT IS IRONIC THAT A MODEL of enlightened horsemanship should be found in cowboy country. To the rest of the world, the American working cowboy has long been a caricature of violence, bravado, and crude horsemanship, thanks mostly to western novelists, artists, and Hollywood filmmakers, but also to the reality of life in post–Civil War America.

In the last quarter of the nineteenth century, being a cowboy (or cow-boy, as it was spelled at the time) didn't require a Harvard education. If you had a pulse and could stay on the back of a horse, you could probably land a job as a cowhand on the big cattle drives of that era. Plenty of cowboys fit the caricature, but there were also thinking individuals who took pride in their horses and worked at developing a light touch.

There was a practical reason to fine-tune this relationship between horse and human. When driving a herd of cattle over varied terrain and through all kinds of weather, your day could go from dull to deadly in a few seconds. The better partnership you developed with your horses, the more likely you were to make it to payday.

Many cowboys had a competitive streak, and when they weren't on cattle drives they liked to test their riding skills and the abilities of their horses. Those who aspired to be the best they could be had no trouble finding role models, for there were always better horsemen around. Each generation since then has produced horsemen who kept this dedication to excellence alive and carried it forward.

Along the way, they've managed to redefine what it means to be a cowboy. The pride, confidence, and machismo are still there, but they are not worn on the sleeve. They are cloaked in a gentility that is increasingly rare in our society today. The modern cowboy tips his hat to ladies and removes it entirely when the National Anthem is played. His language is unconsciously punctuated with "sir" and "ma'am." His movement is often unhurried and deliberate, his manner self-assured but not overbearing. He is often college educated. He may write poetry or prose, dance, and play music. The modern cowboy is not perfect, but he is about as far from the oafish caricature that gave him his name as is possible.

It is somehow fitting that the revolution that brought real horsemanship to the average rider came from this stock. It was a long time coming. Nobody planned it, and its early participants did not realize until much later that they had created something important.

Time has brought clarity on several important points, however, including the question of who actually started the current revolution. Modern horsemen may not agree on much, but virtually all of them agree on one thing. This revolution began with a cowboy by the name of Tom Dorrance.

TOM DORRANCE (1910–2003)

Tom Dorrance was born sixth in a family of four brothers and four sisters, and grew up on a northeastern Oregon cattle ranch that his father, a Canadian named William Church Dorrance, had homesteaded as a young man. At its peak, the ranch ran 750 cattle and 150 horses. It kept the boys busy.

As the youngest brother, Dorrance learned early in life the value of using psychology rather than muscle to get what he wanted. He disliked conflict in any form, and among the brothers he was known as the peacemaker. It became an important part of his way with horses.

According to his brother, Bill, "Tom was easy with the horses, and they all worked for him. He wanted to get along with them. As time went on, Tom figured out how to get a relaxed feel with horses. Not many of his horses bucked, but if one should it wasn't liable to get out from under him. That relaxed feel really felt good to Tom and the horse."

Tom Dorrance worked on the family's Oregon homestead for more than three decades until it was sold in 1945. He never personally owned a horse after that. For the next twenty years or so, he was a nomadic cowboy, working on ranches in Oregon, Nevada, and Montana, and wintering on a relative's ranch in California. At the age of fifty-six, Dorrance took a wife,

Margaret, and he lived the last thirty-seven years of his life with her in California.

Although he lacked a formal education, Dorrance was intelligent, creative, and sensitive. He had unusual powers of observation, a keen memory, and a logical mind. He enjoyed learning. For much of his later life, he worked to perfect a tilt-up automatic gate to make ranch life a little easier. An ingenious invention with fulcrums and balance points, it allowed a heavy gate to be lifted with a single finger.

Countless people and horses benefited directly from Tom Dorrance's uncanny ability to read situations and to be in the right place at the right time,

Tom Dorrance called himself "the horse's lawyer." *(Julie Baldocchi)*

with just the right word or action. He referred to problems with horses as "people problems" and jokingly called himself "the horse's lawyer." But Dorrance was dead serious in his advocacy of the horse's point of view. When his friend and student, Ray Hunt, asked him where he learned what he knew about horses, Dorrance was quick to give credit to his teacher. "Ray," he replied, "I learned it from the horse."

He had to. Growing up on the Dorrance ranch, Tom was expected to get the job done, whatever it took. If he couldn't work out an issue with a horse, he would sometimes consult his older brother, Fred. But Fred died in 1940, drowning in a freak duck hunting accident. After that, Dorrance had only himself to depend upon. He knew he couldn't bully the horse into doing what he wanted. It wasn't his nature anyway. He learned how to make his idea become the horse's idea.

As a teacher, Tom Dorrance was generous with his time but chose his words carefully. He could be direct and to the point or deliberately cryptic and vague, challenging riders to ponder their situations and reach their own conclusions. It was a style perfectly suited for his cadre of dedicated students but left others scratching their heads.

Pat Parelli tells of visiting Dorrance as he lay gravely ill in the hospital. Thinking he might not see him again, Parelli quietly asked the old horseman

When no longer fearful of an object, a horse often becomes curious about it and then tries to dominate it. Ultimately he will become indifferent to it. *(Heidi Nyland)*

if there was anything special he felt Parelli needed to know. "Don't knock the curiosity out of a young horse," Dorrance finally whispered. Over the following weeks, Dorrance recovered enough to go home, but Parelli continued to puzzle over his mentor's words. Gradually he came to the realization that curiosity is the emotion opposite *fear* in a horse. The Parelli curriculum now focuses on developing a horse's curiosity.

Most of today's natural horsemanship clinicians count Tom Dorrance as a major influence. Some knew him and worked with him personally. Unquestionably, his most important student was Ray Hunt, an Idaho cowboy he met at the fair in Elko, Nevada, around 1960. Hunt asked Dorrance for help with his horse, Hondo, and Dorrance agreed. It was a seminal moment for the revolution, for it was Ray Hunt who would later take Tom Dorrance's way to the public.

Where the horsemanship of Tom Dorrance ended and that of Ray Hunt began is difficult to tell today. The former was the teacher and the latter was the gifted protégé, but over time, the distinction blurred. The horsemanship of both men is deep and rich and personal, but some of its basic principles are easy enough to understand. They are embodied in a collection of simple, profound, and often-quoted sayings.

1.   Observe, remember, and compare.
2.   Make the wrong things difficult and the right things easy.
3.   Let your idea become the horse's idea.
4.   Be as gentle as possible and as firm as necessary.
5.   The slower you do it, the quicker you'll find it.
6.   Feel what the horse is feeling, and operate from where the horse is.
7.   Do less to get more.
8.   Take the time it takes.
9.   The horse has a need for self-preservation in mind, body, and spirit.
10.   *The horse is never wrong.*

Like his brother Bill, Tom Dorrance was influenced by the *vaquero* tradition of California and appreciated as much as anyone a finished saddle horse ridden in a curb bit. But he was drawn more to starting horses and working with "problem" horses. For that he used a snaffle almost exclusively. Today, the snaffle bit is emblematic of the natural horseman.

Tom Dorrance inspired a revolution in horsemanship and a multimillion-dollar industry, but he personally profited little from it. In 1987, he published his only book, *True Unity: Willing Communication Between Horse and Human*, edited by Milly Hunt Porter; in 1999, a video, *Greetings from Tom Dorrance,* was released. They were, and continue to be, moderate but steady sellers. He lived his final years in a manufactured home on brother Bill's ranch in Salinas, California. In 2001, Ray and Carolyn Hunt organized the Benefit Tribute to Tom Dorrance to raise money for his mounting medical bills. The event, staged in Fort Worth, Texas, featured a Who's Who of natural horsemanship clinicians, but Dorrance himself was too ill to attend.

After a major stroke, Tom Dorrance passed away at a hospice house in Monterey, California, on June 11, 2003 at the age of ninety-three, with his wife Margaret by his side.

Tom Dorrance was one of those remarkable people who seem to make a lasting impression on everyone with whom they come in contact. He was profiled in both *People* magazine and the *New York Times*. Shortly after his death, in an article titled, "A Tribute to Tom Dorrance," Porter wrote, "I have never felt Tom was about horses. Many people who came repeatedly to watch Tom work were not riders or even horse owners, but were educators, psychologists, or in some other career field. Everyone who came seemed to find something to take home."

Porter's article was published in *The Trail Less Traveled*, a magazine dedicated to natural horsemanship. Ironically, the magazine ceased operation a few months later, after almost nine years.

Toward the end of his life, Tom Dorrance shrank from the role of horse guru, living legend, and elder statesman for the movement he had inspired. He rarely granted interviews, but when he did, he shared his thoughts freely and generously.

Tom Dorrance did not want to be part of the discourse on horsemanship. *(Julie Baldocchi)*

Bill Dorrance, Ray Hunt, and Tom Dorrance. (*Julie Baldocchi*)

Then he asked that he not be quoted. He did not want to be "part of the discourse."

Nor did he want credit for what people were doing with their horses. According to Margaret Dorrance, Tom had a saying: "If it is working, it might have come from me, and you don't need to use my name, and if it isn't working, you might have missed what I said, so then I don't want you to use my name."

Tom Dorrance was a reluctant hero, a man of modest needs and simple habits who for most of his life gave his horse advice freely. The vast commercialization of horsemanship bothered him. To reach more people, and ostensibly to help more horses, many of his ideas were being simplified and slickly packaged by others into mass-consumable, bite-sized how-to chunks for weekend horse enthusiasts. Dorrance had virtually no control over what was happening and certainly benefited little financially.

The loss of privacy that comes with being a celebrity also bothered him and Margaret. They thought about changing their phone number.

Most important, Tom Dorrance simply did not agree with all that was being done under the broad banner of natural horsemanship. Like most good horsemen, he had his own opinions on things, and he resented it when his name was associated with people and techniques he didn't like.

Today, Margaret Dorrance does her best to honor her husband's wishes without denying the world the chance to learn from his remarkable life.

RAY HUNT (1929–)

Without Ray Hunt, the revolution in horsemanship would not have occurred the way it did. Hunt was the pivotal character, the facilitator, the one who started this particular ball rolling.

He has been in the middle of it ever since. To date, he has personally started more than 10,000 colts and, directly or indirectly, he has influenced the horsemanship of millions of people around the world.

Ray Hunt was a thirty-year-old cowhand with a troubled horse when he met fifty-year-old Tom Dorrance at the fair in Elko. Dorrance opened Hunt's eyes to the horse's point of view and gave him some new techniques to try. A few months later, that horse, Hondo, was winning blue ribbons in horse shows and was gentle enough for Hunt's kids to ride. The year was 1961.

Hunt recognized the genius of Tom Dorrance early on and decided to absorb every bit of it that he could. He learned quickly. Dorrance would later say of him, "I have never experienced anyone who could pick up on the slightest clue and build on it in the right direction in such a short time—it is as if he has been doing it all his life."

Ray Hunt took Tom Dorrance's work public and started a revolution in horsemanship. *(Julie Baldocchi)*

In the mid-1970s, when most Western horse clinics were still based on traditional, coercive methods and a philosophy that centered on the human's needs, Hunt began offering the public something different. It took courage for the Idaho buckaroo to fly in the face of common cowboy wisdom. But then, Ray Hunt has never taken much stock in what others thought of him. He is famous for starting each clinic, even today, with the statement, "I'm here for the horse—to help him get a better deal." He makes his priorities clear in no uncertain terms. There will be no coddling, no tiptoeing around delicate human sensibilities. If you get bucked off or kicked or bitten, you obviously did something wrong and that's just too bad. The horse, on the other hand, is never, ever wrong, and Hunt will not back down an inch on that. Ray Hunt is there for the horse. Period.

In 1978, Hunt wrote a classic little book that attempted to put the Dorrance/Hunt approach to horsemanship in writing. *Think Harmony with Horses: An In-depth Study of Horse/Man Relationship*, edited by Milly Hunt, has inspired and puzzled its readers for decades since. Hunt and Dorrance wrestled with the same problem. What they felt, what they knew, and what they did with horses could not be easily put into words. Every horse was different, every person was different, every day was different. There could be no "how-to" matrix of rules—if this happens, do this—because horses and people and life itself were one giant multidimensional swirling mass of change. It was a moving target that was virtually impossible to hit.

According to Hunt, "All the whos, whats, and wheres determine the whys, whens, and hows." Before you can decide on a correct course of action in a particular situation, you have to take into account all the factors that make up that situation. The safest advice he ever gives anyone is simply, "Adjust to fit the situation."

When you get down to it, horsemanship to Hunt and probably every great horseman is mostly about *feel*. How do you describe feel? It's an intangible, maybe king of the intangibles.

Ask a jazz musician how he knows which note to play in an improvised solo. Ask a carpenter how he knows how many strokes of sandpaper are needed on the finish of a cabinet. Or ask Ray Hunt how he knows that a horse is thinking about making a try. The expert draws upon a wealth of experience and intimate knowledge of his subject that become very difficult to verbalize. It becomes part of him; it operates from his intuitive self. It becomes *feel*.

That's why so many of Hunt's answers to questions about horse behavior start out with the same two words: *it depends*. It depends on the *feel* at that moment, and feel comes only with experience.

All that being said, Ray Hunt's book did manage to capture some important essences for us all to ponder. They took the form of a collection of sayings, some his own and some probably originated by Tom Dorrance, presented under the heading of *Equesology*, a word that seems familiar, but does not appear in the English dictionary. These sayings are brilliant in their simplicity and on-the-mark relevance, and form a useful foundation for building a language based on feel.

Some were presented earlier. Here are a few more.

1. Instead of a hard tightness, try to find a soft firmness.
2. Think right down to the ground.
3. If you are going to teach a horse something and have a good relationship, you don't make him learn it—you let him learn it.
4. The right feel and timing bring you the balance.
5. THINK.
6. Ride your horse with your whole body, not just your arms and legs.
7. Notice the smallest change and the slightest try, and reward him.
8. Ride with life in your body.
9. He knows that you know, and you know he knows.
10. *You're not working on your horse, you're working on yourself.*

The last one brings us back to the greater importance of the revolution in horsemanship. It is allowing us to develop better, safer, happier horses, but we are becoming better, safer, and happier people in the process. This is a revolution in horsemanship, but it is also a revolution in realizing human potential.

Ray and Carolyn Hunt reside today in Mountain Home, Idaho.

BILL DORRANCE (1906–1999)

Though only four years older than his brother Tom, Bill Dorrance was born in a different era, the era before Henry Ford changed America with his horseless carriage.

The family's homestead near Enterprise, Oregon, had few conveniences for its ten inhabitants. There was no tractor, no automobile. Horses were

Bill Dorrance doing what he loved. *(Julie Baldocchi)*

used for hauling, plowing, riding, and working cattle. The Dorrances were typical of most rural American families at the dawn of the twentieth century. They relied on the horse for nearly everything.

Sisters Margaret and Lillian grew up to teach school like their mother, Minnie Tinsley Dorrance, while Jean and Ethel did secretarial work. But the brothers, Jim, Bill, Fred, and Tom, all became horsemen, each in his own way.

Oldest brother Jim could sit any horse, bucking or not, and make it look easy. If a horse was a bit edgy and had extra life to him, so much the better. Jim liked it that way. Youngest brother Tom always tried to redirect that energy in a positive direction to get a calm, quiet horse. Bill wanted to train horses from the time he was a teenager and pored over a correspondence course he bought from The Beery School of Horsemanship in faraway Pleasant Hill, Ohio. Fred, probably the most naturally gifted of the four, became a top hand by riding rough string for a ranch in Nevada. Then, around 1930, he became the first of the Dorrance brothers to move to California. Bill was not far behind.

When Bill Dorrance arrived in California in late November 1931, Herbert Hoover was president of the United States and the country was in the throes of the Great Depression. California was not a bad place to be, all things considered. There was ranch work available and a man could work outside year round. No one really *taught* horsemanship back then, and it was seldom even discussed, but Dorrance was observant and noticed that some riders had a better feel with their horses. He learned from each of them. He liked all horses, and wanted to have an easier relationship with them.

It was in California that Bill Dorrance came to understand and embrace the traditions of the colonial California horseman, the *Californio*, and specifically the *vaquero* who worked cattle. He learned to braid his own *reatas* (rawhide ropes) and make much of his own riding tack. Braiding and roping were skills he would cultivate throughout his life.

The vast ranches of California were, in a sense, frozen in time. Automobiles, trucks, and tractors had not yet replaced horses and mules, at least not to the extent they had back east. Producing a horse that could go "straight up in the bridle" was the goal of nearly every horseman. The time-consuming, painstaking California system of bridling reigned supreme.

Bill Dorrance was enamored with all of this and carried its influence throughout his life. He liked the idea of seeing just how far you could take a horse.

He also liked helping people with their horses. Gene Armstrong, an instructor at California Polytechnic State University in San Luis Obispo, would often refer students to Dorrance for help with their horses. They would come for an afternoon and stay for several days. Clinicians Buck Brannaman, Bryan Neubert, and Mike Beck all tell of being helped by Dorrance. According to Beck, Dorrance sometimes mused about what it would have been like to have a school of horsemanship. It was not meant to be. There was always too much work to be done on the mountaintop ranch in Salinas where he and his wife, Marie, raised their three sons.

One of Bill Dorrance's most driven students was Leslie Desmond. Proprietor of a horsemanship school back East, Desmond relocated to California in 1990 and was surprised to find that Dorrance's vast knowledge and experience with horses had not been captured for posterity. No books had been written; no videos had been produced. Nothing. It was through her efforts that Bill Dorrance's only horsemanship book, *True Horsemanship Through Feel*, came to be. The language in this large, beautifully rendered book is simple, but, as with brother Tom's earlier book, there is richness lying beneath the surface for those willing to dig.

The book's editors and proofreaders encouraged Desmond to interpret Dorrance's thoughts and methods to make them easier for the public to understand. She refused. Thus, the book is mostly in Bill Dorrance's own words, giving a strong sense of the horseman and gentle man he was.

Dorrance died in 1999, shortly after its publication, at the age of ninety-three.

PAT PARELLI (1954–)

In the 1980s, Pat Parelli coined the term "natural horsemanship" and gave name to an entire movement. Today, the educational system that

Pat Parelli. *(Photos by Coco)*

bears his name, Parelli Natural Horse-Man-Ship, is used throughout the world.

Born in the ranching community of Livermore, in the San Francisco Bay Area, young Pat Parelli was obsessed with horses from an early age, and by the time he was nine he was working in local stables. Over the years, he had numerous mentors who taught him not only about horses, but also about cattle and dogs and living in harmony with nature. He was a sponge, an eager and talented student who soaked up every bit of information to which he was exposed. Before long, he was formulating his own ideas on raising foals and training horses.

While in high school, Parelli started competing in rodeo. As he puts it, "I rode bucking horses until my brains came in." Under the guidance of his coach, John Hawkins, he won the Bareback Rookie of the Year title in 1972, at just eighteen years of age, with a buck-off average of only 4 percent.

Parelli earned a bachelor's degree in Agricultural Education at Fresno State University. Then he hired on at the Troy Henry Stables near Clovis, California, where his real education in horses began. Henry helped him understand the horse's world and taught him the value of psychology and communication in training horses for performance. Henry also introduced him to his future equine partner, a magnificent Quarter Horse stallion called Salty Doc. One day the two of them would grace the cover of Parelli's breakthrough book, *Natural Horsemanship.*

The public began to hear about Pat Parelli in 1981. His near win on a *mule* at the National Reined Cow Horse Association's prestigious Snaffle Bit Futurity set tongues to wagging. In 1982, after weeks of practice, he hit the road and began teaching and demonstrating what he had learned about psychological horse training. Parelli's vision was to teach people to teach horses. He wanted to create a means for people to use effective, nonviolent communication with the horse instead of force, fear, and intimidation. The public loved it and it brought Parelli to the attention of other master horsemen.

The following year, Tom Dorrance, Ray Hunt, and Ronnie Willis caught Parelli's bridle-less reining demonstration at the California Livestock Symposium. All three became mentors to him in the years to come.

This same year, a co-author of this book, Dr. Robert Miller, met Pat Parelli and wrote a three-part series on him titled, "A New Look at Old Methods." The series ran from November 1983 through January 1984 in *Western Horseman* magazine and introduced Pat Parelli to tens of thousands of Western riders. In 1993, *Western Horseman* published Parelli's book, *Natural Horsemanship*, which remains one of their best sellers. The momentum continued to build, and today the Parelli name is synonymous with natural horsemanship in the United States and around the world.

Although they seldom fault his horsemanship, some critics dislike Pat Parelli's showmanship. He makes no apologies. "I could teach anything, even math, and make it interesting," he says, "because I'm a ham and that keeps people's attention, and because I'm enthusiastic and that's contagious." Out of the spotlight, Parelli is surprisingly quiet and unpretentious. He unwinds by playing guitar, and late-night straw-bale jam sessions are one of his passions.

The Seven Games

Perhaps Pat Parelli's greatest contribution to the revolution in horsemanship—and probably his legacy—is a groundwork routine he calls The Seven Games. Based on the body language horses use to interact with each other to establish leadership, these games create a relationship, calm the horse, focus the human, demonstrate the human's right to be leader of the team, and reinforce the language that the human and horse will use to communicate. They are designed to be done in order, and they prove to the horse that the human understands his world.

The Friendly Game is where the Parelli system starts. *(Photos by Coco)*

Game 1 is *the Friendly Game.* It is all about touching the horse in a friendly, comfortable way all over his body with your hands or with a rope, a stick, a plastic bag, a saddle blanket, or anything at all. It shows the horse that even though you are a predator, you are not going to act like one. When done with rhythm, it also desensitizes him to various stimuli. It is important to smile while playing the Friendly Game and to come back to it between the other games.

Game 2 is *the Porcupine Game.* It is played by exerting steady pressure with the tips of your fingers or a training stick (such as the Parelli Carrot Stick) on different parts of the horse's body to encourage him to yield or move those body parts away from you. Pressure is applied in increasing phases of firmness as needed: pressing the hair, then the skin, then the muscle, then the bone. When the horse responds, the pressure is removed *instantly.* Phases of firmness and instant release of pressure are used in all of the remaining games.

Game 3 is *the Driving Game.* It is like a hands-free version of the Porcupine Game, creating *implied* pressure through rhythmic commotion in the air near the body part to be moved. A training stick may also be used to rhythmically tap the ground as a way of encouraging the horse to move without touching him.

Game 4 is *the Yo-Yo Game.* In this game, you ask the horse to back away from you and then approach you, all through your body language and the rhythmic application of phased pressure through the lead rope.

Game 5 is *the Circling Game.* This is the Parelli version of longeing (sometimes spelled "lungeing"), but there is much more to it. Once the horse has been sent out on a circle and urged into the desired gait, he is allowed—and expected—to continue at that gait without any further pressure. Then, after just two to four revolutions, he is invited back to you, and asked to swing his hindquarters away ("disengage" the hindquarters) in the process. This is more of a mental and emotional exercise than a physical one and gives responsibility to the horse for maintaining gait and motion.

Game 6 is *the Sideways Game.* It teaches the horse to move laterally on both sides. It is done initially with the horse facing a fence to impede any forward motion. Pressure is rhythmically alternated between his front end and hind end in the manner of the Driving Game.

Game 7 is *the Squeeze Game.* In this game, you ask the horse to pass between you and some other object, a fence, a barrel, anything. This teaches the naturally claustrophobic horse to go into enclosed spaces like trailers and stalls.

The Parelli games begin on the ground but have application in the saddle as well. Most of them utilize horseman's tools that Parelli has developed over the years. Most important among these are the rope halter, the 12-foot lead rope, and a training stick he has dubbed the Carrot Stick. These tools existed in some form long before Parelli's time, but he deserves credit for modernizing them, developing creative and effective uses for them, and popularizing them.

Parelli Natural Horse-Man-Ship

As an educational system, Parelli Natural Horse-Man-Ship borrows the best ideas from Scouting, martial arts, and traditional education. It is intended to produce accelerated learning and is influenced by the principles of Neurolinguistic Programming, the practical science of detecting, evolving, and using the conscious and unconscious thinking and behavioral patterns that we constantly experience.

The step-by-step Parelli program advances the student through levels, much like ranks, belts or grades.

There are ten levels. Levels 1 through 3, concerned with basic horsemanship, are really about teaching the human. There is considerable emphasis on developing a relationship with the horse, equine psychology, understanding the prey/predator relationship, and the application of equal amounts of love, language, and leadership. Levels 4, 5, and 6 address

Their annual Savvy Conference draws thousands to Pat and Linda Parelli's International Study Center in Pagosa Springs, Colorado. *(Photos by Coco)*

performance and finesse in the horse. Beyond that is where horsemanship becomes an art form and the levels are less clearly defined. When pressed, Pat Parelli considers himself to be at Level 8 today.

In the mid-1990s, Pat Parelli married his best student, Australian dressage rider Linda Paterson. Linda, who is responsible for most of the written materials used in the Parelli program today, has become a superb teacher in her own right. The Parellis maintain ranches and study centers in Pagosa Springs, Colorado, and Ocala, Florida. The Colorado operation has been accredited as an occupational school by the Colorado Department of Higher Education.

Parelli's first wife, and the mother of his son and daughter, is also a teacher of natural horsemanship. Karen Parelli Hagen and her husband, Jim, operate Natural Hoofprints in northern California.

MONTY ROBERTS (1935–)

Monty Roberts deserves credit for bringing the ideas embodied by the revolution in horsemanship to the masses. His first book, *The Man Who Listens to Horses*, was a bona fide hit with the general public throughout the world, making Roberts a household name and putting nonviolent horse training into the international spotlight.

Born in 1935 in Salinas, California, Roberts was surrounded by horses from an early age. His father, Marvin Roberts, was a respected horseman who used traditional training methods, but from the age of nine, young

Monty Roberts. *(Monty Roberts Collection)*

Monty was drawn more to the psychological approach used by a neighbor, Bill Dorrance.

At thirteen, Roberts tracked wild mustangs in Nevada and developed an understanding of their silent language, a language of gestures he later dubbed "Equus." This became the basis of the nonviolent training technique he calls Join-Up®.

Join-Up®

For many years, Roberts kept his horse training methods to himself and they brought him success in a variety of equine activities. In the show ring, he had eight world champions, including Johnny Tivio, Fiddle D'Or, and Night Mist. He was even better known, however, for producing world-class Thoroughbred racehorses, such as Alleged, An Act, Tobin Bronze, and more than 250 other stakes winners.

In 1986, the methods behind the man came out. A Thoroughbred racehorse trainer, Farrell Jones, happened by one day while Roberts was working with a young horse in his round pen. Jones was so impressed with what he saw that he insisted the world needed to know about it. Demonstrations followed in Kentucky, where Thoroughbred breeders and writers were watching. Articles were written about the work and Monty Roberts's methods went public.

By 1989, England's Queen Elizabeth II, an owner and breeder of Thoroughbreds and other types of horses, had heard about Roberts's methods and expressed an interest in observing him in action. After doing so, she requested that Roberts demonstrate his work throughout the United Kingdom. It was also at Her Majesty's request that Roberts's first book was written and released in England. *The Man Who Listens to Horses* was later published in North America and fourteen other countries. This launched a career in which Roberts has demonstrated his concepts around the world and for many different riding disciplines.

Roberts's training method is demonstrated most often on unstarted or problem (what he calls "remedial") horses. Using a round pen technique honed to perfection over several decades, Roberts's body language first drives the horse away, as a more dominant horse would. Then, when he observes signs that the horse is willing to cooperate—to "renegotiate the contract," as he puts it—Roberts changes his body language to invite the horse in, to bond with him, to "join up." Done by Roberts, the procedure transforms any horse from fearful or defiant to trusting and bonded in 15–20

Monty Roberts's Join-Up® demonstrations draw thousands of spectators. *(Monty Roberts Collection)*

minutes, and, if being prepared for riding, to carrying a rider calmly within 30 minutes. The horse is then ready for more extensive training.

The same principles used to gain trust and respect in the round pen are used to address trailer loading, water crossing, and other typical problem areas for horse owners.

There is a strong philosophical thread running through all of Monty Roberts's work: nonviolence. "Violence is always for the violator," he points out, "never for the victim."

This requires a comment. Roberts would be the first to admit that horses can be very physical with one another. The language of Equus that he observed is a language of physical gestures, often of physical *pressure*—horses routinely kick and bite one another as expressions of dominance—and that can look a lot like violence.

So how can one be in favor of communicating with horses in the language they understand, yet not accept the more physical aspects of it?

Let us offer our own thoughts on this.

Perhaps violence is best defined not by an objective measure of force, say pounds per square inch of pressure exerted, but rather by the mental states of the ones involved. A human that is angry, frustrated, or vengeful when exerting pressure on a horse could very well be committing a violent act, and the horse would certainly pick up on the mental "vibe." Because of the psychological component, it would seem like an attack, an inappropriate and unjust behavior that would probably provoke a *fear* reaction in the horse, a different state of mind than simply feeling submissive to a more dominant individual. On the other hand, the very same physical pressure, applied dispassionately with no intention of hurting or paying back the horse, could be a legitimate training technique that would produce the desired submissive response.

Put another way, violence requires that the one on the receiving end *feel violated*. Hang around horses long enough, and you will probably get kicked at some time or another. It hurts and it leaves a bruise, but you probably won't feel violated. More likely you will feel foolish for not paying better attention. Now consider the same injury received from a thug with a baseball bat in a dark parking lot. *That* is an act of violence. One has a psychological component to it, and the other doesn't. One is an *attack* and the other isn't. This is more than wordplay; there are real differences here.

Monty Roberts's life has had many highlights: as a child he was stunt double for Elizabeth Taylor in *National Velvet* and in other Hollywood films for Roddy McDowell, Mickey Rooney, and Charlton Heston. In his early twenties, he won two National Intercollegiate Rodeo Association Championships, in 1956 for team roping and in 1957 for bulldogging. His Flag Is Up Farms, in Solvang, California, where he lives with his wife, Pat, an accomplished horsewoman and talented sculptress, is a respected breeding operation. It produces top racehorses, performance horses, and halter horses. Roberts has received numerous awards, a certificate of recognition from the CIA, and an honorary doctorate in behavioral sciences from the University of Zurich. He has performed at Windsor Castle and is an accomplished chef.

In the interest of completeness, it must be stated that Roberts's first book, which rocketed him to international celebrity, also sparked a bitter and public family feud over its portrayal of his early life and his deceased father. Although unfortunate, the controversy does not diminish the importance of Monty Roberts to the revolution in horsemanship.

RICHARD SHRAKE (1944–)

"May you always ride a good horse!" is Richard Shrake's signature signoff. And he means it.

Shrake is one of the good guys, a terrific horseman who, in an industry with its share of personality conflicts, is respected and liked by everyone. The feeling is mutual. As a successful show horse trainer and judge, he has played a unique and very important role in the revolution in horsemanship.

Richard Shrake was born in Salem, Oregon, and grew up on his parents' dairy farm. His dad, a former rodeo cowboy from Colorado, kept all

Richard Shrake and Miss Resistance Free. *(Jim Bortvedt)*

kinds of horses on the farm and liked to trade for more when he got the chance. It gave Shrake and his brother, Greg, lots of experience handling a variety of horses of different ages, getting them trained well enough to swap for something better.

At nine, Shrake showed his first pony at a county fair and, by mimicking the other kids in the showmanship and horsemanship classes, finished the day as champion showman of his age division. He just seemed to have a knack for showing, even as a green youngster.

Through his membership in the Salem Saddle Club, Shrake was exposed to several very good horsemen. Somewhat reluctantly, the young cowboy studied with one of them, a German dressage trainer, for three winters, an experience that has benefited him throughout his career. Two of his buddies from the club, Doug Brown and Larry Mahan, went on to fame in rodeo.

In college at Oregon State University, Shrake trained horses on the side to earn spending money. He finished a degree in education at Portland State and soon found himself conducting clinics up and down the West Coast for Carnation-Albers, a large feed and supplement company. By that time, he knew what he wanted to do with his life.

At twenty-three, he put a down payment on eighteen acres in the country outside Portland and started his own training facility, Horsemanship

West. Eighteen years later he sold the property at a handsome profit when the city grew to meet it. Today, a shopping center occupies the land and Shrake's operation has moved east of the Cascade Range, to Sunriver, Oregon.

During its heyday, Horsemanship West had about forty horses in training. Shrake often won awards for having the most students in a show. One year, he took twenty-eight students and their horses to the Junior Cow Palace in San Francisco.

But Richard Shrake felt he needed to prove himself as a competitor if he was to have the credibility needed for a sustained career as a teacher. Over the next few years, he showed against the best horsemen on the West Coast in the open Western division of shows approved by the AHSA (American Horse Shows Association). In 1974, he took Horse of the Year (high point) awards in trail horse, Western pleasure, and stock horse. These national championships gave him the credibility he was seeking. He put the icing on the cake a few years later at the 1979 American Quarter Horse Congress, the world's largest horse show. On a horse named Windjammer, Shrake snagged the most coveted prize of all, the All-Around. There could be no doubt. This man could ride.

Next, Shrake set his sights on becoming the best teacher he could be. In the years that followed, numerous Shrake students won an impressive array of titles at horse shows all across the country. Finally, he felt ready to go for his third goal, becoming a judge.

Richard Shrake has since served as a judge for numerous breed associations. He has judged more than 1,000 shows, including eleven world and national shows, for the American Quarter Horse Association, the American Paint Horse Association, the Appaloosa Horse Club, the International Arabian Horse Association, and the Pony of the Americas Club. He has judged in every state in the U.S. and in Canada, Germany, Switzerland, and Australia. Beginning in the mid-1970s, Shrake has conducted more than 1,400 clinics and seminars, and has appeared at 105 universities and colleges around the world. He originated and coached the United States World Cup Team, and he is the first well-known trainer to work with the BLM (Bureau of Land Management) on their wild horse program.

Richard Shrake has written three books: *Western Horsemanship, Resistance Free™ Training,* and *Resistance Free™ Riding.* He has written articles for numerous horse publications and has two syndicated monthly columns, "Bridle Wise" and "Strides to Success," which are featured in more than 150 American and Canadian publications.

He has produced an extensive collection of videos, currently numbering eighteen, and has nine signature bits in the Richard Shrake Resistance Free™ Bit Collection.

Shrake had many mentors, including Californians Jimmy Williams (considered by many to be America's greatest horseman during his life), Clyde Kennedy, and Arnold "Chief" Rojas (one of the last of the *vaqueros* and one of their foremost historians). In a recent video, Shrake revealed one of Rojas's tricks for gaining a horse's confidence: "Rub the horse's chestnuts, and then let him smell your fingers."

The "resistance free" theme runs throughout Richard Shrake's teaching. From a marketing standpoint, it is a way of branding his product, but it is more than that. It is an expression of his goal, a variation of the Dorrance/Hunt theme of "Let your idea become the horse's idea." Through consistent communication and empathetic leadership, we can transform the horse from a prey animal whose motivations are completely contrary to ours, to a willing partner who is on our team. Can *all* resistance be eliminated? Maybe not, but it is a worthy goal and Shrake urges us to keep it clearly in sight. His efforts to bring these principles to the show world make him particularly valuable to the revolution in horsemanship.

Richard Shrake and his wife, Lee Ann, live in central Oregon where they operate A Winning Way, Ltd. The company produces the Richard Shrake video series and manages the accredited Resistance Free™ Trainer and Instructor Program. Richard and Lee Ann have three grown children.

JOHN LYONS (1947–)

John Lyons has always been different. By the age of twenty-five, long before becoming known as "America's Most Trusted Horseman," he was already a successful distributor, earning a six-figure income selling medical orthopedic implants to doctors and hospitals. But his heart wasn't in it, and one day the young family man decided to follow his dreams, something he has advised others to do ever since.

Born in Louisville, Kentucky, Lyons grew up in the dry desert of Phoenix, where his family moved for his asthma. He was a natural athlete and excelled in baseball and basketball. He planned to be a basketball coach, but after attending the University of Arizona he found himself in sales and he excelled at that too, ending up a few years later in Kansas City, Kansas, drawing top commissions at Richards Medical Supply, an orthopedic manufacturer.

John Lyons. *(John Lyons Collection)*

To this point, Lyons had virtually no experience with horses—unless you count the few times as a ten-year-old that he "borrowed" a neighbor's horse to ride in the desert. Thinking land would be a good investment, he bought a five-acre parcel outside of Kansas City and before long he acquired a horse to go with it. One day it dawned on him that he enjoyed shoveling manure and playing with his horse more than calling on doctors and hospitals. He decided he had to make a change. That was the end of John Lyons the orthopedic salesman, and the beginning of John Lyons the horseman.

Leaving a comfortable job and large income was not easy. Many of Lyons's friends and family were against his giving up that kind of security, especially to do something he knew nothing about.

Undaunted, Lyons moved his family to Silt, Colorado, and tried cattle ranching. The timing could not have been worse. Colorado was experiencing the worst droughts in 100 years, the worst winters, the highest interest rates in U.S. history, and some of the lowest cattle prices ever. With too little start-up capital to weather the bad times, Lyons, like more than half the ranchers in the valley where he lived, went broke. His ranch in foreclosure, the cattle gone, and the debt almost out of sight, Lyons's dream of being in the country was becoming a nightmare.

True to his nature, he refused to give up, and eventually something good came out of it. People began to notice Lyons's natural way with horses and to ask his advice. During his early ranching years, he had also gotten involved in showing horses and had purchased a horse that would become his partner for the next twenty-six years, an Appaloosa stud colt by the name of Bright Zip.

Lyons knew that he needed to know more if he was to become a real horseman. In 1980, he attended a Ray Hunt clinic that opened his eyes about several things. He discovered, for instance, that people really wanted to learn. He saw ways to make that sort of clinic safer for horses and humans. And he realized that he didn't have to be the world's greatest horse trainer in order to help others.

At first, Lyons, too, conducted clinics where he would work with ten to fifteen riders and their horses over a weekend. But the businessman inside saw a better format, one that would reach more people at a lower cost and still be more profitable for him. Thus, in 1988, came the John Lyons Symposium, a three-day demonstration wherein Lyons worked with unbroken and problem horses, and attendees—usually hundreds—watched from their seats. The symposium format caught on, and today Lyons continues conducting them nationally and internationally.

Over the years, John Lyons has developed a large assortment of educational materials and signature products, including books, videos, audios, tack, and a monthly subscription publication, *Perfect Horse.* Lyons serves as spokesperson for a number of corporate sponsors, companies whose products he uses and he feels he can personally endorse. His trainer certification program, now run by his son, trainer Josh Lyons, has graduated many certified horse trainers.

Through skillful marketing and a relentless work ethic, Lyons has proven that training humans to train horses is the best way to help both. He has been honored with many awards over the years, from inside and outside of the horse industry. Lyons has set a standard for achievement in his chosen profession, and many horsemen today try to emulate his success.

John Lyons uses an educational approach to training, based on the model of a schoolteacher and student, and stresses that the human is responsible for what the horse learns. His emphasis is on communication and understanding, rather than force, and the patient application of gentle persuasion techniques. Lyons believes that a horse can and should be taught a *cue* for anything we want him to do. His method for teaching any cue is to plan it out ahead in what he calls a *lesson plan.*

The lesson plan is then carefully executed, taking care to never ask the horse to do something unless it is a virtual certainty that the horse will do it. This is Lyons's way of setting the horse up for success, rather than failure. "The horse only understands what happens, not whether it is right or wrong," Lyons explains. "If you ask a horse to do something and he refuses, you have taught him that that is what you want, and of course, it isn't."

Lyons avoids punishing bad behavior by instead giving the horse a job to do, replacing the negative behavior, in effect, with a positive one. Common sense and logic flow through his work, which is one reason it has become as popular as it has. Another is Lyons's sincere, affable, and unhurried manner. Horses and humans find it easy to trust John Lyons.

At a time when an increasing number of horse enthusiasts and professional performers alike are fearful of getting hurt with horses, Lyons offers hope. Instead of confronting your fear by doing the thing you are afraid of, Lyons recommends doing only what you are completely comfortable doing, even if it is just petting the horse from outside its stall.

"There is a real reason for the fear," he says. "Fear is common sense in disguise. Fear is recognition of loss of control, and it subsides when control returns. That's why you should start where you're in control and build from there." According to Lyons, no one should be ashamed of being afraid. "It is your survival instinct at work. It is your brain doing what it is supposed to do: taking care of you."

John Lyons's three golden rules for training horses are:

1. You can't get hurt.
2. The horse can't get hurt.
3. The horse must be calmer at the end of your training session than he was at the beginning.

John Lyons's champion stallion, Bright Zip, was inducted into the Appaloosa Hall of Fame and honored as the 1994 Breyerfest Horse of the Year. *(John Lyons Collection)*

John Lyons lives in Parachute, Colorado, with his wife, Jody. They have six children. Son Josh is following in his father's footsteps.

A popular fixture in Lyons's presentations for decades, Bright Zip died in 2003 and is buried on the family's Our Dream Ranch.

CHAPTER 4

THE REVOLUTION CONTINUES

By the mid-1980s, there were signs that this revolution in horsemanship might produce lasting change. Public interest was building. Books and videotapes were beginning to show up on the shelves of tack and feed stores. And most importantly, more skilled horsemen were starting to take the message to the public.

The trend continues today as each year more teachers of horsemanship hang out their shingles and open their doors for business. Most have something positive to offer: new perspectives drawn from their own life experiences, new ways of explaining esoteric concepts, new techniques, and new tools. This is a good thing, for it increases the likelihood that the willing student will find a teacher that truly inspires him.

In this chapter, we will meet a few of the horsemen in the revolution's continuing wave, presented in alphabetical order. (A more complete list, with contact information, is contained in the Appendix.) We will also learn why the differences in their techniques really don't matter.

CLINTON ANDERSON (1975–)

Born and raised in Australia, Clinton Anderson's natural ability with horses was apparent by the time he was six years old. At thirteen, he was chosen for a national Polo-Cross team, and by fifteen he was a professional horseman, selling his services to horse owners with trailer-loading problems. Often they had no idea how young he was.

Originally from Australia, Clinton Anderson now calls the United States home. *(Charles Hilton)*

"My dad would drive me to a job," he explains, "and when the customer saw us, he just assumed Dad was the one he'd hired. I kind of enjoyed that."

Anderson spent two years as a full-time apprentice with nationally acclaimed clinician and trainer Gordon McKinlay of Rockhampton, Queensland, and under McKinlay's guidance he worked with more than 600 horses, including brumbies, the wild horses of Australia. From there, he apprenticed with another well-known Australian trainer, Ian Francis, before starting his own training facility at the tender age of eighteen.

As time went on, Anderson became more taken with the sport of reining and arranged an apprenticeship in America with the legendary Al Dunning. It was on this trip that he met and married his wife, Beth.

Returning to Australia, Anderson came within one point of winning Australia's 1997 reining futurity, and the next year he moved to America for good. Aggressive marketing and a brutal schedule of appearances followed, and by 2001 he was headlining horse expos and had launched the first weekly made-for-TV horse training program on satellite television. His show remains one of the network's most popular offerings today.

An outstanding trainer and rider, Anderson is an even better teacher of horsemanship. His rapid-fire, Aussie-flavored delivery and straightforward, tell-it-like-it-is approach keep audiences of all ages rapt during his presentations. Nearly all of his demonstrations are with young or problem horses he's never seen before.

In addition to mentors McKinlay and Francis, Anderson has been most influenced by the work of Australian Kell Jeffery, Americans Ray Hunt, Pat Parelli, John Lyons, and Dr. Robert Miller, and show horse trainers Dunning, Bob Avila, and Andrea Fappani. The list grows every year. "The key is to keep learning," he says.

Anderson places a great deal of emphasis on groundwork, and he has numerous exercises designed to get the horse's respect by gaining control of its feet, getting the horse to move forward, backward, left, and right upon cue. He delays mounting a horse for the first time until he's absolutely sure there is nothing more he can do from the ground.

In the saddle, he makes extensive use of lateral flexion exercises to calm the horse and ensure that he remains in control. He advocates strongly that all riders practice the one-rein stop, or what he calls "the emergency hand brake stop," which is discussed in detail in our chapter on riding. Anderson calls his system of training Downunder Horsemanship.

In December 2003, Clinton Anderson's abilities were put to the test in a colt starting contest staged at the Cowtown Coliseum in Fort Worth, Texas. Called El Camino del Caballo ("The Road to the Horse"), the event matched Anderson and skilled fellow clinicians Curt Pate and Josh Lyons with three virtually untouched three-year-old geldings, all by the same Quarter Horse sire. After three hours of round pen training over two days, the trainers were judged on the performance of their horses on an obstacle course. Anderson won with a nearly flawless performance, capped off by *standing* on his young horse's back, cracking a whip and flapping a yellow rain slicker while the audience cheered.

In the past, few clinicians have successfully bridged the gap between the worlds of natural horsemanship and competitive horse showing. These activities typically attract different audiences. However, Anderson continues to compete seriously in reining. Being willing to play their game has won him the respect of an increasing number of upper-echelon performance horsemen, including world champions Avila (reined cow horse),

Clinton Anderson demonstrates his Downunder Horsemanship technique at the Road to the Horse colt-starting competition in 2003. This three-year-old Quarter Horse gelding had just three hours of training on it. *(Charles Hilton)*

Fappani (reining), Martha Josey (barrel racing), and Cleve Wells (Western pleasure). Each has publicly acknowledged the wiry Aussie's talent and the efficacy of his training methods. At a certain level, a good horseman is just a good horseman, regardless of how he spends his days. Clinton Anderson is clearly at that level.

Clinton and Beth Anderson are currently building their own 115-acre equestrian center north of Columbus, Ohio.

BUCK BRANNAMAN (1962–)

Dan Brannaman received his first taste of celebrity at the age of five when he and his older brother, Bill, won a talent contest on a local Spokane, Washington, television program. From then on, they were known respectively as Buckshot and Smokie, the Idaho Cowboys, purveyors of trick roping and riding. Shortly after, they joined what is now the Professional Rodeo Cowboys Association, and began performing at rodeos across the United States.

Child stardom peaked for them in the early 1970s when they appeared in a TV commercial for Kellogg's Sugar Pops cereal. Millions of Americans saw Buckshot and Smokie, alias the Sugar Pops Kids, performing their rope tricks and eating their favorite cereal on national television. The two young boys would have given it all up in an instant for a normal home life.

Dan "Buck" Brannaman was born in Sheboygan, Wisconsin, but grew up in Idaho and Montana. His early life, as related in his autobiography, *The Far-*

Buck Brannaman. *(Emily Kitching)*

away Horses, was marred by regular beatings from his father, Ace Brannaman, a brutal and unfulfilled man who lived vicariously through the show business successes of his sons. After the death of Buck's mother from diabetes in 1973, the violence escalated until local authorities intervened. The Brannaman brothers were placed in a foster home with a kind and loving couple, Forrest and Betsy Shirley, who raised them as their own.

After high school, Brannaman worked on a number of ranches and became more and more confident in his ability with horses. One day, while in Bozeman, Montana, to see a ranch manager about a job, he had some time to kill and caught part of a horsemanship clinic presented by Ray Hunt. Appearing with Hunt was his teacher, Tom

Dorrance. Seeing the two master horse-men changed the cocky young cowhand's life. He'd never dreamed that horses could be handled so effectively and so lightly. From that moment forward, Brannaman made it his mission in life to be just like Ray Hunt.

Before long, Brannaman became Hunt's protégé and friend. The older horseman and his wife treated Branna-man like family. He learned all he could about horsemanship and working cattle from Hunt and the Dorrance brothers. The ranch roping style they used came easy to him. As children, the Brannaman brothers had been mesmerized by Will Rogers's 1925 film, *The Roping Fool*, and Buck found as he began to do his own clinics that the public also enjoyed rope handling. He made it his special trademark and later held two titles for trick roping in the Gui-ness Book of World Records.

Brannaman was a third-year ac-counting major in college, at the top of his class, when his advisor heard about his unusual ability with horses. Calling Buck into his office, he suggested that the young man forget college and pursue his horse career, which is exactly what he did.

Buck Brannaman found himself in the public spotlight again in 1995 when it became known that he had been the real-life inspiration for the title character, Tom Booker, in *The Horse Whisperer*, the first novel by British producer and screen-writer, Nicholas Evans. A bestseller in twenty countries, the book was subse-quently made into a hit movie directed by

A master rope handler who holds two Guiness world records for trick roping, Buck Brannaman now teaches ranch roping. *(Buck Brannaman Collection)*

and starring Robert Redford. Brannaman was hired to keep the movie authentic from a horse training standpoint.

When Redford asked him for his honest opinion of key scenes in the book, Brannaman replied, "If you want to get it right for the people who know this approach to horses, I'd rewrite the horse scenes and start over." Redford took his advice. Dialogue was also reworked under Brannaman's direction to make it ring true to real cowboys.

At one point, the movie portrayed, in a dramatic way, a training technique that is often misunderstood: laying a horse down. Brannaman addresses this in his book.

> The scene became somewhat controversial because many people thought we were being unkind to the horse. Nothing could be farther from the truth. Laying a horse down is a technique I learned from my teachers, and I've used it over the years with horses that are really troubled. Under the right circumstances, it can save a horse's life by helping him into a frame of mind where he can trust the human. In many cases, this will be the first time in his life that he's been able to do so.
>
> . . . When the horse lies down and finds that your response is different from what he expected, you have an opportunity to bond that you never could have gotten any other way. Then, after the horse gets up, you have the further opportunity to accomplish things with him without much of the defensive behavior that has inhibited his ability to change.

When not traveling doing clinics, Buck Brannaman lives on his 1,200-acre ranch in Sheridan, Wyoming, with his wife, Mary, and their three daughters.

CRAIG CAMERON (1949–)

For most of Craig Cameron's horse-training career, he has been proving people wrong. For years, he has claimed that he can start any horse and have it riding quietly in about an hour. "That's impossible," the skeptics scoff beforehand. "You must have ridden that horse before," is what they say afterwards. He just smiles his trademark smile and shakes his head.

Craig Cameron is a true Texas-born and ranch-raised cowboy, and that is all he has ever wanted to be. Throughout the 1970s, he was a professional rodeo cowboy, specializing in riding bulls. He left rodeo to become a full-time horse trainer, making a name for himself at the Hickory Creek Ranch in Giddings, Texas, where his work with outlaw horses caught the public's attention. They wanted to see more, and that led him to develop the one-hour demonstration for which he is now known.

Craig Cameron grew up in an era when horses were "broken" and from his first exposure to these rough and dangerous methods, he knew they weren't right. He would be well into his thirties before he saw an alternative that really worked, however. "The first real horseman I met was Ray Hunt," he says. "He and Tom Dorrance taught me about working through understanding, adapting to each situation, and giving the horse the time he needs to develop his trust."

They also taught him how to use the horse's sense of self-preservation instead of fighting it. "You have to give a horse a reason to change,"

Craig Cameron. *(John Brasseaux)*

Cameron explains. "You have to allow him to get scared so he can find out he doesn't need to be scared." The trick, of course, is to keep both of you from getting hurt in the process. That's where feel, timing, and experience—things Craig Cameron possesses in abundance—come in.

As for the specific techniques he uses, they differ only slightly from those of his colleagues, but in his hands they are particularly effective. In the round pen, for instance, Cameron does not "free longe" the horse; he uses a rope or long lines to remain in contact with the horse at all times. To develop the respect of the horse, he practices "sending and bending." Bending is Cameron's term for disengaging the hindquarters of the horse. "When you control the hindquarters, you control the horse, whether on the ground or in the saddle," he says. He also makes masterful use of hobbles of various types to teach the horse patience and to yield to pressure.

Today, Craig Cameron still enjoys conducting demonstrations of colt starting and problem solving, and teaching his methods to others. Some of this is on the road, but a great deal takes place at his Double Horn Ranches in Bluff Dale, Texas, and Lincoln, New Mexico. Both ranches are steeped in

The press has called Craig Cameron's Cowboy Boot Camp the "ridingest clinic of all." *(John Brasseaux)*

the history of the Old West, offering guests a pleasant respite from the pressure and pace of modern life.

Most unique among Cameron's course offerings is his Cowboy Boot Camp, a four-day total immersion program that has riders in the saddle for up to eight hours a day. The analogy to military boot camp is tongue-in-cheek, but only slightly. The press calls this "the ridingest clinic of all." Inspections are conducted, merits and demerits are handed out, and Challenge Trails test the mettle of horse and rider. There is an air of structure and purpose at Cowboy Boot Camp that hails back to the days of the U.S. Cavalry. The biggest difference is that everyone is having fun and can opt out of any activity if they so choose. Cameron's purpose is to provide an "education vacation."

In a high-profile profession where egos often run rampant, Craig Cameron is remarkably humble, positive, and happy with the life he leads. He also makes no claim to having all the answers. "Horsemanship is an art form, a lifetime endeavor," he says. "You have to always be willing to change, whether you're a horse or a human."

His good nature and wry sense of humor have prompted comparisons to Will Rogers, the iconic American humorist, trick roper and cowboy. Cameron's first book, written with industry veteran Kathy Swan is called *Ride Smart: Improve Your Horsemanship Skills on the Ground and in the Saddle.*

Craig Cameron lives in Bluff Dale, Texas, with his wife, Dalene, and his stepson.

PETER CAMPBELL (1964–)

Peter Campbell doesn't hesitate a moment when asked who influenced his horsemanship most. "Tom Dorrance," is his answer. They met in 1988—

Campbell was twenty-four and Dorrance eighty—and four years later they partnered up for a series of horsemanship clinics in Canada. It was a rare and special opportunity to work in public with his mentor.

Peter Campbell was born on St. Patrick's Day 1964 in serene and scenic Banff, Alberta, Canada. To the south, America was reeling from President Kennedy's assassination four months earlier, and the country's military presence in Vietnam was beginning to divide the country. Then there was Beatlemania. Just weeks before, the British quartet had stormed America and seized the hearts and minds of the country's young. So much was happening so fast.

In the midst of all of this, Ray Hunt was busy learning all he could from Tom Dorrance, laying the groundwork for a revolution in horsemanship in which Peter Campbell would become an important player.

At the age of twelve, Peter Campbell developed an interest—some might call it an obsession—with

Peter Campbell. *(Peter Campbell Collection)*

horses. Over the next dozen years, he learned everything he could. He studied horsemanship and worked cattle horseback for ranches in Alberta, Nevada, California, and Oregon and for the renowned Gang Ranch in British Columbia. In 1988, he began conducting clinics in the United States and Canada.

For Campbell, it's important to let the horse know you understand his world. "I want the horse to understand he can have his self-preservation and still respond to what we're asking him to do," he explains. "The horse will tell us what we need to do to work with him if we only listen, understand, and feel as the horse does."

Today Campbell conducts more than thirty horsemanship clinics per year throughout Canada and the United States, and two exclusive clinics at his ranch in Wyoming. Besides the principles of natural horsemanship, Campbell likes to teach the *vaquero* horsemanship of California and is considered an expert on the California tradition of creating a bridle horse.

Peter Campbell regularly contributes his thoughts to magazines, and radio and television programs. He has produced a video series titled *Willing Partners.*

Campbell lives with his wife, Trina, in Wheatland, Wyoming.

LESLIE DESMOND (1954–)

Leslie Desmond's most influential mentor was a retired cavalryman who had lost his left leg in World War I. When Desmond met him, Ivan Taylor was in his mid-nineties and running a little stable on the banks of the Battenkill River behind the fairgrounds in Manchester, Vermont. Desmond's work with Taylor inspired her to release her first instructional videos on horsemanship for children.

Leslie Desmond grew up in rural New England, where she was exposed to traditional horsemanship. She competed in jumping and gymkhana events, and for twenty years coached people of all ages in riding and horse care. Along the way, she developed a reputation for being able to help troubled horses, and racehorses, ponies, draft horses, jumping horses, and various show horses were brought to her.

In 1990, she moved her riding school to California and released *Horsemanship Videos for Children,* a three-volume video series. This how-to series was well-received and was later renamed *American Horsemanship for Young and Old.*

In California, Leslie Desmond met master horseman Bill Dorrance who, in his mid-eighties, still operated a cattle ranch on Mount Toro near Salinas. Bill Dorrance, his younger brother Tom, and Ray Hunt were well known to serious horsemen in the area.

Although he still rode and roped with men half his age, Dorrance was beginning to think about his own mortality. The horsemanship school he

Leslie Desmond now teaches horsemanship in Sweden. *(Klaus Guni)*

had considered starting had never materialized, and now he was toying with the idea of a book.

"I'm happy to share what I've learned," he said. "When you've passed on, especially, it's always nice to leave something useful for others."

Desmond was in the right place at the right time, for both of them. "Thanks to Ivan, I was struck by the immense value of the knowledge that Bill Dorrance offered us," she explains. "It was an honor to be asked to write that book."

By the time *True Horsemanship Through Feel* was published in 1999, the public was ready for it and it made Desmond's name familiar to horsemen throughout the United States and Europe. Today, she contributes articles to horse publications on both continents and has students in America, Germany, Sweden, Norway, and Australia. When not globetrotting, she now resides in Sweden, home base of her company, Diamond Lu Productions.

BRYAN NEUBERT (1952–)

Bryan Neubert was born into a ranching family in the rugged mountains of Salinas, California. Horses were essential to the operation, and he started riding before he can remember. A horseman could hardly have picked a better place to grow up.

At fifteen, school friends invited Neubert to their neighboring ranch to do some roping. That day he met their dad, Bill Dorrance. Although forty-six years his senior, Dorrance eventually became Neubert's best friend, often calling on the telephone just to chat about the horses they were each working with.

Through Bill Dorrance, Neubert met Tom Dorrance and Ray Hunt before he was out of high school. Over the years, he worked for and with all three men on numerous colt starting projects. Neubert was an eager student and a hard worker, and the older men took to him, happily sharing their knowledge.

It was Tom Dorrance who taught him the most. "Tom was as close to my idea of a genius as any man I've met," Neubert recalls. "One thing he

Luke and Bryan Neubert, with Tom Dorrance, taking a break at a clinic. *(Bryan Neubert Collection)*

Bryan Neubert gentling a horse in 1996. *(Bryan Neubert Collection)*

always emphasized to me was the importance of straightness in a horse—moving straight and being straight mentally with you." It was all part of Dorrance's golden rule: Make your idea become the horse's idea. In 1976, Dorrance took on a sizable colt starting job, and Neubert offered to work with him for free just to learn what he could. Within a few weeks, the ranch owner was insisting on paying him.

Before his death, Tom Dorrance gave Neubert's children a little piece of history. It was his first Wade tree saddle, designed by Dorrance and built on a tree he'd obtained from his old friend Clifford Wade. The saddle was the prototype for those used by most of the natural horsemanship clinicians working today, including Neubert.

Public awareness of Bryan Neubert increased dramatically with a February 1996 feature in *Western Horseman* magazine titled "Taking the Wild Out of Mustangs." In 1997, he released what is still one of the best colt starting videos available, *Wild Horse Handling with Bryan Neubert.* Using a young, wild horse fresh off the Nevada range, the two-hour video shows in great detail the entire process of building a horse's trust and confidence, teaching it to tolerate handling by the human, mounting, and riding for the first time.

Neubert has also made a video on another of his passions, one he shared with his friend Bill Dorrance. *Introduction to Rawhide Braiding, "The Cowboy's Craft" with Bryan Neubert* is for the beginning or intermediate braider and teaches a method of making reins, romals, bosals, quirts, hackamores, reatas, and hobbles.

Today Bryan Neubert conducts clinics on colt starting, problem solving, working cattle, and advancing in performance. Still, he doesn't particularly enjoy the notoriety he has gained. "I just want to be the most effective cowboy I can be," he says.

Bryan Neubert lives in northeastern California with his wife, Patty. Their two sons and daughter all ride horses for a living.

LINDA PARELLI (1958–)

Before Pat Parelli came into her life in 1989, Linda Paterson was a talented, but frustrated dressage rider in Australia. A chance exposure to one of Parelli's videos in a tack store led to attending a clinic and the life-changing realization that the problems she was experiencing with her horses were because of her, not her horses. She became one of his top students and, in 1995, his wife.

A better match of complementary personalities and skills could hardly have been made. A superb rider whose joy in riding is contagious, Linda is also a fine writer with a great deal of experience in developing effective educational and motivational materials. Her ability to translate Pat's vision and enthusiasm into a concrete learning system accounts to a large extent for the speed with which the Parelli system is spreading around the world.

Linda Parelli was born in Singapore and was enamored with horses from the first moment she can remember. When she was twelve, her family moved to Australia, where she began her long love affair with riding and jumping. As an adult she was introduced to dressage and it became a special passion. At the time she met Pat Parelli, she was advancing in the competitive world with an ex-racehorse named Siren, but the gelding was becoming duller and duller. Her other horse, a hot Thoroughbred named Regalo, was out of control and dangerous. Her fateful visit to the tack store was to purchase yet another gadget to help her control her horses.

What she saw in the Parelli tape was the epitome of what she had dreamed of obtaining with her own horses: fiery performance and total harmony, wrapped up in one. She was hooked on the Parelli system from that moment forward and by 1993 had moved to the United States to become more involved with it.

As Linda learned, she wrote. Her notes would evolve over several years to become the backbone of the Parelli home study program, a multimedia, self-paced set of courses comprising three levels: Partnership, Harmony, and Refinement.

Today, Linda Parelli is both student and teacher. She is at Level 4 in Parelli Natural Horse-Man-Ship and is one of a handful of the more than 150 certified Parelli instructors in the world to hold a Parelli Five Star Premier rating. She is contributing original concepts to the

Linda Parelli. *(Photos by Coco)*

program, such as *fluidity*, a way of synchronizing with a horse by mimicking his movement, "getting all your joints moving," as she puts it. "Cantering with your arms" is one exercise she has developed to help riders get the idea.

Linda Parelli matches the colorful and entertaining style of her husband with an equally engaging clarity of speech and self-effacing grace. Far from causing intellectual whiplash, the cowboy and the lady together offer a cohesive and inspirational educational experience to dedicated students and casual observers alike.

And it's fun.

Linda Parelli has encouraging words for would-be horsemen: ". . . it doesn't take talent, it doesn't take bravery, and it doesn't take years to get there. It takes heart, desire, and access to the right educational system."

GaWaNi PONY BOY (1965–)

As a youngster, GaWaNi Pony Boy, a mixed blood Tsa-la-gi (Cherokee) Native American, was more interested in dirt bikes than the family horses. Later, at the Berklee College of Music, he pursued a dream of fame and fortune as a jazz pianist. Ultimately, however, teaching proved to be his calling.

Pony now teaches elementary and middle school children about Native American culture by touring the United States giving presentations in school gymnasiums. He appears dressed in full Native regalia, his long black hair trussed in the traditional manner, with an authentic teepee and pinto pony as visual aids. Hordes of kids sit cross-legged on hardwood floors, hanging on his every word.

At horse expos and clinics, and in his writing, Pony teaches horsemanship, combining the natural principles of the revolution with the philosophical grounding of his Native American roots. His first book, *Horse Follow Closely*, was a bestseller, an appealing marriage of his horsemanship philosophies and stunning photography by Gabrielle Boiselle. He followed it up with a children's version, *Out of the Saddle*, a collection of essays by women titled *Of Women and Horses*, and a series of frequently asked questions with his answers, the *My Horse* series.

The horse training principles he uses are easy enough to understand: Listen more. Talk less. Let the

GaWaNi Pony Boy. *(Barbara Simmons)*

horse teach you instead of trying to teach the horse. One of the first exercises Pony gives students is taken from an old Cheyenne custom for getting to know a new horse: simply spend time with him. A whole day, if possible, doing nothing, asking nothing, just observing the way the horse lives and acts. Learn what motivates him as an individual before asking him to do something for you. It is a surprisingly useful way to spend a day, something that most busy horse owners would never otherwise consider doing.

Articulate and sincere, Pony is also modest about his ability to train horses. "My strength is in teaching horse owners how to better understand horse behavior," he explains. He sees this as a gift he was meant to share.

Pony's training techniques, which he calls Relationship Training, have much in common with those of other natural horsemanship clinicians. He uses many of the same tools, including a round pen. Although he no longer wears his fringed and beaded Native costume at horse events, GaWaNi Pony Boy's teaching still retains a distinct flavor of its own and draws appreciative audiences in the United States and abroad.

GaWaNi is pronounced "gah-wah-NEE." It is a name that has been in his family for generations and means "he is speaking."

GaWaNi Pony Boy and his family live in St. Augustine, Florida, where he spends his spare time deep-sea fishing, SCUBA diving, and being a leader with Christian Surfers United States, a national ministry to the surf culture. He is also playing music again, this time strictly for his own enjoyment.

MARK RASHID (1956–)

Mark Rashid (pronounced "RASH-id") just might be the most sensitive cowboy you ever meet. Besides being a horseman, he is a guitarist, singer, and songwriter, and his writings on horsemanship have a highly personal storytelling style that has proven an ideal vehicle for communicating his original take on the horse–human relationship.

Rashid was born and raised in Fond du Lac, Wisconsin. At the age of ten, he met his mentor, a wise old horseman by the name of Walter Pruitt. For years, young Rashid pedaled his bicycle to Pruitt's modest farm to clean stalls and learn what

Mark Rashid. *(Mark Rashid Collection)*

he could about horses from the old man. And learn he did. Stories of this formative period in his life are sprinkled throughout his writing.

Later, Rashid got a great deal of hands-on horse-training experience working as a wrangler on Colorado guest ranches. "Dude string" horses presented a variety of challenges, but in time Rashid had them all working well and much more safely for the city slickers who rode them.

Mark Rashid is quiet and easy-going, a likable man with a handlebar mustache and a bit of an Old West air about him. He is fond of saying that he is "just trying to get along," but the fact is that he is actively moving the practice of horse psychology forward.

Rashid's concept of "Passive Leadership" challenges the usual view of man's role in the horse's world. Instead of seeking to become the alpha leader to your horse, Rashid recommends modeling your role after the "passive leader" in the herd.

The passive leader is the horse that leads by example. He does not force herd members to follow him. They follow because they want to. Nor does he challenge the alpha leader's position. In the dominance hierarchy of the herd, he falls somewhere in the middle. He avoids confrontation with other herd members by figuratively (and sometimes literally) sidestepping their advances. The passive leader is confident and independent and, like Rashid himself, just tries to get along. Buck, Rashid's own ranch horse and star of his latest book, led him to formulate this original concept.

Prolific and unusually talented as a writer, Rashid has produced four books: *Considering the Horse*, *A Good Horse Is Never a Bad Color*, *Horses Never Lie*, and *Life Lessons from a Ranch Horse*. He also has a video series, *Finding the Try*.

When not on the road teaching horsemanship, Mark Rashid lives in Estes Park, Colorado, with his wife, Wendy, and their three children.

DENNIS REIS (1958–)

Dennis Reis was born in Marin County, California. At the age of twelve, he was given a blood bay gelding by a friend of his father's. The horse bucked and bolted and embarrassed him. It wouldn't trailer and was almost too uncontrollable to ride, so the boy had to walk it to horse shows, with his father driving slowly behind, emergency flashers flashing. It mattered little. Young Dennis Reis had a horse, just like the TV cowboys he admired.

By the mid-1970s, Reis was putting his bucking experience to good use on the rodeo circuit. He twice made it to the National High School Rodeo Finals in bareback and saddle bronc riding, respectively, and became a member of the Professional Rodeo Cowboys Association at sixteen. He worked as a colt starter on a thoroughbred ranch and a trainer's assistant on a reining and cutting horse ranch.

Most importantly, he met an older cowboy who shared his deeper interest in what made horses tick. Pat Parelli had already made a name for himself in rodeo and had landed a job with a respected performance horse trainer, Troy Henry. Parelli shared with Reis what he was learning about psychological horse training, and the two teamed up for a trip to Australia.

Over the years that followed, Dennis Reis saw how Parelli began teaching what they had learned and he longed to do the same. But Reis was different. Where Parelli was gregarious, talkative, and seemed supremely confident, Reis was shy, introspective, and had a stuttering problem. It took several years before he felt ready to give it a try, but in 1989 Dennis Reis conducted his first clinic. To say he was nervous would be an understatement. "I was talking so fast," he relates, "I think I gave a ninety-day clinic in the first five minutes." With time, he developed his own style and his own following.

Today, Dennis Reis is an articulate and inspirational teacher of what he calls "Universal Horsemanship." He has a number of unique offerings. For instance, in 1997 he began an annual women-only extended clinic. "Many of my students are middle-aged women who absolutely love their horses but have fear issues," he explains. "This type of clinic allows me to focus better on their needs." Reis also puts on a "Day of the Horse" extravaganza at Las Vegas's Excalibur Hotel during the National Finals Rodeo each December. It gives rodeo attendees and Las Vegas conventioneers alike an eye-opening look at the power of natural horsemanship.

Featured prominently in recent years has been Ty

Dennis Reis. (*Dennis Reis Collection*)

Dennis Reis teaches a horse to flex laterally, a good exercise for body and mind. *(Dennis Reis Collection)*

Murray, the most successful rodeo cowboy of all time (nine individual world championships, seven all-round world championships). After retiring from rodeo and being exposed to Reis's work, the legendary cowboy came to the startling realization that he could not *ride*. He could stay on the back of a horse better than any human alive, but he turned to Reis for help in developing the finesse of a real rider.

The Reis team is working tirelessly to have the horse recognized nationally with its own day. The Day of the Horse is now a reality in California, and petitions are being circulated to make it a nationwide day of honor.

Dennis Reis is an example of how far someone truly dedicated to self-improvement can go. He sees the revolution in horsemanship, as so many of its participants do, as a revolution in the development of human potential. The horse is the vehicle, and the goal is a better human being as well as a better horse.

Dennis and his wife, Deborah, live at the Reis Ranch in Penngrove, California, where they conduct clinics and manage their rapidly growing teaching business.

WHY DIFFERENCES DON'T MATTER

Horse owners who become seriously involved in the revolution in horsemanship often become disciples of a single clinician. That's fine. All of the leading clinicians are competent horse trainers and effective teachers. Their techniques are based on scientifically correct behavior-shaping principles, and emulating a good teacher is one way for a student to learn.

The techniques these horsemen use do vary, however, and it is difficult for some students to keep these differences in perspective.

A clinician may use a particular technique because it is what he was taught by his teachers. If it worked well for him, he might not have tried other ways. Or maybe he tried many ways and concluded that this was the best. Or maybe it was just easier for him than other methods. Regardless of the reason, he perfected the technique and made it an effective way to accomplish a task. Now it is something that he thoroughly understands and can teach enthusiastically. Is it the only way to get the job done? No.

A clinician may also use a particular technique *just to be different*. For most of us, horses are a hobby, but for a professional clinician, it is his livelihood and he has to do whatever he can to make his product, which is his teaching, unique and valuable to the customer. If every clinician said and did things in exactly the same way, there would be little reason to pick one over another when it came time to spend your hard-earned money. You would also lose entirely the benefit of multiple perspectives.

The most successful and popular clinicians are very savvy businessmen, which is good for all of us because it ensures that the educational materials and equipment we need to progress in our own horsemanship will continue to be available to us. These clinicians are skilled at building their own followings, much as professional sports teams do. The logo-emblazoned products that many of them offer are calculated to aid in building a team mentality.

Again, that's fine. However, it is a mistake for the student to assume that other clinicians are wrong because their techniques are different.

It is an even bigger mistake for clinicians to foster this attitude of rivalry among their students. It is a disservice to the horse industry for clinicians to voice criticism of their colleagues, whether it is based on a sincere belief that their competitors are doing things incorrectly or because of jealousy, insecurity, or the need to elevate their personal egos.

It is very tempting to do, and sometimes it begins innocently enough. Students of horsemanship often want to hear why they should spend time and money on learning one approach instead of another. The clinician is sometimes put on the spot in front of a large audience and is asked to compare his methods to others.

It is analogous to saying to a car dealer, "Tell me why I should buy your Chevy instead of that Ford across the street." Students of horsemanship are consumers just the way car buyers are. The smart car salesman will respond, "That Ford is a fine automobile, but let me show you what makes this Chevy different." Not better. Just different. Both automobiles will get the buyer where he needs to go. In the end, it doesn't really matter which is chosen. It comes down to personal preference, and that is the way it should work when choosing a system of horsemanship to follow.

Let us take a brief aside to comment on another aspect of this rivalry issue: the Internet. Never before in the history of man has there been such a fertile environment for the planting and nurturing of information and misinformation, for spreading truths and half-truths and for generating support or bias on virtually any subject. On the Internet, any person with an opinion or an agenda (and time on his hands) can present himself as an expert on any subject.

When it comes to natural horsemanship, the threads, or ongoing discussions on a particular point, are laced with both valuable information and dangerous—and in some cases slanderous—untruths. Clinicians are seldom directly involved in these discussions but their views and methods are fodder for many a passionate interchange. The goings on in cyberspace are best taken with a grain of salt. The Internet may be the greatest communications advance of all time, but there are still imperfect human beings using it.

The point of all of these comments is that there isn't necessarily one way to do things correctly. There may be several ways, and what works best for one person, or on one horse, may not be best for another person or another horse.

Let's give some specific examples:

When starting a green colt in a snaffle, some clinicians use a martingale. Some do not. It doesn't matter. Either method, used correctly, can produce a well-reined horse.

Some teach lateral flexion by tying a rein to a stirrup. Others will tie a rein to the tail. Some will only teach it from the saddle and others from the ground. What matters is the end result, a horse that will flex laterally. None of the methods mentioned inflict pain. All are acceptably humane.

Some clinicians teach a horse to pick up a forefoot by pushing on the shoulder to get weight off the desired foot. Others pinch the chestnut, or the tendon of the lower leg. All of these methods work. It doesn't matter.

Clinton Anderson likes a rope halter. (Charles Hilton)

Monty Roberts prefers a flat halter. *(Monty Roberts Collection)*

Backing up can be taught from the ground or from the saddle. It can be taught by wiggling a long lead rope to create discomfort, by tapping on the chest, by causing the feet to move independently with the reins, or by combining any of the above. These are all acceptable methods. What matters is that the horse learns to back up.

Groundwork is begun in the halter. Most of the clinicians today are using rope "cowboy" halters, and even here opinions vary as to the exact style, texture, and design of the halter.

Curt Pate likes the halter to come up behind the jaw, and it works well for him. Other clinicians use a halter that does not come up behind the jaw.

Clinton Anderson wants two knots on the bridge of the nose to increase the sensation the horse will feel in these places.

Monty Roberts doesn't use a rope halter. He has designed a flat halter with different points of attachment so that it can serve as an ordinary halter or a "come-along" or even as a sidepull to teach the elements of reining. He calls it his Dually Schooling Halter.

Steve Edwards doesn't like to use a halter on green mules. Instead, he fashions a lariat into a "come-along."

All of the above work in the hands of their respective clinicians, and they work on similar principles. What matters is a well-halter-trained horse.

Some clinicians begin to ride in the snaffle, and the kind of snaffle varies with the clinician: plain, full-cheek, D-ring, Doctor Bristol, mullen mouth, etc. It doesn't matter. The choice depends upon the trainer and the horse. They all work if you know how to use them.

Stroking a horse is a form of positive reinforcement. *(Mark Rashid Collection)*

Some clinicians want the bit low in the mouth, while others want a wrinkle at the corner of the lips.

Most of the clinicians are actually starting colts in the halter, emphasizing to the student that turning, stopping, and backing can be conditioned without inflicting discomfort upon the mouth, and that the function of any bit, therefore, is simply as a signaling device.

Some clinicians combine leg aids with reining early on. Others delay introduction of seat and leg aids until later. The end result is what matters.

Some use spurs initially, others add them later, and occasionally spurs are not used at all. All agree, however, that the spur is a signaling device, not a weapon to be used for punishment.

All of the clinicians involved in natural horsemanship do a lot of rubbing and stroking to reinforce the horse positively. Some rub here. Others rub there. Some rub anywhere and everywhere. Most do not pat or slap the horse. Although most horses will tolerate some slapping, it does not aid in relaxing the horse as does stroking.

Some clinicians use food treats as rewards during training. Some use them only when training sessions are completed. Some feed treats by hand. Some put the treats in a feed bin or bucket. Some believe in never giving food treats in any way at any time.

Some clinicians twirl the end of a rope to get the horse to move forward. *(Charles Hilton)*

Some prefer to use a whirling rope to act as an extension of the arm and communicate one's intentions to the horse. Others use a flag, a stick, or a stick with a string attached. (Most do not call this a "whip" because of its inhumane connotation.) The sticks may be called "carrot sticks" or "handy sticks" or "wands" or "flags" or "canes" or just "sticks."

Most clinicians use the round pen. Some don't. It doesn't matter. It is how we communicate our intentions and how effectively we control the feet and movements of the horse that determines if it sees us as a leader.

In riding, some clinicians squeeze with both legs only when they want to encourage forward movement. Others use the same cue, with the bit held steady to block forward movement, as a way of asking for a backup. The horse can be quickly conditioned to any sensory signal. They learn, and they learn quickly.

Of all the techniques central to natural horsemanship, the one that may elicit the most disagreement is the initial bonding process. Ray Hunt and Buck Brannaman call it "hooking on." Monty Roberts calls it "Join-Up." Other clinicians give it no special name but most still perform some variation of it. The differences between them are not as important as the similarities and that they accomplish the desired result. All are based on the principle that controlling movement in the horse, either by causing it or by inhibiting it, and controlling the direction and the velocity of such movement, results in dominance. This is the way horses establish which horse leads and which horses follow. Horses, being natural followers of herd leaders in order to stay alive in the wild, do indeed "hook on" to whatever

Buck Brannaman drives horses away with assertive body language. *(Emily Kitching)*

When Brannaman relaxes his body, the horses stop running and one seems ready to "hook on." *(Emily Kitching)*

creature they come to regard as a leader. Moreover, the relationship increases in intensity as the subordinate horse learns that being close to the leader ensures peace and comfort, and therefore increases its desire to "join up" with the leader.

Once that relationship is established, the skillful trainer enhances it. The more the horse is "hooked on" and "joined up," the easier it is for the person to control its movements. The more the movements are controlled, the more respect the horse will develop for the person. The result is achievement of that elusive goal: *complete respect devoid of fear.*

But a student seldom has anything approaching the skill of the experienced trainer. He has difficulty seeing and understanding the horse's responses, reacting quickly enough with the correct level of energy, and using his tools in a coordinated and effective way. The result in such cases is frequently frustration, anger, fear, impatience, and aggression, all natural human reactions, and all counterproductive in building a relationship with a horse.

Lapses of attention or uncoordinated or inappropriate responses interfere with the establishment of conditioned (trained) responses. If we continue pressure when immediate relief from pressure is called for, the lesson is spoiled. Conversely, when pressure is needed, and we relax the pressure, the lesson is again spoiled.

This is *why* so many people who can't do what the clinicians, with their experienced and disciplined responses do, end up thinking that the method doesn't work, or that it only works for the teacher, or that the teacher has some mystical, mysterious gift of influencing horse behavior.

It is the precise method of obtaining "Join-Up" or "Hooking On" or "Bonding" or "Partnership" or whatever you want to call it that causes some clinicians to most vociferously condemn others.

Remember, control of motion can be accomplished in a variety of ways.

You can *cause* it rapidly, in a round pen, as Monty Roberts does, and the horse will soon begin to demonstrate submissive signals. Roberts ignores these until the horse has exhausted its biological "flight distance" and is pleading for leadership. He then abruptly assumes a completely nonthreatening posture, draws the horse to him, strokes it to comfort it, and the horse then wants to follow him anywhere. With a halter-broke but otherwise green colt this usually takes five to ten minutes.

Many other clinicians modify this procedure, usually in a round pen, by responding to the early submissive signals the horse gives by removing the pressure, and then resuming it when the horse wants to leave or takes its attention off of the clinician.

This method takes longer, but the end result is the same. The horse bonds with the human and wants to follow that leader. Which method is superior?

It doesn't matter! Not to the horse!

Once it decides that with the leader is the safest place to be, whether that took five minutes or an entire day, the relationship is established.

Moreover, exactly the same results can be obtained by *preventing* movement. Hence the effectiveness of hobbles of the one, two, or three-legged variety.

In the Pacific Northwest, certain tribes of Native Americans start colts by driving them into deep water and, while they are swimming, transferring to their backs from a trained saddle horse. Horses can't run away while swimming. They come ashore in a submissive state of mind looking for leadership.

During the closing years of the twentieth century, a very controversial method, the isolation chute, was introduced as a means of gentling captured mustangs. The horses were run into a chute with their head extending through an opening at one end. Then sand was poured into the chute, completely submerging the mustang except for its protruding head. Later, wheat was substituted for the sand because it was lighter and less likely to interfere with the horse's respiration. Completely immobilized, the horse's head was then handled, rubbed, and stroked. When the horse was released from the chute, a definite transformation had taken place. The formerly frightened and wild mustang was now subdued and quiet. Submission had occurred, but the horse still had to be trained.

Obviously some of the methods of inhibiting movement are more extreme than others. Immobilizing one leg is less traumatic than dropping a horse to its knees or completely immobilizing it on its side. The enlightened concept is to use the *least* pressure necessary to obtain the desired result, even though it is often human nature to seek the method requiring the most pressure.

Most horses will respond to conservative means of controlling movement. Yes, a horse can be made to move by striking it forcefully with a whip, but simply shaking a stick or rope will usually suffice.

Similarly, restraining one leg will produce a submissive attitude in most horses relatively quickly. It is usually not necessary to cast them and render them helpless on the ground.

Each clinician should use whatever method works best for him or her and teach that method, but never close the mind to an alternative.

Unquestionably, some methods are superior, especially in the hands of an experienced advocate, but that doesn't mean that somebody else's method is *wrong*.

There are many traditional methods that *are* wrong in the sense that they are based upon unnecessary coercion and the use of unjustifiable force, but the clinicians involved in this revolution are all using technically correct methods which utilize minimum coercion and end up with a horse that is gentle, obedient, respectful, but not fearful.

These clinicians are worthy of our respect. Every one of them has something to offer, and the wise student will take what he can from each, weave his own tapestry of understanding and technique, and put in the hands-on time to become proficient with it. In doing so, he will become his own horseman just as each of the clinicians has. Instead of looking for things to criticize, we urge the reader to look for things to embrace.

CHAPTER 5

WHY NOW?

THE REVOLUTION IN HORSEMANSHIP that occurred during the final decades of the twentieth century was remarkable not only for how it redefined the horse–human relationship, but also for the fact that it occurred when it did.

The horse was no longer key to man's survival, as it had been for thousands of years. Since the introduction of the internal-combustion engine, horse populations had been steadily decreasing and generations of city dwellers had little or no experience with horses. In a sense, the horse had become irrelevant to modern human life.

Even more remarkable, this abrupt change in long-established, traditional methods of handling horses was not introduced by academic behavioral scientists, not by pontificating philosophers or clergymen, not by the disciples of classical European horsemanship indoctrinated with the lore and experience of centuries, but by a few cowboys from the northwestern United States.

Initial skepticism toward this revolution by those few cowboys' own contemporaries, by English horsemen, by dressage aficionados, and especially, by other nations' horsemen, has rapidly diminished.

There is no really satisfactory name for the kind of horsemanship the revolution has introduced. The various clinicians teaching it have labeled it as they have personally seen fit, much the way manufacturers brand their products. A few examples include "resistance free horsemanship," "universal horsemanship," "new age horsemanship," "progressive horsemanship," "downunder horsemanship," "renaissance horsemanship," "outside-the-box horsemanship," and "natural horsemanship."

The last one has caught on most widely around the world, and although all of these labels are both descriptive and appropriate, natural horsemanship is the most well known.

Just what does natural horsemanship mean? From whose point of view is this supposed to be natural? The kind of horsemanship we are talking about isn't natural to mankind. Not at all! We must be *taught* these methods, and only those among us who are most dedicated, most eager to learn, most open-minded, and most willing and able to resist our normal human emotions will be able to master the methods. No, natural horsemanship is meant to be natural for the horse. And therein lies its efficiency.

Today we can all learn what was once known only to the exceptional horseman: how to communicate with another species using the means of communication that that species has been genetically endowed with. We can speak to the horse in a language he understands and thereby maximize the relationship between horse and human. We can get the horse to do what we want him to do, not because he is forced to do so, but because he wants to.

But why now? Why didn't this happen a century ago when our society had become totally dependent upon horsepower for transportation, for agriculture, for commerce, and for military might? Why did it wait until the waning years of the twentieth century and the dawn of the twenty-first, when the horse had been relegated, for the most part, to the role of a recreational animal in prosperous, industrialized nations? And why did it catch on in those nations, such as the United States, Canada, Western Europe, Australia, and New Zealand, but make only meager inroads into Second and Third World nations?

There are several factors involved.

BEHAVIOR AS A FIELD OF STUDY

The science of psychology—the study of behavior—has become accepted by society at large. Unlike the disciplines of anatomy and physiology, which have been studied for millennia, the scientific study of behavior is but a century old, and a majority of the most significant aspects of behavioral science have been understood only in quite recent times. Early in the twentieth century, most physicians received no training in psychology. Only recently have some veterinary schools included animal behavior in their curricula.

In generations past, most people were embarrassed to reveal that they had received psychological counseling or therapy. What we now call Post-Traumatic Stress Syndrome in combat-weary soldiers was known as "shell shock" in World War I and "battle fatigue" in World War II to make it less humiliating for soldiers to receive the help they needed. But by the late twentieth century, treatment for mental issues was commonplace and openly discussed. Prozac®, the anti-depression drug, became one of the most widely prescribed medications in modern times.

Science now recognizes that much behavior is preprogrammed in the DNA of each animal species, and that other behaviors are the result of learning—of environmental experiences. The link between mental state and behavior in all species has become much better understood, and a whole technology of behavior shaping has been discovered.

EDUCATION

Most horse owners today are educated. That wasn't true a century ago when a majority of those who worked with horses had little education. Indeed, many were illiterate, a situation that still exists in many parts of the world, and abusive horsemanship is commonplace where ignorance reigns.

Education opens one's eyes to how little one really knows and how much more there is to learn. It is a humbling experience. In fact, humility and open-mindedness about new ideas are directly proportional to one's knowledge and education. It is only the ignorant person who believes he knows it all.

Today's horse owners are more receptive to new ideas because they are more educated to begin with and are interested in continuing their growth.

THE INFORMATION EXPLOSION

Information today is disseminated instantly, whereas in previous times it may have taken months or years for new ideas to reach the public. Today's horse owners read. They subscribe to magazines. They are on the Internet. They avidly buy videotapes, watch televised horse programs, and listen to horse radio. Most importantly, the clinicians that are furthering this revolution are traveling all over the world, taking the information directly to the people. The horse-owning public sees what they do, marvels at it, and wants to learn *how* to do it.

Today any individual who really wants this information has virtually instantaneous access to it and can be assured that it is current. Information is a valued commodity today and is marketed as such. Competition exists between sources, and quality control is paramount. It is no longer a challenge to get information quickly. The challenge now becomes applying it slowly, for the horse does not operate at the same fast pace that technology does.

THE HORSEWOMAN

Possibly the most significant factor in the speed with which this revolution has spread is the fact that, for the first time in human history, women dominate the horse industry. The clinicians who pioneered this movement will tell you that without the prevalence of women in their audiences, they probably could not have stayed in business.

Historically, women have had an inconsequential role in horsemanship. Dealing with horses was the man's job, just as cooking and cleaning fell to the woman. During the nineteenth century, some women began to ride for recreation but they were from the upper strata of society where such pleasures were affordable (and they usually rode sidesaddle). Other than that, with rare exceptions throughout history, a woman rode as a passenger and whenever possible, in a carriage of some sort. The emancipation of women in the twentieth century combined with an elevated standard of living to create what is now a very common phenomenon—the female pleasure rider.

Women are more involved in horsemanship now than at any time in history. Clinician Linda Parelli fields questions. *(Photos by Coco)*

If this has been fortuitous for the equine industry—those who sell tack and riding habit, horses, horseshoes, and horse products—it has been a *blessing* to the horse. Why? Because most women are nurturing by nature and try to avoid conflict. They are less aggressive than most men, less intimidating in their stance, speech, or movements, and less inhibited about crooning to or petting animals. These are exactly the qualities to which horses are most responsive.

Yet, these qualities, which are less intimidating to the horse and less likely to precipitate the desire for flight, can also cause the horse to be less respectful and to feel dominant to the woman.

Perhaps this is the reason that the clinicians who began this revolution were all men. As time goes on and more women master the techniques, however, female natural horsemanship clinicians are becoming more common. Linda Parelli, Lee Smith, Julie Goodnight, Karen Scholl, Tammy Yost-Wilden, Leslie Desmond, and Australia's Wrangler Jayne Glenn are but a few.

Out of all this we have become aware of what is required to become a master horseman, a person who can obtain that ideal relationship between horse and human: total respect and no fear. Note the leading clinicians: See how kind they are to the horse, how considerate, how patient. The horse does not fear them. But note, too, how *persistent* they are, how *assertive*, how effectively they control the horse's movement. From this they gain respect. Complete respect. Zero fear.

Famed nineteenth-century horse tamer Dennis Magner summed up the requirements of a good horseman this way: "the delicacy of touch and feeling of a woman, the eye of an eagle, the courage of a lion, and the hang-on pluck of a bull-dog."

In modern parlance, you might say that the ideal horseman is a man who is in touch with his feminine side or a woman who is in touch with her masculine side. Both masculine and feminine traits are needed for effective communication.

DECREASED ACCEPTANCE OF VIOLENCE

Another reason that the revolution in horsemanship occurred when it did is that most people were tired of violence. In the latter third of the twentieth century, violence was in our faces like never before. Wars, assassinations, rapes, random murders, prison riots, psychopaths, domestic violence, and drive-by shootings were crammed down American throats nightly from the moment the age of television began, first in black and white and then in color. Was it a more violent time for mankind? Absolutely not. But never before did the violence seem so close at hand, so personal. Images from the war in Vietnam especially were relentless and inescapable, as were the calls for peace, love, and harmony. Horses were an escape from the violence that was all around Americans, and it was only natural that horse lovers would be drawn to nonviolent training methods.

THE URBANIZATION OF SOCIETY

In 1923, a quarter of the American population lived on farms. Today, the figure is less than 2 percent. Moreover, the urban population no longer resides in smaller cities, but in megalopolises. The early twentieth century saw only one megacity in the United States, New York. Now there are dozens. Many urban dwellers are so far removed from the soil and from animal life that they completely lack a perspective of nature and the cycle of life and death that defines it. Children's textbooks, even in the cities, once described farm animals and farm life. Today it is assumed that children can no longer relate to such subjects. Millions of children grow up with a perception of animal life as it is depicted in cartoons, anthropomorphically, with the animals thinking and talking and behaving in a human-like manner. We have endowed even the urban house pet, the dog or cat, with a surrogate human role.

Veterinarians are keenly aware that most pets today, unlike those in previous generations, have become surrogate people: children, companions, partners, slaves, and occasionally masters. The horse, once primarily a beast of burden, a transportation machine, has now become primarily a companion animal, fulfilling a completely different role in the human psyche. It is inconceivable for many horse lovers today to treat a horse as an object. As a society, we have become ready for the revolution in horsemanship, wherein the horse is treated with respect, consideration, and compassion.

THE RELATIONSHIP

Riding or driving is no longer the overwhelming object of horsemanship. The *relationship* with the horse is for many people the most important thing, and they are accordingly very receptive to training approaches which emphasize this aspect.

According to Eitan Beth-Halachmy, a senior California clinician and the founder of Cowboy Dressage, many horse owners—perhaps a majority—

care little about lead changes and collection. He observes that trailer loading, ground manners, leading, and standing tied quietly and compliantly are more important to such people. Their riding is often limited to simply enjoying the out-of-doors on occasional quiet trail rides, and all they need is a gentle, well-mannered, and trustworthy mount.

Beth-Halachmy, a rancher who immigrated to the United States from Israel decades ago, has also observed that for those horse owners who do compete in horse shows, endurance racing, rodeo, and other equine sports, a growing cultural change in American society affects their interest. The drive for money and ego gratification increases their competitiveness. We see this not only in equine sports but also in all kinds of sports and recreational activities, even in Little League and certainly in college and professional sports. Many competitors, therefore, are not satisfied with merely competing; they want to *win*, and they willingly spend the

For many modern horse owners, it's all about the relationship. *(Shawna Karrasch Collection)*

money and time necessary to improve their horsemanship and give them a competitive edge. Attending natural horsemanship clinics, they hope, will give them that advantage.

Conversely, the growing corruption in the sport of showing horses has turned off many former competitors who have found what they consider to be a better outlet for their desire to do things with their horses; namely, getting deeply involved in natural horsemanship. They attend clinics, buy videotapes, books, and horse magazines, and join clubs and groups dedicated to this kind of horsemanship. Their passion leads to their buying logo clothing and other items to signal their involvement, and many clinicians sell such items to help finance their businesses and foster further followers.

The corruption within the horse shows due to politics is not the only factor that has discouraged many from participating in showing, a traditional sport that is inherently conceived to improve the quality of horses bred and the techniques used in training. More important to an increasing percentage of horse owners, many of whom own show-quality horses, are the often brutal and sometimes illegal practices imposed upon show horses. Unfortunately, such practices exist in all of the show disciplines.

Even though many show people are quick to condemn such practices in other disciplines, they often ignore equally unsavory practices in their own backyards. Some examples of things that drive people away from showing horses are as follows:

The soring of Tennessee Walking Horses is designed to generate more exaggerated "action" or leg movement from these magnificent show horses by making it painful for their feet to touch the ground. Federal regulations outlaw this sadistic practice, but the appreciative roar of a show crowd when they see the "Big Lick" and the financial incentives that go along with pleasing the public have kept the practice alive.

American Saddlebreds are still mercilessly shod for increased leg action. Atropine, a dilating drug, is often used in the eyes to give them a large, dark, and soft look at the expense of the horse's ability to focus. Ginger is often applied to the anus, causing a temporary irritation and the desire to lift and carry the tail higher than normal.

Many of these practices have spilled over into other breeds such as the Morgan, which is also shown in this style of competition.

Hunters and jumpers are still "poled" over jumps by some trainers. The horse is rapped on the ankles as it goes over a jump to teach it to jump higher. The poles used sometimes have tacks on them.

Excessive mouth contact, to a brutal degree, is very common in the dressage world.

Reining horse trainers wanting quick results have been known to use electric reins, barbed wire reins, and handshake buzzers. One even used a live chicken to flog the horse's neck when teaching the turn.

The "peanut roller" gaits of Western pleasure horses are a gross caricature of the working stock horse's way of traveling. Producing it involves abusive training techniques, and the excessive weight upon the forehand due to the lowered head position is, according to respected veterinarians, a major contributor to forelimb lameness. Fortunately, changes are being made in Western pleasure in direct response to public disgust with these practices.

ANIMAL RIGHTS ACTIVISM

The Animal Rights Movement has caused a change in the way we as a society regard the use of all animals. Granted, there is a fanatical fringe to this movement, typified by such organizations as PETA (People for the Ethical Treatment of Animals) who seem to oppose almost *any* use of animals by humans, but the fact remains that these radical activists have caused needed changes in our society. There were and still are many abusive practices in farming, circuses, zoos, animal shows, scientific laboratories, and breeding kennels.

Animal rights groups have aroused public cognizance of such problems, often by exaggerating and even lying to get their points across. Hosts of laws have been passed in recent decades to enforce animal welfare regulations. Some of these regulations are illogical and represent a backlash to improper practices being allowed to flourish for generations.

The Animal Rights Movement was probably fostered by the much older Human Rights Movement, which has been around in spirit since 1215, when King John of England signed the Magna Carta. Worldwide, legislation against human rights violations has become common, protecting children, women, minorities, and the disabled. So, we see *cultural* changes that were once unimaginable—slavery was legal in the United States only a century and a half ago—and are now accepted as a matter of course.

The same attitude now prevails in our society toward animals. Child and wife beating, once commonplace, are now illegal. So is animal beating. What we accept as "common sense" or "common decency" was, not too long ago, a crazy idea. The world does change, however slowly. We no longer put people in stocks or flog them as punishment. We don't burn people at the stake for heresy or adultery, at least not in *our* society. These cultural

The revolution in horsemanship has encouraged some riders to enter horse shows. *(Heidi Nyland)*

changes mark the advances in a moral society, and compassion toward animals is part of the change.

Let us leave the question of whether animals actually have "rights" for others to debate. Activists who support that belief have helped to effect positive change in our treatment of animals, including horses, and that must be recognized as one of the underlying reasons the revolution in horsemanship occurred when it did.

Many of the reasons we have listed for the belated onset of the revolution in horsemanship are interrelated. Thus, the educational level of today's typical horse owner and the information explosion are connected. The increasing female dominance of the horse industry, too, is intimately related to society's new commitment to animal welfare.

In an opposite manner, some horse people are drawn to natural horsemanship because they think it will enhance their chances of winning in competitive equine sports, whereas others are drawn to it as a kinder and gentler substitute for those very same activities.

CHAPTER 6

WHY IT WORKS
AND WHY IT'S BETTER

IN THE PREVIOUS CHAPTER, we learned why the revolution in horsemanship occurred when it did. One important reason was the increased acceptance of behavior as a field of study. In this chapter, we'll take a closer look at equine behavior and discover why natural horsemanship works so well and is superior to many other approaches.

UNDERSTANDING THE HORSE'S MIND

The behavior of any individual is determined by two factors. There are genetically predetermined behaviors that are present at birth, and there are behaviors that are the result of learning experiences which occur throughout life, but which are particularly profound early in life.

We'll first consider the genetic behaviors of the horse, those that are fixed in the DNA. Later we will explore the behaviors that result from learning *after* the birth experience.

Genetically endowed behaviors are the result of natural selection. Like anatomy (the *shape* of an individual) and physiology (the *function* of that individual), behavior is essential for any organism to cope with the habitat in which it finds itself.

Take the dolphin, for example. Once a land mammal, it had to adapt to a water habitat. Anatomically, it did this by assuming a fish-like shape. Physiologically, it had to adapt to swimming underwater for long periods of time without breathing and to withstanding pressure at great depths. It also had to develop a unique acoustical system in order to communicate and to hunt for food beneath the surface.

Similarly, the dolphin's *behavior* had to conform to the needs of living in an aqueous environment.

The horse, originally a small, multi-toed, swamp-dwelling creature, also had to adapt to a changing environment as rain forests dried out and converted to drier grasslands. When the habitat changes, the things that live in it must adapt to the changes or suffer extinction. The reason so many species are endangered today is because the massive population of human beings on Earth, by far the most abundant large mammal to have ever lived, is altering the environment in many ways. Certain species, being highly adaptable, can survive these changes. Thus, the crow, the coyote, the English sparrow, the rat, and the cockroach thrive, whereas other species are threatened with extinction.

The horse adapted well. It learned to graze on the prairies rather than browse on leaves in the forests. It became perpetually aware of the predators that loved to eat horses. As the modern horse evolved, it was not only surrounded by such present-day predators as the wolf, the cougar, and the jaguar, but by myriad others such as the saber-toothed tiger, the dire wolf, the cave bear, and lions larger than today's African variety. Acute awareness, strength in numbers, a willingness to follow an experienced and competent leader, and, above all, speed allowed the horse to survive in its natural habitat.

Horses, present on this planet for much longer than our own species, even survived domestication. Only about a dozen species of mammals have ever been successfully domesticated by man, and none has been as challenged as the horse by its conqueror.

Horses often have been regarded by mankind as stupid creatures; beautiful, swift, useful, strong, but stupid. This impression has been due to differences between the species. Yet those differences are nature's wisdom.

There are ten distinct characteristics of the horse's mindset and associated behavior that must be appreciated if we are really to understand this creature. Some of these are very different from those in our own species. This is the reason that mankind has had difficulty in establishing optimum communication methods with horses, and why it has taken so long for this revolution in horsemanship to occur.

Characteristic #1: The Horse Runs When Frightened

There are a variety of methods of defense. One can fight, or one can run away. One may hide, or even play dead. The armadillo and the tortoise have primary defense strategies built into their anatomies, but so does every other creature. Consider the skunk, the porcupine, the rhinoceros, and the scorpion. The anatomy of every creature reveals its ultimate defense mechanism. The teeth of the wolf or the tiger, the horns of the buffalo or the yak, the fangs of the viper, and the coloration of the sage hen all reveal means of survival.

When we look at the horse, we see a running machine. The horse sprints to stay alive, and its anatomy, its physiology, and its behavior are all designed to facilitate survival by running away. The horse's cardiovascular system, its musculoskeletal system, its feet, and its nervous system are all designed to facilitate flight.

It is difficult for us to identify with this characteristic of the horse, because we are not flight creatures. Indeed, humans are relatively slow-moving creatures. As a predatory species, our speed did not contribute to our hunting efficiency, nor did it serve to protect us against other carnivorous predators. It was our superior brains and tool-making skills that enabled us to survive.

The flightiness of the horse is so basic to its character that the other nine behavioral characteristics all exist because it is a flight animal—the only domestic animal whose primary defense in the wild state is flight. Lacking horns or other weapons, the horse always depends upon flight to survive a life-or-death situation. Yes, horses can kick, strike, and bite, but unlike other prey species such as sheep, goats, and cattle, whose horns in the wild serve as their ultimate weapons, the horse runs.

The flightiness of the horse is the reason it so often injures itself or others. When frightened, run! Run first, and ask questions later, if at all.

Those of us who do not understand the horse's true nature might ascribe this flightiness to stupidity. Horses run through barbed wire fences, into automobiles, and off cliffs, so they must be stupid, right?

We forget that in the horse's natural habitat, there were no such objects. They lived on open grassy plains. No cars. No fences. No trains. No box stalls. No bulls to fight or urban crowds to subdue. No cavalry charges, and no overloaded wagons.

Yet, ironically, it is the horse's flightiness that has made it so useful to us because we have harnessed that instinct and directed it down the racetrack, into the harness collar, after the steer, over fences, around barrels, against the enemy, through the buffalo herd, up mountains, and around the chariot course.

Because the art and science of horsemanship involves Equidae other than horses, a few words about related species' behavior is appropriate here.

The ass, also known as the donkey, or in Spanish as the *burro*, has been domesticated for thousands of years. It may surprise readers that this species and other equines originating in the Old World such as the zebra and the onager are probably more highly evolved species than is the horse. Horses, after all, developed in North America, and took eons to migrate to other continents by way of the Bering land bridge. Examination of the anatomy of these related species actually shows them to be even more adapted to a foraging environment than is the horse. They are less susceptible to most (but not all) of the afflictions of horses. The coloration of the zebra is certainly a highly specialized and late development designed to confuse the vision of a predator when the animals are in close groups.

The zebra has been a difficult animal to tame, but not an impossible one by any means. In recent years, zebra foals have been successfully imprinted by humans and trained immediately after foaling, a subject that will be discussed later. Zebra have been trained to ride throughout history, but their temperament is notoriously refractory.

Recently, zebra hybrids have become popular. Zebra are crossed with either horses or donkeys, and the offspring are known, unofficially, as "zorses" or "zedonks." Attractive animals, their resistant personalities make them more novelty than practical mount.

Most species of wild asses evolved in mountainous terrain. One exception is the Somali Wild Ass, which evolved on arid plains and can run at racehorse speed.

Therefore, the blind flightiness of the horse is not typical of ass behavior. When asses sense danger, they decide among three options: to flee like a horse, to stay put because they feel safe where they are and refuse to move (hence the reputation for stubbornness), or to attack (hence the value of burros to protect sheep against smaller predators like coyotes or stray dogs). They are therefore decision-making, judgmental creatures and much less reactive than is the horse.

When jackasses are bred to mares to produce mules, or vice versa, to produce hinnies, the resultant hybrids inherit their anatomy, physiology, and behavior from either or both parents.

Thus, the typically reduced reactivity or flightiness of mules makes them less inclined to run at top speed for us (although there are notable exceptions), seemingly wiser, and hardier due to hybrid vigor. They are less inclined to the blind flightiness and panic of horses, but their canniness and ability to make choices and decisions creates a different set of problems for the horseman to solve. It is the donkey's reduced flightiness that gives mules the behavior that is different from typical horse behavior. There is a profound observation in the mule industry: Mules *must* be trained the way horses *should* be trained.

Nowhere has the revolution in horsemanship been received more warmly and enthusiastically than in the rapidly growing American mule industry. We will discuss mule training in greater detail later.

Characteristic #2: The Horse Is Highly Perceptive

Because it is a flight creature, the horse must be more aware of its surroundings than prey species equipped with other kinds of effective defenses. The rhinoceros, for example, may serve as prey for the hungry lion. Its eyesight is notoriously poor, but armed as it is with a formidable weapon—its horn—and possessing a very aggressive disposition, it doesn't need especially keen eyesight. It and other herbivorous species may serve as prey, but that doesn't mean that they lack aggression or are not extremely dangerous. For instance, most hunters regard the plant-eating Cape buffalo as Africa's most dangerous game species, even more dangerous than the predatory, meat-eating lion. Among domestic animals, *none* compares in ferocity with the Spanish fighting bull. Even the young heifers of that breed will attack unprovoked.

But a flighty animal like the horse or the zebra must detect danger early enough to escape through flight.

Horses possess the same five senses we do, that of sight, smell, hearing, taste, and touch, but the senses differ from ours. It is important that we understand the differences. The hearing of horses is much more acute than ours. Like dogs, horses can hear a range of sound beyond that which can be heard by humans. Moreover, they have movable pinnae (the external part of the ear) that aid in locating the source of sound. Thus, horses hear things we cannot, and they react to them, often with flight.

Our sense of smell is exceedingly weak. How can we possibly identify with a dog, which can smell the ground and know who was there an hour ago? Horses, too, have

Horses are extremely perceptive, but their senses differ from ours. *(Heidi Nyland)*

very good olfactory powers and even possess an olfactory organ that we do not. They have, in their mouth, a vomeronasal organ, also known as the Organ of Jacobson. It is an accessory olfactory organ, connecting with the nasal cavity. This is why horses exhibit the Flehmen response (lifting their upper lip to enhance their sense of smell). It adds to their olfactory powers. Horses smell things that we don't, and they react accordingly.

The tactile sense of the horse bears special mention. We have all seen horses react to a fly landing on its hair—not its skin, but its hair. Imagine how sensitive those nerve endings must be to detect such a minor stimulus. The horse has this exquisite sense of touch over its entire body surface. No wonder well-trained horses can detect the slightest change in seat or body position of a rider, even through a saddle and pad. Horses are so sensitive that they can detect the proprioceptive (balance) changes a rider's body unconsciously makes if the rider's visual focus changes, even if the rider makes no conscious body movements. In other words, if the rider looks to one side, even without moving the head, the rider's body will automatically make proprioceptive changes anticipating a move in that direction *and the horse will feel it*. That's why riders are instructed to maintain visual focus when they are riding, such as looking to the next jump or fixing the eyes on the cow when cutting.

Horses sometimes panic at tactile stimuli to which they have not been desensitized, such as the touch of a curry comb, the weight of a saddle, the pressure of a girth, or the touch of a spur. Reacting quickly to unfamiliar stimuli of any kind is what has kept the horse extant for so many years.

The eyesight of horses is very different from our own, and it often leads us to misunderstand their reactions to visual stimuli.

We have excellent color vision. Horses do not, seeing colors more or less in pastel shades. On the other hand, the horse can see very well at night. It must—big cats usually hunt when the sun goes down. Humans don't need good night vision—we are supposed to sit around a fire in a cave at night.

Moreover, the horse's eye can detect movement more efficiently than ours can. A slight movement in the grass may mean approaching death. That's why horses get nervous on windy days. Everything is moving.

The human eye has excellent powers of accommodation due to its highly elastic lens. Even if you don't move your head, the lenses of your eyes will change shape as you look from a near object to a faraway one.

The horse has a less elastic lens than we do. In order to change focus it has to alter its head position. When a horse is grazing, its eyes are focused on the grass in front of it. Then, if it hears a suspicious sound, it must elevate its head in order to focus on infinity. This serves three purposes. It is fast: when the horse whips its head up, the change in focus is instantaneous; there is no one- or two-second delay which may cost it its life. The movement also alarms the other horses nearby. Finally, with the head up, the horse is in a position to take flight if necessary.

Similarly, when a horse is being ridden, its eyes are focused on what is directly in front of it. As it approaches water, mud, or a log, the horse would like to be able to lower its head to see what it will be stepping in or over, which a good rider will allow.

Horses have very large and prominent eyes. Their eyes are placed laterally, near the sides of their heads, as in other prey species such as deer, sheep, antelope, cattle, rabbits, ducks, geese, and chickens. This gives them a very wide field of vision, and excellent peripheral vision. When grazing, horses have blind spots only directly in front and directly behind them, but by moving the muzzle from one side to the other just a little bit, they can see everything around them.

This wide field of vision comes at a cost, however. Because the horse's eyes are set laterally, it does not have good depth perception. It does have some straight ahead, but not compared with ours. That's why horses are often confused and intimidated by a shallow ditch or stream.

Since their eyes are placed laterally, each eye sends a separate message to the brain. This is the reason a horse may see something with the left eye and be unafraid of it, yet panic when it comes into view on the right side. This is a common phenomenon. It is discussed later in this book under "cellular compartmentation."

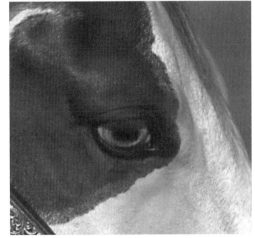

Predatory species—those that must hunt prey—have their eyes placed in front of their heads; dogs, cats, owls, hawks, and humans have frontal vision. Both eyes see the same thing and send the same slightly overlapping picture to the brain. This binocular (two-eyed) stereoscopic (overlapping) vision gives excellent depth perception, needed by hunters of all species. A hawk dropping down on a rodent needs accurate depth perception. So do an eagle scooping a swimming fish from out of a river, a tiger intercepting the flight of a running gazelle, or a primitive human hunter throwing a spear at moving game.

Horses see very differently than we do. (*Heidi Nyland*)

Aboreal creatures also need good depth perception. A gibbon swinging from branch to branch high in the rain forest needs perfect depth perception. That's why primates developed binocular stereoscopic vision.

Horses collect and process visual images from the environment differently than we do. Combine that with the survival instincts of a highly evolved "run first, think later" species, and the result is behavior that sometimes seems stupid to us. Horses are not stupid. Horses are simply *different* from us. Their eyes and reflexes are those of a species that evolved in open grasslands plagued by hungry carnivorous predators, and which survived by running away.

Characteristic #3: The Horse Reacts Quickly

The horse has extremely fast reaction time. Species that survive by running away from danger must have faster reaction times than those equipped with weapons, such as horns. That's why horses are faster than cattle. Both are prey species. The bovine facing a lion may run, but it may also turn and fight. The horse *must* run. That's why a good cutting horse can outmaneuver a frightened cow or the highly trained horses used in bullfighting in Portugal are able to outmaneuver the aggression of an angry bull.

The reaction time of even an old horse is so much faster than that of a young and athletic human that working around horses is potentially dangerous, especially for the inexperienced. If a horse wants to kick or strike you, not to intimidate you but to actually harm you, you will not be able to avoid it. We just can't move fast enough. We are not flight creatures. So where we position ourselves when working with horses, and having the experience and knowledge to be able to read their intentions, are paramount to staying safe.

Characteristic #4: The Horse Learns Quickly

The horse is the fastest learner of all domestic animals and, in fact, is one of the fastest learners in the animal kingdom. Unfortunately, horses will learn undesirable behaviors just as quickly as desirable ones. This is why novices should not train horses. It requires expertise. The rapid learning of the horse is like a powerful tool that can be both useful and dangerous.

For example, a horse may rear up on his hind legs when he is first taught to back up or to longe. This is especially common with very young horses. It isn't usually an act of aggression; it is more often an attempt to find the right answer, the response that will cause the pressure exerted by the trainer to go away.

A good trainer may be able to read a horse well enough to keep that from happening in the first place, but if it does, he simply ignores the rearing and keeps applying the pressure. The horse cannot rear for long and will soon try something else to relieve the pressure. Eventually, it will move in the correct direction and when that happens, the trainer instantly removes the pressure. The horse learns very quickly to find relief from that sort of pressure in the future by performing that sort of movement.

A novice trainer who is intimidated by the rearing will remove the pressure far too early. He may even drop the lead rope and run for his life. The horse learns that all it has to do in the future to get rid of that sort of pressure is to rear up on its hind legs. Instead of teaching the horse to back or longe, the trainer has taught it something quite different: rearing.

Horses learn with remarkable rapidity. Fixing a specific behavior such that it will be reliably performed upon cue typically takes only three experiences. This seems to be the magic number of repetitions a horse needs to learn basic behaviors, assuming he is taught in a flawless fashion.

Speed of learning is a measure of an animal's intelligence and on that score, the horse rates very high.

Characteristic #5: The Horse Has an Excellent Memory

Any animal that stays alive by running away had better have a good memory. Those with poor memories don't survive. The memory of the horse is infallible. Its ability to retain information is awesome. When traumatized, the horse's memory of the incident will last a lifetime. Behavior manipulating techniques may override the reaction to the memory but will not erase it. It lies there, dormant, waiting to be recalled with sufficient provocation.

Memory, another measure of intelligence, would require us to rate the horse very highly. Its retention is equal to that of the elephant.

Horses seem to classify all of the experiences they remember into one of two categories: things to run away from and things not to run away from. Problems arise when horses categorize harmless objects, including plastic, horse trailers, electric clippers, water hoses, and veterinarians, as things to run away from.

Characteristic #6: The Horse Craves Company

All domestic animals, with the exception of the cat, are, in the wild state, herd animals. That is, they live in groups.

Horses are herd animals. They have a psychological need to be with others of their kind. Steens Kiger and his son, Donner, bond over a corral fence. *(KMR/Rick Littleton)*

In nature, some species are basically loners. They can and do enjoy the company of their own kind, but they don't need them to survive. With the exception of the African lion, all existing species of cats are loners. So are bears and many other species of mammals and birds, reptiles and fish. This pattern exists throughout the animal world, even among insects.

Other species, however, normally live in groups. This may be advantageous for procuring food. Dogs and wolves, for example, are pack hunters. Together they can pursue, harass, and eventually bring down game that they could not kill alone.

In prey species, there is often protection in numbers. A single musk ox could not easily survive an attack by a pack of wolves, but a group of them, gathered in a circle with horns presented outward, would have a much better chance.

Horses depend upon running away from danger to survive, and many eyes, ears, and nostrils have a better chance of detecting danger than a solitary pair. A group of horses in flight has better odds of surviving hunting lions. That's why wild horses all run together when they flee. The predators have the best chance of obtaining a meal if they can isolate a straggler, or one slowed by old age or illness.

THE POWER OF THE GROUP

A horse is sometimes said to be herd bound, buddy sour, or barn sour. He may want to race back to the barn or follow too closely in a group of trail riders. He may be drawn, as if by a magnet, to the gate of an arena or become agitated and distracted anytime he is separated from his companion horses for training. These are all symptoms of the need and desire of horses to be with their own kind.

Are they problems? Not to the horse. They are perfectly normal behavior for the horse, which evolved over millions of years as a herd animal. However, they do pose safety hazards for us humans and interfere with our ability to use our horses the way we would like, and from that standpoint, they are problems to be solved.

The herd is a source of safety and comfort for the horse. We need to change that mental association slightly. We need him to believe that when we are around, he will be even *safer* and even *more comfortable* with us.

This is done by application of the predominant principle used throughout all of natural horsemanship: making the right thing easy and the wrong thing difficult.

It starts by letting the horse be where he wants to be, whether it is at the barn, with a group of horses on a trail ride, or at the arena gate. He is then required to *work* there, in other words, to move his feet. This might mean trotting circles around the other horses on the trail ride, or practicing rollbacks in front of the gate, or lots of backing at the barn. When the horse shows signs of tiring from this work, he is taken away from the place he wanted to be and allowed to rest for several minutes.

The wrong thing (being with other horses) has been made difficult and the right thing (being away from other horses) has been made easy.

With repetition, the horse eventually associates being with his buddies, while a human is handling him, with work. It is with the human that he gets the most comfort. Horses have another instinct that comes into play here: conserving their energy. Some might even call it laziness. However you characterize it, the horse will choose rest over repetitive exercise every time.

This training technique also reinforces the human's leadership role. Any time you can get a horse to move his feet, you are controlling his movement and asserting your position as the dominant member of the team.

Of all animals that live in groups, the group is most important to the flight creature. The group leader is thus all-important to the horse.

Wild horse bands are usually led by an older mare, probably not as a matter of gender but of seniority. The oldest and most experienced horse in the band will be a mare, because old stallions are a rarity in breeding herds. Once past his prime, a stallion will be run off by a younger competitor, and he will end up in a bachelor band. (However, in domestic herds, we often see geldings, which obviously do not exist in the wild, assume herd leadership.)

Horses instinctively know that following a herd leader and being close to her gives them the best chance to survive. In other words, horses *need* leadership. They *need* company. They feel insecure in the absence of leadership and a group. This is why horses are so commonly "herd bound" and "barn sour." They feel unsafe away from their group.

All horses can be led—even an alpha, a natural leader. How leadership is achieved will be considered shortly. For now, suffice to say that horses crave a group.

In the absence of other horses, a surrogate or substitute will do. Horses can surrogate-bond with any other creature: goats, cats, chickens, or people. Humans do the same thing. Like most primates, we are group creatures. We surrogate-bond. Isn't that why we adore our dogs, cats—and horses?

Characteristic #7: The Horse Communicates with Body Language

Even though we humans communicate primarily by vocalization, we also communicate with body language. The body language of each species is genetically endowed, the reason why, even when we are with a person who speaks an entirely different language, we can still communicate by observing one another's body language. We instinctively read anger, indifference, rejection, acceptance, or submission, unless the other person deliberately conceals his attitude by avoiding these instinctive body positions.

Horses vocalize, of course, but their major means of communicating with each other is body language (it is safer for a prey species not to be too noisy). If we are to really understand horses, we need to learn their body language. It is true that in time, they learn ours, but it gives us a tremendous advantage if we can learn theirs and utilize it, not only to understand what they are saying, but also to tell them what we want them to know.

Natural horsemanship has made coercion unnecessary in horse training because it uses the natural equine body language. We cannot duplicate that language because we are not horses, but we can mimic it.

Certain postures of the horse are relatively easy for us to interpret. Ears laid back in anger, a head held high in the flight position, teeth bared and the head held low in a menacing snaking position are all familiar examples.

However, the language of submission is a bit subtler, and varies greatly from species to species. We have observed that submission is signaled by assuming a position of the greatest vulnerability for the species involved.

Consider the human being. The club has been mankind's primary weapon for tens of thousands of years. The human is a tool-using species. Therefore, in all human cultures, past and present, the *bow* is a submissive act, presenting the back of the head to the club. We bow in deference, bow in respect, bow in prayer, and nod "yes" in acquiescence.

Dogs lie on their backs, fold their paws, and expose their throats and abdomens to a dominant individual. This is a most vulnerable position for a species whose teeth are its only weapon.

The bovine defensively or aggressively lowers its head, presenting its horns. But submissively, it elevates the nose, laying the horns back, a vulnerable position for a horned species.

The horse, which uses aggression by kicking, striking, biting, rearing, and bucking only when flight is either impossible or an inadequate defense in the horse's mind, is most vulnerable when it is grazing or drinking. With its head down, the horse cannot use its keen senses of vision, hearing, or smell most effectively. This is especially true at the water hole where the footing is often bad. That's why the lion hunts at the water hole, and it's also the reason that the dominant horses drink first while the subordinates watch for danger. If danger appears and the band flees, nature decrees that the dominant individuals hydrate themselves first. Survival of the dominant is nature's plan.

How does a horse signal submission? It does something no other domestic animal does. It simulates feeding or drinking. It lowers the head and makes licking and chewing movements with the mouth. It assumes a vulnerable position.

How far a horse lowers its head depends upon how certain it is that the individual challenging it is a leader. If uncertain, it may merely give a subtle nod. If more certain, it will bow strongly. If overwhelmed with submissiveness, it will drop its muzzle to touch the ground, often several times.

Similarly, the mouth movements will vary with the degree of submissiveness. If uncertain, the subject will merely loosen its lips. In a flight mode, the lips are clenched firmly. Keep in mind that the horse cannot breathe through its mouth. Horses breathe only through their nostrils.

If definitely submissive, the horse will lick and chew quite obviously, and if positively overwhelmed, the horse will do what baby foals do when they feel threatened: open and close the mouth repeatedly. This is, unfortunately, called "snapping" (or "clacking") in the United States where it has a connotation of aggressiveness, whereas in reality such mouth movements in horses of any age announce, "I'm just a helpless nursing baby. Please don't hurt me. You are the boss."

Characteristic #8: The Horse Must Know Who's Boss

Unfortunately, the terms "dominance" and "dominate" have developed negative connotations due to popular usage in recent times. We tend to think of whips and chains. We associate the words with world figures like Adolph Hitler and Saddam Hussein. These were, of course, dominant individuals, and they were also cruel, but domination does not necessitate cruelty. Great religious leaders, great statesmen, great teachers are also dominant people, and they may be very kind and considerate.

Dominance means *leadership*. Horses seek and need leadership. In your relationship with a horse, it is absolutely essential that you be dominant. You must lead the horse, not vice versa.

Species that live in groups and have a group leader have what is technically known as a *dominance hierarchy*, an order of authority. In horses, alone of all domestic animals, the dominance hierarchy is established by the leader controlling the movements of its peers.

Horses look for leaders. *(Emily Kitching)*

Aside from the fact that the horse is a flight creature, nothing is more important than this fact. It is the secret of natural horsemanship, and we will repeat it to emphasize its importance: *Leadership is determined in horses by the ability to control the movement of the subordinate horses.*

Movement can be controlled in two ways. It can be caused and it can be prevented. The leader will, often with a subtle movement, cause the other horses to move. When they move away, however slightly, they are, in effect, saluting and saying, "Yes, Ma'am! You are in charge!"

Conversely, the leader may block the movement of the others. When they stop moving, they acknowledge their subordinate role.

As surrogate leaders, humans can cause the feet of a horse to move—or we can inhibit movement. Done correctly, the horse will soon recognize our authority and signal, with its body language, "Okay! *You* are in charge. I accept your leadership. I feel safest when I'm with my leader. I *want* to be with you."

Again, this is the secret of natural horsemanship. It explains why the use of force, pain, and coercion have been less effective than the revolutionary methods displacing so many traditional aspects of horse training.

The feet are the horse's survival. Control the feet, and you control the horse's attitude. The end result using these methods is maximum respect and minimum fear. Isn't that the relationship we desire with the horse, absolute respect and no fear? Fear elicits in the horse the desire to flee. We want a partnership devoid of fear, but commanding complete respect because *we* have to make the decisions when working with horses.

Characteristic #9: The Horse Can Be Rapidly Desensitized

Curiously, the horse—this timid, flighty, claustrophobic creature that can so easily detect any threat and so quickly react to it—can be desensitized to frightening but harmless stimuli more quickly than any other domestic animal.

Why?

A creature like the horse reacts to any unfamiliar sensory stimulus, such as a novel visual stimulus, a new sound, an unfamiliar smell, or the touch of something never before experienced, with flight. If it did not quickly desensitize to such stimuli once it determined them to be harmless, it would never stop running. It would never have time to eat, drink, rest, or reproduce. So, the easily frightened horse, once it is convinced that what frightened it is harmless, soon ignores it. This is why horses are so useful in battle, for hunting, in polo, rodeo, jumping, gymkhana, herding cattle, and

Monty Roberts desensitizes a horse to the look, sound, and feel of an electric hair dryer, and to handling its ears. *(Monty Roberts Collection)*

for police work. It is why they can be taught to tolerate the chaos of parades, riots, traffic jams, and pull carts and pack dead elk.

Yes, many horses are afraid of harmless things, including plastic, flags, electric clippers, fly spray, trailers, farriers, and veterinarians. But that's because they were not effectively *desensitized* to such things and often were, in fact, *sensitized* to them with a bad experience. Usually it was the initial experience. Remember . . . horses don't forget.

A very important part of horse training—and special attention is given to this aspect in natural horsemanship—is the meticulous desensitization of the green horse to the innumerable things it will experience in life, things that it must not react to with fear and flight. In today's world, this must include automobiles, trucks, plastic, all kinds of noises, bicycles, motorcycles, llamas, pigs, kids on roller skates, dogs, and fireworks.

Characteristic #10: The Horse Is a Precocial Species

Lastly, but very importantly, horses are a *precocial* species. This means that, like so many other prey creatures, including sheep, goats, cattle, deer, ante-

Horses can be desensitized to stimuli that would otherwise cause fear and flight—even helicopters. *(Dennis Reis Collection)*

lope, elephants, chickens, turkeys, duck, geese, and pheasant, they are born, or hatched, fully developed. They are small, of course, but their senses are fully functional. They are neurologically mature enough that they are soon able to be on their feet, run from danger, follow mother and their group, and, above all, *learn*.

Other animals are helpless at birth. These are called *altricial* species. Their senses are inadequate, their development is incomplete, and they have limited learning ability. Examples of altricial creatures include dogs, cats, bears, eagles, hawks, owls, and humans. Note that the examples cited are all predatory species. Mother is able to protect and defend the young.

Because we are an altricial species, as is the animal most familiar to us, the dog, we humans have for the most part assumed that newborn foals have limited learning power. That's why, in most cultures throughout history, we have delayed training foals. Varying with the culture and the era, this commonly and arbitrarily was at weaning, or specific ages, such as one, two, or three years of age.

In the western United States and Canada, right into the middle of the twentieth century, it was very common not to do any training at all until the age of four or five, and they were called "colts" at that age.

Of course, learning is possible in any species at any age, so very useful horses were produced by such methods, but it is understandable why so many of those horses were notoriously unpredictable in their behavior, and why so many cow horses would buck every time they were mounted. The bucking horse became symbolic of the West. Starting mature horses, and doing so with hasty and crude methods is not the best way to produce a gentle, safe, dependable mount.

Today, as part of the revolution in horsemanship, foal training at a very young age is popular, and a later chapter in this book explores the topic further.

HOW HORSES LEARN

We have discussed the inherited behavior of the horse; those genetically programmed responses that helped this animal to survive in its natural habitat of open grasslands, constantly threatened by the presence of large, predatory carnivorous species. We understand how the horse's flightiness, fast reaction time, keen memory, speed of learning, and its exceptional awareness all contribute to its chances to survive and reproduce. We can see how its desire to be with other horses, to seek a leader, to find its place in the dominance hierarchy, and its predetermined body language are all essential factors in the probability that it will survive.

All of this is present by the time the horse is born, but much more lies ahead that will affect its behavior throughout its life. From the moment it is born, the horse begins to learn.

In fact, learning is possible even before the foal is born. Recent studies have shown that the human, an *altricial* species, is capable of limited prenatal learning. Late-term human fetuses can learn to recognize certain sounds, for example, such as music, or the sound of a specific voice. Sound travels well through placental fluids.

A precocial species such as the horse is capable of even more complex prenatal learning. There is good evidence to support this, but from a practical standpoint, we are more concerned with *postnatal* learning, what is learned *after* the foal enters the world.

As we have already stated, learning is possible throughout life, but especially for horses, what is learned in the first hours and days of life is critical. In the wild, the mare constantly controls the movement of the foal, licking it, caressing it, nudging it this way and that, chastising it when it does the wrong thing (endangering itself or the herd), nourishing, and, above all, protecting it.

As a result, the foal learns who its mother is, respects her, is programmed to follow her and to learn more from her. It learns to keep up with her and mimic her gait, learns who the other horses are in the band, and learns what to flee from.

As a domestic animal, the horse became useful to early man for several reasons: the flight instinct can be channeled, so that humans could avail themselves of the horse's speed, strength, and agility. The horse quickly accepts surrogate bonding, learning to accept humans as dominant leader horses, whether that dominance is acquired by gentle, persuasive means, or by traditional coercive means. Both work, but as we have learned, the former work more effectively because they minimize the fear factor that causes horses to prefer to escape their human masters. The fact that horses can be so quickly and completely desensitized to frightening but harmless stimuli also made the horse an ideal domesticated animal.

In order to be useful to us, horses must be *trained*, and horse training involves a number of behavior-shaping and behavior-modifying procedures, described as follows.

CONDITIONED RESPONSES

Most of the things we teach horses consist of conditioned responses. When we condition, we seek to establish predictable behavior that is fixed by reinforcement. There are two kinds of reinforcement: negative and positive.

Most horse trainers primarily (but not exclusively) use negative reinforcement. This is a scientific term, one of the four quadrants of *operant conditioning,* and will be discussed in greater detail later. Negative reinforcement does *not* imply punishment. What it means is that we create discomfort for the horse. The discomfort may be physical or psychological. Then, when the horse exhibits the behavior we desire, we remove the discomfort and immediately and profusely give the horse comfort.

Let's consider a couple of examples.

We ask a green horse to turn to the left by reining left. The horse may be in a snaffle, a hackamore, a halter, or a side pull. It doesn't matter. The pressure is uncomfortable to the colt. He has no idea how to escape the discomfort, so he tries this way and that to no avail. Finally, he moves ever so slightly to the left. The trainer instantly stops the pressure. Repeated promptly and consistently, the horse soon learns to obtain comfort by turning left in response to that particular cue. This is an example of negative reinforcement utilizing *physical* discomfort.

A clinician often uses a round pen to teach a horse to look to him and eventually come to him. He starts with causing the horse to take flight by

As early as 1972, Dr. Jim McCall was using body language to control a horse in a round pen. He called it "tackless training." *(James McCall Collection)*

creating *psychological* discomfort. This can be done by tossing a rope or a longe line at the horse, by slapping the ground with a whip, by waving a flag, by flapping his arms, or causing any similar commotion. The horse then moves briskly around the pen in an effort to escape the psychological discomfort. Initially, the horse does not look at the trainer. It may, in fact, look to the outside of the pen, as if ignoring the source of its discomfort in the hope it will go away. Eventually, however, it does look at the trainer and when that happens, the stimulus is removed. The horse soon learns that if it faces and approaches the trainer, it is rewarded with psychological comfort. This is an example of negative reinforcement using psychological discomfort.

Note that in either case, the horse is not *hurt*. Pain is not inflicted. The horse experiences discomfort, but it is not extreme. This is where natural horsemanship differs from most traditional methods. What we have learned, finally, is that it isn't necessary to be extreme. Horses want comfort, and will seek it even if the discomfort we use to alter their behavior is quite mild. We don't need to whip them. Annoyance from a piece of fluttering plastic may be all we need. We don't need bits capable of inflicting torturous pain. Horses will respond to a simple halter, and if we understand how to condition the response, we can fix it.

Both negative and positive reinforcement are reward systems. The difference is that with negative reinforcement we give the horse comfort by stopping discomfort, whereas with positive reinforcement we simply give the horse an immediate reward when we obtain the desired behavior.

In training animals, food is the most common positive reinforcer. Everything that eats can be trained. In some species, such as sea mammals, training is done almost exclusively with food used as a positive reinforcer.

Many horse trainers oppose the use of food in training, believing that to do so will "spoil" the horse and teach it to bite. That negative reinforcement is so effective in training horses is another reason trainers do not use food. But horses can be very swiftly and effectively trained using food treats. In fact, some of the best horse trainers in the world do so.

Circus horses are commonly trained using food for positive reinforcement. Arguably the best circus horse trainers in the world, Fredi Knie and his family, of Switzerland's National Circus, generously reward their subjects with treats. So do many of Europe's classical horsemanship schools, such as Vienna's Spanish Riding School.

Stroking and verbal praise can be used as a reward in training horses. *(John Brasseaux)*

Hollywood Hall of Fame stuntman, Rodd Wolff, a master of the dying art of teaching a horse to fall on cue, always has a carrot handy to reward a horse for a good tumble.

Clicker training and target training, which are discussed in some detail later in this book, use positive reinforcement with food and achieve magnificent results.

A more common form of positive reinforcement used in training horses is petting and praise. Horses and dogs, being group animals, seek acceptance. Moreover, the horse is a mutual-grooming species. Horses encourage bonding by nibbling and rubbing one another. Therefore stroking, with or without verbal praise, can be used as a reward in training horses.

All the founding clinicians involved in the revolution in horsemanship use a lot of stroking to reward desired behaviors. They vary where they stroke, however. Bill Dorrance said to rub the belly. Richard Shrake usually rubs the withers and the dock at the root of the tail. Monty Roberts rubs the face. Others rub the neck, and many rub anywhere. The fact is that horses *like* to be stroked and rubbed. They appreciate it. As always, the reward must immediately follow the desired behavior for optimum effectiveness.

Traditional horse trainers did not historically do a lot of stroking. They obtained the results they desired with negative reinforcement, perhaps followed by *patting*, which the horse learns to tolerate but which is not a natural reward. Patting is a human expression. Today you still see a lot of horse patting—even slapping—in the show world. The rider who does this means well but simply does not know any better. He is exuberant over a good performance and, because a slap on the back is a friendly way to congratulate a human, he thinks it must mean the same to a horse. This is precisely the mindset that natural horsemanship endeavors to change. Horses are *different* from humans.

Today's clinicians typically use negative reinforcement (relatively mild discomfort rather than a painful stimulus) and then stroke the horse briefly but generously to positively reinforce the desirable behavior obtained. Buck Brannaman, in his book *Groundwork*, repeatedly advises us to pet the horse in conjunction with every new procedure learned. In *Think Harmony with Horses*, author Ray Hunt says, "Think! Feel! Don't forget the recesses; give your horse a break—reach out and rub his neck." The best place to stroke the horse, whether on the neck, the belly, rump, or forehead, varies with the individual. It's up to the human to find that special spot where touching is most enjoyable to the horse.

DESENSITIZATION

Because they are flighty, horses must be desensitized to a wide variety of sensory stimuli if they are to be useful to us and safe. The importance of desensitization is clear when we look at the statistics for horse-related injuries to humans. Most are caused by *gentle* horses experiencing unfamiliar stimuli. Most occur while the person is on the ground, or mounting or dismounting, rather than from being thrown when riding. That's why it is so important to thoroughly desensitize horses to every possible frightening stimulus during their training.

Many of the videotapes produced by clinicians today are devoted to problem solving, and most problem solving includes desensitization to one stimulus or another. The methods of desensitization vary, and the student of horsemanship will benefit from studying as many as possible. The methods are not always intuitively obvious to a human.

For example, how many of us desensitize under the tail so that the horse can have its temperature taken without a fear reaction, which could result in somebody getting kicked? How many desensitize the feet so that if the horse gets caught in wire it will stand quietly and not panic and tear itself up? How many people routinely include desensitization to fly spray, water hoses, and electric clippers as part of the training? How many horses are trained to willingly accept deworming paste medication, or simple dentistry, or, in the case of geldings, to allow cleaning of the sheath, or the udder in mares? These are all important things, along with many, many others.

There are two primary ways to desensitize horses. One is called *flooding.* In flooding, we repeatedly expose the horse to a frightening stimulus until it *habituates.* This means that, not having been injured, the horse finally accepts the stimulus and soon is unaware of it.

An example of flooding is the time-honored Western method of "sacking out" a bronc. The colt is restrained so that it cannot escape. It is then stroked repeatedly and energetically with an empty feed sack, or a blanket, or a slicker. At first terrified, the colt eventually ignores the sack and may even start to enjoy it. It keeps the flies away and is like another horse's tail.

Flooding pushes the horse past its threshold of tolerance for a particular stimulus and ignites the horse's natural fear reaction, the desire to run away. For the method to work, the handler must be able to prevent flight and keep the horse from getting into position to use its secondary defense mechanisms, kicking and striking. This can be done with just a halter and lead rope, but it takes considerable skill in controlling a horse's feet from the ground.

This method works, and it works rapidly. The problem is that it is dangerous, especially for novices, and is only recommended for experts. Unless one is really experienced, it is very easy for the horse or the handler to be seriously injured.

An exception where flooding is practical and safe is in the desensitization of a newborn foal lying on the ground. It has no choice but to lie there if restrained, and in about an hour the foal can be barraged with flooding stimuli. Done correctly, the foal afterwards has learned to have its feet handled preparing it for the farrier, every body opening examined preparing it for the veterinarian, prepared to accept halter, bridle, saddle, girth, fly spray, electric clippers, paper, plastic, ropes, and a variety of other scary things. Meanwhile, interestingly, it bonds strongly with the handler. It is vital when doing this *not* to stop before habituation occurs. If the stimulus is stopped while the foal is thinking flight, it will tend to fix the flight reaction. Instead of desensitizing the foal we will have sensitized it, exactly the opposite of our goal. Training horses of any age is not for impatient people.

The other primary method of desensitization is safer and more common than flooding. It takes longer to perform but is less likely to cause a wreck, and is suitable for use by novice and veteran horse handlers alike. It is known as *progressive desensitization.*

Safety comes first when Monty Roberts desensitizes a horse to having its legs touched. *(Monty Roberts Collection)*

Today's clinicians typically employ progressive desensitization in their colt-starting demonstrations. Using a coiled or uncoiled rope, a plastic flag or glove attached to the end of a stick, a sack, a blanket, or anything else that might bother the horse, the trainer gently but persistently teaches the horse that such things, though unfamiliar, will not harm him. The way in which this is done is often called "*Advance and Retreat*" (or "*Approach and Retreat*"). The trainer brings the stimulus close enough to the horse to cause a mild fear reaction, then retreats. He does it again, getting a bit closer, and retreats. Eventually, the horse accepts the stimulus.

The retreat part of this method is very important, and it also happens to be completely counter to the instinctive behavior of humans, especially males, and most especially, young males. We humans are hunters, and it is not predatory to retreat. Most natural horsemanship clinicians today are male, and many of them are relatively young. It is a tribute to them that they have been able to learn how and when to retreat in order to reassure a frightened green horse. It is compassionate. It is intelligent.

The approach part of the method is calculated to create psychological discomfort but not all-out panic. The retreat should occur before the horse attempts to flee. The timing is important. It takes experience to know when the horse is on the verge of taking flight and when the frightening object, whatever it may be, should be backed off. It is also important to understand that the retreat is *temporary.* As soon as the fear response subsides, the frightening object is reintroduced and usually it can be brought just a little closer each time. Pushing the horse too far, which is the result of human impatience, inexperience, ineptness, or anger, may spoil the lesson.

The experienced handler knows how to approach this line without crossing it, but if that does happen and the horse reacts with panic to the stimulus, the handler turns it into a flooding session. He has no choice. As with newborn foals, removing a stimulus when the horse is trying to flee will fix that behavior. Instead of desensitizing the horse to the stimulus, it sensitizes him to it. This is why so many horses—most horses, in fact—are fearful of certain objects or experiences. They have been *taught* to be afraid by a handler improperly attempting to cure their fears.

One of the greatest tools for desensitizing horses is so commonplace today that it is completely taken for granted. It is given freely with virtually every purchase we make. It accumulates with its own kind in closets, cupboards, and drawers, waiting to be put to additional uses, and it is so plentiful on the landscape as to constitute a large part of the litter problem in industrialized countries. It is plastic.

Plastic didn't exist in the world in which the horse evolved. It didn't exist until the late twentieth century. It rustles. It moves. It makes sounds like something sneaking through the grass. It moves in the wind. It reflects light in a way that in nature only occurs over water. No wonder horses instinctively fear plastic.

Desensitizing horses to plastic is a good example of the process, utilizing retreat to give the horse confidence.

Have an assistant, mounted or afoot, drag a sheet of plastic *away* from the horse being trained. The horse being desensitized can be led or mounted. Follow the plastic at a safe distance, stopping from time to time. Be patient. Gradually you will find that the horse gains confidence and eventually will come up close to the plastic, smell it, and investigate it. Progressively, curiosity replaces fear. The desire to dominate is not far behind, often resulting in pawing or biting at the plastic. The last stage is indifference. The point will come when some food treats can be placed on the plastic spread out on the ground and the horse will eat off of it.

This is an example of the way clinicians today are using progressive desensitization rather than the traditional flooding process (sacking out a restrained horse) to produce virtually "bomb-proof" horses. Mounted police units have found such methods to be the best way to train police horses, which must remain calm and obedient in chaotic traffic conditions, noisy crowds, and even in riots.

Learning Must Be Generalized

With desensitizing, a horse learns, with surprising speed, to tolerate the specific stimulus being used, in a specific location by a specific person. But to be really useful, learning must be *generalized.*

Learning experiences become generalized by being repeated in multiple locations, and in a variety of ways. Otherwise, you end up with a horse that behaves well in one particular arena, with one rider. Training must include several different blankets of different texture, several sheets of plastic of different colors (especially black and white, which horses see most vividly), in different locations, and wielded by several different people.

Horses, though intelligent, cannot think as we do, reasoning that "Oh, it's a sack of a different size and color, but it's just a sack and it won't hurt me because the last one didn't."

To a horse, a novel (new and unfamiliar) stimulus is a whole new ball game, and until learning becomes generalized, the instinctive reaction to a novel sensory stimulus is to run away.

That's why, when the automobile was invented, some old, gentle well-broke carriage horses went berserk the first time they saw one. Some communities outlawed automobiles because they caused so many wrecks.

PHOBIAS

There are certain kinds of learning that require little or no reinforcement. Those experiences that occur during the critical learning times in newborns trigger this sort of automatic learning. As mentioned earlier, a prey species must quickly learn to follow and obey its mother and be a part of the herd if it is to survive. This is an example of normal, natural, instant learning.

But even when older, at any stage of life, certain profound experiences can elicit a learned reaction with a single experience. In a flight animal like the horse, this is what commonly occurs following a very traumatic experience. Let's look at some examples.

1. An inept trainer attempts to load a horse in a trailer for the first time. The horse, a claustrophobic prey species, is understandably afraid to go into the trailer. The human quickly resorts to force by whipping the horse. The horse is thinking, "I'm afraid to go in there. I'm afraid I'll get hurt."

   The horse is then hurt, which validates the fear, and the result, immediately, is a horse afraid of trailers. This same process is what produces most "spooky" horses, which shy at every suspicious object.

2. A horse that has never seen a pig before suddenly confronts one, whirls in fear, and runs through a barbed wire fence. With one expe-

rience, a fear of pigs is created, even though the pig itself did not cause the injury.

3.   A colt is being shod for the first time. The owner has failed to teach the colt to quietly and gently allow all of its feet to be picked up and tapped with a tool and the sole stroked. It doesn't know the farrier, and the whole scene is frightening. The farrier attempts to work on one foot. The colt understandably struggles because it is afraid. The farrier loses his temper and hits the horse with his rasp. The horse has been thinking, "I'm afraid I'll get hurt!" He gets hurt. Now he is afraid of farriers and farriery. This problem can even apply to a single foot being worked on if the traumatization occurs when that particular foot is involved.

There are horses that are angels on three feet and in terror of a fourth foot being shod; horses which love to have one ear handled but will react violently if the other ear is touched; horses terrified of one veterinarian but who love—or at least tolerate—another vet.

It is incumbent upon us, the supposedly more intelligent species, to understand how horses think and how they learn; how fast they learn, both desirable things and unacceptable things, and how long these things are remembered. Forever!

The horse is bigger, faster, and stronger than the human. The human must be smarter. *(Photos by Coco)*

One of the most important lessons the clinicians who teach and practice natural horsemanship have taught the scientific world is this: *Unacceptable behavior can be changed.* It can be changed permanently, *even though the memory of what caused the unacceptable behavior is indelible.* It can be changed without the chronic use of tranquilizers, antidepressants, and other behavior-modifying drugs. We can't afford to put horses on Prozac® or Ritalin® or Valium® or any of the dozens of other behavior-altering drugs now in daily use for people and dogs.

Modern clinicians consistently take horses with horrible behavior faults—terrified horses, vicious horses, severely hyperactive horses—and in remarkably short time change these horses permanently.

Horses are very different from humans, but many of the behavior-modifying principles that work with horses also work with people. Those who must deal with human behavior problems—psychologists, psychiatrists, counselors, teachers, and parents—should take note, and many do. The revolution in horsemanship has implications far beyond the horse.

All the leading clinicians are aware of and point out to their audiences and students that mastering natural horsemanship will enhance the ability to get along with our friends and neighbors, our employees or employer, our customers, our dogs, our children, and our spouses.

Indeed, the revolution in horsemanship is much more. It is a revolution in relationships.

CHAPTER 7

REVOLUTIONS
IN RIDING

"Riding," according to Pat Parelli, "is simply the act of not falling off." If we go with that tongue-in-cheek definition, it follows that really good riding is nothing more than being really good at not falling off. The revolution has proven again that a lot more is possible when horsemanship is taken to the horse's back.

Sit down on a Saturday afternoon and watch an old western. Any of the "B" westerns from the 1940s and '50s will do. You'll see some pretty amazing examples of not falling off—except when the script called for it—from those old movie stuntmen. Many of them were very good athletes, and they could make riding look exciting and highly physical on film. Horsemanship taken to the horse's back is something much more—and in a sense, less. It appears effortless. There is little extraneous movement. Good horsemen seem to be one with their horses. They feel as if their horse's legs are their own legs. The centaur, the half man/half horse of Greek mythology, is a fitting symbol of this union.

The revolution in horsemanship has instilled in us the desire to take everything in this relationship between horse and human to the highest possible level, and that includes riding. The way we do that is by infusing the simple act of riding with real horsemanship. The result is more than not falling off; it is harmony, fluidity, and ultimately, *unity* of body and mind.

Ironically, the horse's own adaptability has kept the bar relatively low when it comes to our riding. Horses are capable of performing upon command the most impressive of maneuvers even if taught and cued in a crude manner. You don't need this special relationship, this unity we're talking about, to get a horse to do useful and fairly complicated things.

History is full of examples, and we can see it today in the show world. In nearly every equine breed or riding discipline, professional horse trainers use harsh training techniques to get the results they think will impress a judge, excite an audience, and keep the horse's owner coming back for more training. Some horses have such spirit and courage that they can rise above this kind of abuse and deliver stunning performances in the show ring. We can only imagine what would be possible if these horses were really committed to the team.

IT STARTS ON THE GROUND

Riding is not the same as horsemanship. Horsemanship encompasses the entire horse–human relationship, and a great deal of that relationship takes place with the human's feet flat on the ground. It is from the ground that we feed our horses, clean their stalls, groom them, clip them, lead them, load them in trailers, unload them, deworm them, doctor them, clean their hooves, saddle them, and bridle them. Equine husbandry, or what we often simply call horse-keeping, is practiced entirely from the ground.

When a good rider is not also a good horseman, what's usually missing is a foundation built on the ground.

The revolution in horsemanship has placed strong emphasis on groundwork because that is where the human gains the respect of the horse and establishes his right to be leader of the team. Once that right is estab-

Respect is gained by first controlling a horse's movement from the ground. Here Clinton Anderson changes a horse's longeing direction from clockwise to counterclockwise. *(Charles Hilton)*

lished, a language must be built so the horse understands the requests that are made of him. Again, this is best done from the ground. The last place in the world you should be is on the back of a horse you can't control, and it doesn't matter whether that's because of your lack of leadership or the horse's lack of understanding. You can get hurt either way.

Probably the biggest mistake man has made in trying to conquer the horse is trying to force our way of thinking on him. The revolution has made it clear that we should be doing just the opposite: we should be learning to play by the rules of the horse's world.

Horses and humans are similar in some ways, but very different in others. Normal human beings can tolerate being alone. Indeed, many of us cherish our alone time and jealously guard it. As we've already learned, horses hate being alone. They are herd animals. It is programmed into their very DNA to seek the company of other animals, even outside of their species, if necessary. One of the saddest sights to a real horseman is that of a single horse standing alone in a field. There is never any joy or life in the demeanor of such animals.

When we team up with a horse, we are, in effect, creating a small herd, a herd of two. Once they are part of a herd, horses immediately feel the need to decide who is going to be the "boss hoss." Among themselves, this takes the form of dominance games, whereby they try to get each other to move. Control of movement, remember, is how horses decide who is dominant over whom, who will lead and who will follow.

Somewhere inside every horse is a natural follower, *but only if a more qualified leader is present.* This is a crucial point to understand. It is why the very same horse can be wild and disrespectful with one human, but attentive and well behaved with another. The difference is how he perceives the human's leadership capability. Fortunately for us, most horses have no problem relinquishing leadership of the team to a human being, but only if that human can prove to them in the language they understand that he or she is up to the job of leading and protecting both of them, *every single day.*

In your job as leader of your team, there are no days off. You win the job and hold onto it in the same way, by how you act around the horse. The language of action is what he understands. Are you confident in your manner without being overbearing? Are you observant of what he is telling you? Do you give him a fair chance to do what you ask before increasing the pressure on him? Do you have clear boundaries of acceptable behavior and space, and instant consequences for violations of either? Are you consistent about when and how vigorously you enforce the rules?

If you are all of that, chances are good that your horse considers you the boss hoss. Chances are good that he seems relaxed, respectful, attentive, and responsive when he's around you. Then, and only then, should you consider riding that horse.

The revolution in horsemanship has not only clarified our understanding of the role of leadership in horsemanship, it has given us tools to make us better leaders and more efficient ways of communicating our leadership qualities to our horses.

DICTATORSHIP VS. PARTNERSHIP

Leadership comes in different flavors. An iron-fisted dictator is a leader who is 100 percent the boss. Followers have zero say in the relationship, and the dictator doesn't really care what they think or feel. Such leaders often oppress those they lead.

But there are also absolute leaders who do have consideration for the welfare and points of view of their followers. Let's call this kind of leader a benevolent dictator. This might be represented as a 75/25 split in terms of influence. The benevolent dictator has 75 percent of the control or influence and the followers have 25 percent. The benevolent dictator is still very much in charge, but he has empathy for the point of view of his followers and does nothing to hurt them or even make them uncomfortable as long as they give him obedience.

In the early stages of the relationship, especially with a horse that has never had a good human leader, it is crucial that the human assume the role of a benevolent dictator. It must be crystal clear to the horse that he may not make his own decisions while he is with the human handler. Once the relationship has matured under these terms, it may evolve gradually to resemble a *partnership*.

Partnership is a word that is thrown around a lot in talk about horsemanship. Let's stop and think about the real implications of this idea.

In a partnership, there are *expectations* as to how each partner will behave. There is a contract, an understanding. Neither partner is free to do whatever he wants whenever he wants. Each has responsibilities to the other. When we have a partnership with a horse, we say to him, "I will care for you and protect you. I will make the decisions for both of us. I will be fair in what I ask of you. In return, you must give me absolute obedience." It's not a bad deal for the horse. In fact, it is just the kind of deal he looks for his whole life.

A human partnership is never a perfect 50/50 split. There is always one partner who puts a little more in, who feels a little more need to control the outcome, who is more qualified to lead, or who has more drive and energy to make things happen. This is not a bad thing; it is perfectly normal, and helps avoid stalemates and standoffs where nothing gets done. In business, the more dominant partner is often the older or more experienced partner, hence the term *senior partner* and the implication that there is more power and control given that person. The theoretical split of power might be something like 51 percent for the senior partner and 49 percent for the other partner.

This is the kind of partnership to which you can aspire with a horse. You must establish the ground rules for the relationship from the position of benevolent dictator, but once that is working well, you can move easily and smoothly toward the senior partner role.

Will you ever have to go back to being more assertive, more controlling, more of a dictator? Of course. Your horse wants proof every single day that you are still a competent leader and won't get him killed.

He may even ask for proof rather than waiting for you to offer it. He asks with little tests. Will my human let me get away with crowding him a bit today? Okay, what if I turn my hindquarters toward him? And what if I pin my ears and act aggressively? Without clear, consistent, instantaneous response from the human, the horse may conclude that at least that day there are no boundaries for his behavior.

A horse understands that a leader who doesn't establish and enforce boundaries in space and behavior is no leader at all and deserves exactly what other less dominant horses would get in the herd: regular reminders of who is really in charge. This may take the form of biting, kicking, bolting, striking, refusing to move, or pushing, to name just a few. Ultimately, all of these behaviors have to do with movement, either causing movement of the subordinate or inhibiting it. Done to other horses, these produce discomfort. Done to us frail humans, the same acts can be deadly.

This is normal horse behavior. As clinician Clinton Anderson puts it, the horse is simply "showing you his union card."

THE PRE-RIDE CHECK

The most effective strategy to establish and reestablish your right to lead is a preemptive strike. In other words, showing the horse before he asks to be shown. You demonstrate that today, like yesterday and the day before, *you* are the one who's going to be in charge.

The receptivity a given horse demonstrates toward your being leader will vary from day to day. In human terms, we might characterize these as mood swings. A horse may seem grumpier, more skittish, or antsier today than yesterday. Maybe it's the weather (windy days often bring up a horse's flightiness). Maybe it's pent-up energy from too much of the wrong kind of feed and too little exercise. Maybe it's impatience to be fed. Regardless of the cause, these attitudes threaten your safety. The solution is to prove that you are the leader and that everything else in that horse's life is unimportant.

Remember, you cannot simply usurp the role of leader. You can't announce one day, "Okay, from here on out, I'm in charge." Leadership of the horse–human team is not conferred by the simple fact that you were born a human and the horse was born a horse. Neither does leadership come with the ownership papers when you buy a horse or with the receipt when you get a horse back from a trainer. Leadership has to be earned by each person who handles the horse, and that comes from action.

A nicer term for our "preemptive strike" would be the pre-ride check. Some clinicians call these groundwork exercises, or drills, or lessons. The Parelli System has formalized them into the Seven Games. Clinician Frank Bell calls it his Seven Step Safety System. Whatever form it takes, the pre-ride check begins with a few moments of bonding, of touching in a friendly manner, either with your hands, a soft rope, or a training stick. This is to remind the horse that you are his friend and your touch feels good. It also gets you relaxed and into a nonaggressive posture.

Next comes a series of requests for the horse to move in certain, specific ways of your choosing: forwards, backwards, left and right. These are done with more assertive body language on your part and they escalate in intensity, if necessary, until the desired result is achieved. When the horse responds and allows you to control his movement, he is saying, "Okay, you can be the boss today."

What if he doesn't respond? You cannot allow that to happen. Once you place your request on the table, you must be prepared to go the distance, to wait as long as

Before riding any horse, it's important to be able to control him effectively from the ground. Richard Winters asks a horse to pass between him and a fence. By pointing and looking in the direction he wants the horse to go, he "opens the door." *(Richard Winters Collection)*

Winters sends the horse out on a 12-foot line. *(Richard Winters Collection)*

it takes, to turn up the pressure as much as it takes to get compliance. If you don't, you have taught the horse exactly what you did not want to teach him: that if he resists long enough, you will give up. This is why smart horsemen are very careful to ask in such a way that they are virtually assured of getting a correct response. No one wants to go to battle with a horse, and good horsemanship dictates setting the horse up for success rather than failure. One of the cardinal rules of natural horsemanship is to ask the horse "as gently as possible, but as firmly as necessary." Notice that failure to get the response is not an option.

On the ground is where all of these little dramas should play out. Groundwork is a systematic, consistent way of building and reinforcing the language of communication and the leader–follower relationship that must exist between horse and human. Groundwork also gets a horse used to specific physical sensations, to sounds and sights that require a certain response from him, whether a human is working him from the ground or from his back.

Groundwork teaches him to move away from pressure. It may be the feeling of a little pressure at his girth, which tells him to move in the opposite direction. It may be the feeling of a slight pull on one side of his mouth, that tells him to flex his neck to that

Winters challenges the horse to follow his feel over uneven terrain. *(Richard Winters Collection)*

side. It may be the sound of a cluck or kiss, or the general feeling that you have raised your energy level that tells him to give you more forward movement. It may be the sound of "whoa" or "easy" and a relaxing of your energy that tells him to slow or stop.

In some ways, the pre-ride check is like a pilot's preflight check. It can uncover problems that would send you crashing to the ground, just as the pilot's check can. It doesn't take long; in fact, some horsemen get so good at it that an observer would hardly know it's happening. It may just look like the rider is moving the horse around a little to make mounting easier. But the horse knows because he has been asked in no uncertain way to perform on the ground, to respond to the rider's requests. The rider will not mount until the horse is clearly willing to be a follower and ready to comply with the requests the leader gives him.

THE INDEPENDENT SEAT

The revolution has taken riding to higher levels not only by improving and clarifying the relationship between horse and rider, but also by giving the rider ways to improve the mechanics of riding. To this end, great emphasis is placed on developing balance and equilibrium on the horse's back, and obtaining an independent seat.

What is the independent seat? The seat, in this discussion, is not only your buttocks but also your upper legs, the part of your body that presses continually against the saddle (or if riding bareback, the horse's back). This is your greatest natural riding aid for the simple reason that it has the most contact with the horse. Your calf, your heel, your hands on the reins, these allow you to influence but a tiny fraction of the equine "real estate" that your seat can influence. And always bear in mind that the horse is capable of detecting the slightest sensation on his skin. If you look to the left or to the right, the horse feels the subtle change in your seat. If you shift your weight slightly forward or back, he feels it. If you sit taller in the saddle, or relax into a slouch, he feels it. He thus senses your intentions, your wishes for him, through your seat. These become part of the language of riding, and they can become so subtle that only the two of you know it's happening.

Now, what about the independent part of the independent seat? It means that the rider's seat becomes one with the horse and moves independently of the rest of the rider's body. This is possible because of the design of the human skeletal system, and especially the pelvis.

Improving balance on the ground aids in developing an independent seat while riding.
(Photos by Coco)

Consider all the ways you can bend at the waist. You can bend to the left and right, forward and back. You can stand up straighter or slouch lower. In all of this, your pelvis remains fairly stationary, even though the rest of your body may have moved dramatically. The pelvis is a flexible junction, a multidirectional shock absorber when you are riding. Rigidity of your pelvis is the enemy of good riding. A loose and flexible pelvis—a "neutral pelvis" in the words of Connected Riding creator, Peggy Cummings—allows for this all-important independent seat.

The value of having an independent seat has been known and taught by great riders down through history, including Xenophon, who noted that ". . . the rider should accustom himself to keep his body above the hips as supple as possible; for this would give him greater power of action, and he would be less liable to a fall if somebody should try to pull or push him off."

PASSENGER LESSONS

So how does a rider develop an independent seat? A good way to start is by taking what many clinicians now call "passenger lessons." Instead of trying to control where the horse goes, the rider lets him go where he wants to go. The only rule is that the horse must not change gait. Other than that, the rider provides no direction. He is just a passenger.

As a practical matter, a passenger lesson is best done in a riding arena or other enclosed space. In the beginning, it's enough to simply hold the reins loosely. As the rider gains confidence, he may want to drop them on the horse's neck or over the saddle horn (if they are loop reins or knotted split reins) and let his hands drop to his thighs. Once that is mastered, the next step is to ride with feet out of the stirrups, then with eyes closed, and finally, bareback.

During a passenger lesson, a horse will often want to go to the gate or to a portion of the arena near other horses. These are "magnets" for him, and it is perfectly normal for him to be drawn to them. The rider does not try to stop him, but simply urges him back to the correct gait when he tries to stop and hang out. Natural horsemanship uses the same sort of solution for horses that don't want to leave the barn ("barn sour" horses) or horses that don't want to leave their herd ("herd bound" or "buddy sour" horses). The principle is to keep the horse working when he's near the "magnet" and allow him to rest only when he is some distance away from it. The wrong thing is made difficult and the right thing is made easy. Remember, horses are basically lazy creatures. This is not a fault in their design; it's how they preserve their energy for when they really need it.

If the rider does not have access to a riding arena or does not feel confident enough to relinquish control to the horse, an approximation of the passenger lesson can be obtained by having a helper longe the horse and rider in a circle. Longeing eliminates the unpredictability of a true passenger lesson, but is still worth doing, especially as a first step.

BAREBACK, YOGA, AND TAI CHI

There is no question that physical fitness, balance, and body awareness play significant roles in a rider's success. One of the simplest ways to improve all three requires no special training or equipment. Just ride your horse bareback.

A saddle, especially a big Western saddle, can be a crutch. It is too easy for the rider to brace against the stirrups, lean against the pommel or cantle, or grab the horn. There is little need to develop balance. Riding bareback forces one to get in rhythm with the horse's movement, to develop equilibrium while in motion. Otherwise, the rider will slide right off.

Pat Parelli has for many years included a bareback and bridleless demonstration in his public appearances. Pat races around the arena, performs spins and sliding stops, and jumps various obstacles with only a handful of mane to steady himself. His students are encouraged early on to ride bareback. Going bridleless comes a bit later.

A good compromise for the rider who finds his horse's bare back too uncomfortable is the bareback pad. Bareback pads soften the effect of a bony back on a rider's sensitive bottom and minimize sweat and dirt that transfer from the horse's back to the rider's pants. Some pads have a leather loop approximately where the saddle's horn would be, giving insecure riders a place to grab in an emergency.

Exercise, especially stretching, is helpful for any rider and it becomes more beneficial as we age. Entire exercise regimens have been developed specifically for riders. For example, *The New Total Rider: Health & Fitness for the Equestrian*, by Tom Holmes, integrates a physical exercise program, a nutrition strategy, and a sports psychology program. *Yoga for Equestrians: A New Path for Achieving Union with the Horse*, by Linda Benedik and Veronica Wirth, contains ground and mounted exercises derived from the practice of yoga.

Tai Chi, one of the "internal" martial arts, has been adapted to the needs of riders. The slow, controlled, and highly focused movements of Tai Chi help riders maximize balance, recognize and release tension, and create

Pat Parelli encourages his students to ride bareback early on. *(Photos by Coco)*

harmony, grace, and suppleness between horse and rider. James Shaw's video *Tai Chi for the Equestrian: Cross Training for Riders* demonstrates these movements. Centered Riding instructor Suzanne Sheppard also incorporates elements of Tai Chi in the clinics she does with her partner, natural horsemanship clinician Bob Jeffreys.

VISUALIZATION IN RIDING

Visualization in riding has two different meanings. One has to do with how you use your visual organs, your eyes. Riders today are encouraged to look not at their hands or the horse's head, but at the horizon or some object well in front of them that serves as a target. At other times, they are advised to use a "soft" eye, a concept popularized by Centered Riding creator, Sally Swift, to not focus on anything at all.

This tends to happen naturally as one becomes more comfortable with the movement of the horse, just as it does when learning to ride a bicycle.

But there is a reason to master this skill early. Looking down when riding changes your center of gravity on the horse's back, moving it farther forward and making it that much harder for the horse to lift his front end. It's easy to forget how heavy the human head is. Even tilting it down slightly to look at the reins moves your center of gravity forward a few inches.

Riding is one activity where you can easily get in your own way. Keeping your eyes up keeps you more relaxed. Looking down tends to cause you to tense up, which is normal, but still the opposite of what you want. When we tense up, especially as the result of fear, we humans have the instinctive desire to pull our limbs together and tuck the head, an approximation of the fetal position. This is nature's way of protecting our vital organs. Ironically, though natural for us, this position sends the worst possible message to a horse. It makes him want to go faster, to escape what feels to him like a predator tightening its grip on his back. This is particularly important to bear in mind when riding. Relaxation in the saddle is absolutely key to becoming a good rider.

The other meaning of visualization has to do with what visual images are playing through your brain as you ride. Sally Swift, creator of Centered Riding, is the most well-known proponent of visualizing various scenarios to put your body in the proper posture and position. For instance, a very effective image for riders is the "puppet on a string." Imagine that you have an eyebolt sticking out of the top of your head and a string attached. You are dangling from that string like a puppet. Visualizing this image causes many riders to sit up straighter, without tensing up, an appropriate posture for forward movement.

Another image is seeing yourself as a scoop of ice cream melting down over the saddle. This causes you to collapse and totally relax on the horse's back, an appropriate posture for slowing your horse, or simply standing still with him.

Visualizing yourself in the act of riding, doing it correctly and successfully, is a form of self-programming that can have a tangible positive effect. *Mental Equitation*, by James Arrigon, and *Focused Riding*, by Robert and Beverly Schinke, explain the technique in detail. Experts tell us that the subconscious mind cannot distinguish between reality and imagined events. Thus *thinking* through a good riding session is, to the subconscious, no different than having *lived* through a good riding session. It can increase one's confidence, decrease one's anxiety, and aid in relaxation and balance. Strangely, it can even improve the physical performance of the rider. The connection between mind and body is that strong.

THE DRIVE LINE

We have all been taught that you kick a horse to make him go faster and pull back on both reins to make him slow down or stop. Many horses learn to respond correctly to these cues, and in some riding disciplines they are still prevalent. The revolution has taught us, however, that both are counterintuitive to the horse and are likely to fail in an emergency situation.

Let's first look at kicking. If someone were to poke you in the side, your instinctive reaction would be to contract your body to form a ball, that fetal position where your internal organs are most protected and you feel the safest. When you kick a horse in his side, he has a similar instinctive reaction. He contracts his body, too, by elevating his back and shortening his stride. This is the opposite of lengthening his stride and increasing his speed. If you needed to move your horse quickly out of the way of an oncoming car, for instance, kicking wouldn't be the best way to do it. You *never* see jockeys kicking their horses to get them to run faster.

What is the correct way to ask for more speed? A really good rider seems to just think more speed and get it. In reality, the horse picks up subtle cues from the rider, cues the rider may not even realize he's giving. Leaning in slightly, rotating the pelvis forward a few degrees, tensing the core muscles, actively pushing with the seat rather than passively following the horse's motion—all communicate a general increase in the rider's energy and the expectation of an increase in speed. For less gifted riders, asking for more speed may take something more deliberate like contracting the muscles of the rear end ("smiling with all four cheeks" according to Pat Parelli), or squeezing slightly with the calves on the horse's side. This is the closest you will come to kicking the horse.

If that doesn't work, do *not* kick! Turning up the pressure must take a different form. Some suggest flapping the legs with rhythm on the horse's side. Others suggest an audible cue, such as a clucking or kissing sound. If that doesn't work—and this is a key point—physical pressure is applied *behind* the drive line, usually in the form of some kind of spanking.

It would be convenient if your horse came with his drive line clearly marked with a bright yellow dotted line. But he didn't, and you can put away the spray paint because you can't add one, either. The drive line is not a perfectly definable location. It is approximately where the horse's center of gravity lies, but even that isn't 100 percent accurate. In fact, the only way we can define the drive line at all is by describing how a horse responds to pressure in front of it and behind it.

For a general reference, let's say that the drive line is approximately where the front girth of a Western saddle would go, about 4 inches behind the front leg. It is almost never any farther back, but it may be as far forward as the slope of the horse's shoulder. The triangular-shaped region between these two reference lines is a gray area, sometimes acting as if it's in front of the drive line and sometimes behind.

Round pen training, where the horse is free to move about a 50-foot (more or less) round corral in response to the trainer, makes extensive use of the drive line. Canadian clinician Chris Irwin describes the technique best. Imagine a laser beam coming straight out of your belly button. When you face the horse, if that beam hits him behind the drive line, he will be encouraged to go forward. If you change your angle slightly so the beam hits him in front of the drive line, it encourages him to slow down, and ultimately to change direction.

The drive line works similarly when riding. Pressure applied behind the drive line encourages forward motion in a horse, so spanking him on the rump or flank with the end of your reins or a riding crop gives him a clear signal to increase his speed. Most Western riders slap first one side, then the other to make the pressure even and the forward movement straight.

You may also be able to use the same sort of signal in front of your legs in that gray area mentioned earlier. You will probably get less of a response that way, however, because it is, in fact, a gray area. The signal is not as crystal clear to the horse. Some riders prefer using this area because their hands can stay closer to the normal riding position and they feel more secure in the saddle.

As a way of turning up the pressure even more gradually, some riders slap first on their own legs or on the saddle or saddle blanket. The horse still feels the increased energy emanating from the rider and sees the motion out of the corner of his eye. This is often sufficient to get the desired response.

English riders use the same principle when they close their legs behind the horse's girth to create or maintain impulsion, i.e., controlled forward movement. Tapping with a riding crop behind the drive line further clarifies the rider's intent.

What about pressure applied in front of the drive line? When we ride, we exert pressure in front of the drive line by using the reins and sometimes our feet. The action of the reins and bridle applies pressure on the poll, the bridge of the nose, the mouth, the chin, or all of the above, all of which are well in front of the drive line. When there is more pressure to one side than the other, the horse turns. Even pressure on the face causes the horse to flex at the poll and tuck his face in. In combination with pressure from the rider's feet in front of the drive line, the horse will back up. In combination with leg pressure *behind* the drive line, the horse will collect or compress his frame, elevating his back in the process and bringing his haunches more underneath him.

As we said before, a horse can learn to slow down and stop when a rider pulls back on both reins, but this is not a fail-safe cue. Why? Because horses can brace against the bit and keep right on going. A racehorse, in fact, will *increase* his speed when the jockey takes a firmer hold of his mouth. This is because of a phenomenon known as "opposition reflex" or, technically, *positive thigmotaxis*, moving into a source of pressure. This phenomenon is seen in many species in the animal kingdom.

THE ONE-REIN STOP

The revolution in horsemanship has elevated to the highest level the importance of safety for the rider. For one reason, many riders are older and don't bounce like they used to or heal as quickly from injuries. Roy Rogers, America's beloved King of the Cowboys, said in his twilight years, "When I was young and would fall off a horse, I might break something. Now I splatter." Feeling safe is a prerequisite for feeling confident as a rider.

To feel safe, a rider must believe that he can stop the horse and regain control, no matter what happens. Bolting and bucking are twin terrors to the novice rider because they represent loss of control.

The one-rein stop is a time-honored way of regaining control in almost any situation. It's variously known as the emergency hand brake stop, disengaging the hindquarters, untracking the horse, and doubling the horse. These all refer to exactly the same thing: pulling the horse's head around to one side and holding it there until he stops moving. It is most often called the one-rein stop because you are pulling on *one rein only*.

This takes some strength, but not as much as you might think. Horses have tremendous power to move their heads up and down, but far less to the left and right. The key thing is to pull back on one rein and hold on until the horse has stopped and you can safely dismount, if you so choose.

Why does the one-rein stop work? The secret lies in one of its more descriptive aliases, "disengaging the hindquarters." In order to run off or buck, a horse's hind legs, the source of his power, must be on parallel tracks. In other words, they must both be able to move straight forward. They are engaged in the same way that a car is in gear. The one-rein stop unbalances the horse and forces him to step over with one of his hind legs. This "untracks" him, or takes his hind legs off of parallel tracks. It disengages him or puts him in neutral gear. Keeping his head pulled around keeps him in this neutral position. All of this forces him to think about his feet and is a very clear reminder of who is in charge, of who controls his movement. When you give him all of this to think about, he has no room left in his brain to think about bolting or bucking.

Many natural horsemanship clinicians teach the one-rein stop and some insist that their students practice it at all gaits until it becomes almost a reflexive action. Anytime the rider feels he has lost control of the horse, he is encouraged to use the one-rein stop. Ironically, once the rider is confident that he can stop the horse and get off, come what may, he relaxes and becomes a better rider, making the likelihood of needing to use the one-rein stop much less.

Why not just explain this to students? Why make them practice it over and over until they don't even have to think about it? Two reasons. One, timing is important. In an emergency, the longer you wait to react, the more dangerous things become. In a full-out bucking or bolting episode, adrenalin is flowing in both horse and rider. Neither is likely to be thinking clearly. A one-rein stop executed in a panic on a horse at a dead run could cause horse and rider to fall. Second, it takes space to do the one-rein stop because the horse travels in an arc as he slows down. If you and your horse were bolting down a narrow trail, this could be a problem.

The quicker the rider can apply the technique, the better. If it has been practiced and is an instinctive response on the part of the rider, a horse will take no more than a few steps before he is asked to flex his head to one side and control is once more established. Note that horses learn this, too. And when they feel the familiar sensation of the one-rein stop, they often click out of panic mode. They know the leader is back in charge.

The one-rein stop can be used whether riding in a curb or snaffle bit. The snaffle must be of the full-cheek variety or be used with a chin strap to avoid pulling through the horse's mouth.

MOUNTING FROM THE OFFSIDE

Traditionally, we mount horses from the "near" or left side. Most traditions start for logical reasons, and this is no exception. Most people are right-handed, and right-handed soldiers always carried their swords on their left

CELLULAR COMPARTMENTATION

The failure of a horse to transfer what he has learned on one side to the other side has long been recognized and accepted by horse trainers. The assumption has been that horses' brains are somehow different in this respect from those of other mammals, such as humans. Dissection has proven that to be incorrect. The cross-hemispherical neuropathways of a horse's brain are no different from those of other mammals.

Then why can't a horse make the correlation? Why can't we just teach him on one side and let him figure out the other?

According to horse trainer Willis Lamm, who works with Dr. Corrine Davis, a research veterinarian at Stanford University, the current theory is called "cellular compartmentation." Untrained horses will not transfer what they learn, to a significant degree, from the left side to the right side, from low to high, from front to back, from any compartment or "box" to another. This is believed to be a survival mechanism that operates at the cellular level.

According to Lamm, "As a prey animal in a hostile world this tendency to think in terms of 'It (the stimulus) is okay here, but prove to me first that it's okay over there' is key to early detection of real threats, and therefore to survival." Interestingly, with training, especially the sort of bonding and desensitization that occurs during a pre-ride check, the horse relaxes and the rigid compartmentation is diffused, making it easier to teach him new things and help him correlate past experiences. Perhaps it is a simple matter of the horse learning to trust the human.

hips. Mounting from the left side prevented the soldier from jabbing himself in the side with the sword hilt as he swung a leg over.

There is absolutely no reason to limit ourselves to mounting on the left side. It is better for the horse's back, in fact, to alternate sides, and the aging rider will enjoy the break it gives his left knee. Perhaps even more important from a safety standpoint, practicing mounting from the offside (far side or right side) will prepare you and your horse for situations where that is the only practical way for you to mount.

Imagine you are on a narrow mountain trail with a steep drop-off to the left. It wouldn't be safe or practical to dismount and remount on the left side. But what if your horse had never been exposed to your mounting from the right? To him, it would be much like the very first time you climbed on him! Remember, a horse doesn't correlate experiences on his left side with identical experiences on his right, at least not in the same way or to the same degree that we do. This is why we must always work both sides evenly; we are, in effect, teaching both sides—educating both hemispheres of his brain—individually.

HELMETS

Compared to the human's body size, the human brain is quite large and, unfortunately, vulnerable to injury. Life is never the same after one's brain has been damaged. Wearing a helmet while riding may be the ultimate no-brainer, yet, in some circles, including virtually all Western riding activities, it is still not common. Why?

The number-one reason is tradition. The cowboy hat is the symbol of all that is Western. Having the right style of hat with just the right shaping is very important to the real cowboy and the weekend wannabe alike. Functionally, the cowboy hat is hard to beat. It keeps the sun out of your eyes and the rain off your neck. It makes bald spots and bad hair days unimportant. If it gets beat up and dirty, it looks all the more authentic. And of course, it is pure Americana.

But all that functionality and style counts for nothing in a riding accident. The cowboy hat provides virtually no protection for the skull. If it doesn't fly off, it crumples upon impact. The authors of this book, and undoubtedly many readers, know of people who died as a result of riding accidents where a helmet would have made a difference.

In some states, laws mandate wearing helmets while riding motorcycles or snowmobiles. Most children on bicycles wear helmets now, where just ten years ago it was a somewhat rare sight. Motorcycles and bicycles share roads with cars and trucks, drunk drivers, distracted drivers, and careless drivers, but at least cars and trucks operate in a highly predictable manner. Horses do not.

Sometimes a helmet is seen as a sign that the rider lacks confidence in his ability with horses, or is a pessimist or lacks courage. All of this, of course, is nonsense.

Wearing a helmet is common sense for any rider.

Some horse show classes have long traditions regarding headgear, and participants are reluctant to go against tradition by wearing a helmet. However, time spent in the show ring is minimal compared to time spent in training or pleasure riding when a helmet could be worn.

At this writing, few clinicians actively involved in the revolution in horsemanship wear riding helmets in public or make a point of recommending them. However, there are signs that change is afoot. Some clinicians don helmets before stepping onto young or problem horses. Frank Bell, GaWaNi Pony Boy, and mule clinician Steve Edwards are prime examples. And in his Join Up demonstrations, Monty Roberts insists that the initial ride on a horse be done in a helmet. Even those clinicians, such as Curt Pate, who have not yet made the change themselves often say they believe in helmets and recommend that students wear them.

Wearing a helmet is common sense for any rider. *(L. Hanselmann/NARHA)*

Rodeo cowboys, especially bronc and bull riders, have in recent years adopted safety equipment such as protective vests and neck collars. Some bull riders even wear safety helmets. Yet most bucking stock riders wear soft cowboy hats. They are not in the business of teaching, so it is difficult to criticize them for their choices. However, like clinicians, they are in a position to positively influence recreational riders.

Western-style riding helmets have been marketed in the past but failed to gain any real acceptance due primarily to their bulky appearance. Let's hope that someday alternative materials will be available that allow helmets to retain the look of a real cowboy hat while providing real protection for the cowboy noggin.

CHAPTER 8

THE COWBOY ENIGMA—
RODEOS AND RANCHES

IT WAS UNEXPECTED THAT MANKIND'S long relationship with the horse would undergo a revolutionary change in training methods, popularized by a few cowboys, late in the twentieth century. There is an even more surprising aspect to this phenomenon.

Most of the men who took this approach to the public were at one time rodeo contestants.

RODEO COWBOYS

Rodeo is a rough-and-tumble, American-born sport. It is fast and furious, and it can be dangerous for man and beast. It's not for sissies. Yet rodeo has produced numerous great horsemen who now support and teach gentle, humane, and noncoercive methods of training horses, men who preach a philosophy of compassion, kindness, and justice in the way we approach the job.

It's not as contradictory as it first seems.

Young people, both male and female, are initially attracted to the sport of rodeo because they want to be around animals. They want to work with animals, play with them, and involve their lives with them. The fact that rodeo is highly competitive, physically challenging, dangerous, and exciting doesn't deter young people from becoming involved—it attracts them!

The risk to animals in rodeo is greatly exaggerated by its opponents. Any injury to an animal is regretted by participants in the sport, and the rules attempt to minimize the risk of injury. With rare exceptions, rodeo

Some rodeo events, like team roping, require a partner-ship between horse and rider. *(Heidi Nyland)*

Others, like saddle bronc riding, are bucking contests be-tween man and beast. *(Heidi Nyland)*

people *love* animals. They lavish attention upon them. Visit the behind-the-scenes area of a rodeo grounds, and you see dogs in cars, campers, pickup trucks, and motor homes. You see sleek, well-groomed horses, and in the bucking horse and roping stock corrals you see well-fed and well-cared for horses and cattle. They are well-cared for because they are financially valuable, if for no other reason.

Rodeo events consist of either a partnership between man and beast, as in the timed events such as roping, steer wrestling, or barrel racing, in which the horse is essential to the athlete's success, or in "rough stock" bucking contests between man and beast as in bronc or bull riding.

Non-rodeo people are often unaware of the esteem with which the contestants regard great bucking stock. Many of these animals are themselves talented athletes, of considerable monetary value, and often surprisingly old. There have been illustrious bucking horses still competing in their late twenties, and even into their thirties, which is quite old for a horse. Bucking stock live a good life, are well-fed, and only occasionally required to perform.

The partnership between a timed event competitor and his horse is very close. A successful performance in the arena may take only a few seconds, but it represents months and often years of training, practicing, and conditioning. It isn't surprising that young animal-oriented people select rodeo. But it isn't easy. There is a physical risk involved. The odds of financial success are slim. Rodeo contestants *pay* to enter a rodeo, and only a few winners come out ahead financially. All the rest lose.

Remarkably, the sportsmanship traditional in rodeo exceeds that of all other professional sports. Competitors advise and help one another, often share winnings, often share horses, and the displays of braggadocio, temper, bravado, strutting, and egomania seen so commonly in other sports are extremely rare and frowned upon in rodeo. Although most of today's contestants are not from a working cowboy background, the cowboy's traditional ethics and mores still predominate in the sport.

Considering all of the above, it isn't that surprising that some rodeo cowboys, when they got too old to compete successfully, especially in the rough stock events, became horse trainers. Working with animals was their life. So, when such people turned to horse training rather than rodeo as a livelihood, during the last decades of the twentieth century, it was inevitable that some of them would be intrigued by, and become involved in, natural horsemanship.

Bill Smith, of Thermopolis, Wyoming, was one of the top ten saddle bronc riders in the world for sixteen years. He was three times PRCA

Three-time PRCA World Champion saddle bronc rider Bill Smith, of Thermopolis, Wyoming, showed his talents at the 1975 National Finals Rodeo. *(Bill Smith Collection)*

Mel Hyland of Alberta, Canada, was twice PRCA World Champion saddle bronc rider. *(Mel Hyland Collection)*

Pat Parelli competed in bareback bronc riding for more than ten years. *(Pat Parelli Collection/Photos by Coco)*

Dennis Reis was a professional rodeo cowboy at sixteen. *(Dennis Reis Collection)*

Richard Winters roped calves and rode bucking horses in rodeo competition. *(Richard Winters Collection)*

(Professional Rodeo Cowboys Association) world champion. Today he does natural horsemanship clinics all over the United States.

Mel Hyland, a Canadian, was twice PRCA world champion saddle bronc rider and is now a busy clinician.

Pat Parelli, before he became a world-class clinician, was one of the top bronc riders in the country.

Dennis Reis, a Northern Californian clinician, was a professional bronc rider by the age of sixteen.

Californian Richard Winters went to school at Hartnell College at Salinas in order to compete on their successful rodeo team. He rode saddle broncs and roped calves. Today he is a dynamic, crusading spokesman for natural horsemanship.

Texas clinician Craig Cameron rode bulls professionally in his youth.

Doyle Parker of Montana and J. C. Bonine of Texas, both former bronc riders, are today clinicians.

Harry Whitney, a respected clinician now living in Wickenburg, Arizona, entertained in rodeo with animal acts and Roman riding, and performed pickup work.

Monty Roberts was twice National Intercollegiate Rodeo Association champion. Today he is teaching horsemanship full time and is known around the world for it.

Larry Mahan, who was six times PRCA World Champion All-Around Cowboy and held the title of most successful rodeo contestant of all time for twenty-five years, is today involved in a wide variety of activities, but one of them is serving as a clinician teaching this kind of horsemanship.

Alfonso Aguilar, a Mexican veterinarian and a charro (elite horseman of Mexico) since the age of nine, spent a decade in the United States learning natural horsemanship. Although Aguilar was not a rodeo contestant, he was a superb roper who has competed frequently. Today he is actively teaching natural horsemanship, not only in Mexico but all over Europe as well.

Buck Brannaman, in addition to dabbling in high school rodeo competition, has been a professional trick roper since childhood and has participated in countless rodeos in that capacity.

The great rodeo cowboy, nine-time PRCA world champion, Ty Murray, has become a student of clinician Dennis Reis's Universal Horsemanship. In 2003, during the National Finals Rodeo in Las Vegas, Nevada,

Ty, along with his parents, participated in Reis's Day of the Horse exhibition performance at the Excalibur Hotel arena. Murray has become an articulate and effective spokesman for the revolution in horsemanship.

How ironic that these former rodeo contestants, engaged in a sport that many uninformed people regard as inhumane, were instrumental in eliminating the coercive brutality that has typified traditional horse training techniques since mankind first domesticated the animal.

Yet, it is understandable. These men loved the horse, and they knew the horse better than most so-called horse lovers do. This combination of love and respect for the animal, combined with real understanding of its nature, is what created the revolution in horsemanship.

THE SPORT OF RODEO

The sport of rodeo itself has had significant effect upon Western horsemanship in North America, some positive and some negative.

Rodeo is a truly American sport, evolving in the late nineteenth century when Western cowboys began to compete to display their riding and roping skills. Several communities claim title to originating rodeo, but the first real modern rodeo was held in Prescott, Arizona, in 1888.

Like so much of the North American cowboy culture, rodeo has Mexican roots. The word rodeo, pronounced "RO-dee-oh," is an anglicized corruption of the Spanish word spelled the same way but pronounced "ro-DAY-oh." It means an encirclement; hence, a cattle roundup.

During the early twentieth century, the sport became increasingly popular in America, coinciding with the popularity of "Wild West Shows," which were entertainment spectacles featuring riders and ropers and marksmen, and reenactments of warfare and cattle drives. Although the Wild West Show faded into relative obscurity before World War II, rodeo has become increasingly popular.

Inevitably the sport and its stars influenced the entire cowboy culture and Western horsemanship in general. Some of the innovations were not conducive to the riding art. For example, a saddle seat with a high rise beginning at the pommel and sloping toward the cantle is advantageous to saddle bronc riders and calf ropers. Thus this became the style in most Western saddles from the 1930s right up to the end of the century. This high rise put the rider's center of balance *behind* the horse's center of balance, a point not conducive to optimum horsemanship. Not until Ray Hunt became a clinician popularizing the Wade tree saddle with its more level seat, did a change come in the saddlery industry. A majority of today's clinicians use the Wade tree and it will be discussed in more detail later.

Cantles, too, have changed. In the late 1940s and '50s, calf-roping saddles began to lower cantle height in order to facilitate dismounting in this timed event. Calf ropers then dismounted on the near side and crossed under the rope to throw the calf from the offside of the horse. The low cantle, often only an inch in height, was thought to speed the dismount. Today, calf ropers dismount from the offside, a seemingly obvious timesaver but which, like most innovations, nobody had thought of earlier, and cantles on roping saddles became respectably higher. For general Western horsemanship, the natural horsemanship clinicians have repopularized saddles with 3-, 4-, and even 5-inch cantles. Even Clinton Anderson uses a sort of hybrid Aussie-cowboy hornless saddle with a noticeable cantle.

The timed events of roping and steer wrestling require that the horse travel and stop with a low head carriage. Thus, the tie-down became universally popular with competitors in these events, but it should not be required in other horsemanship activities. It is an excuse for poor training and poor horsemanship. Nevertheless, because of rodeo's influence, the tie-down became very widespread in Western riding outside of rodeo. Today that trend is being reversed by the natural horsemanship movement.

Timed rodeo events also popularized rather severe leverage bits, gag bits, and mechanical-leverage hackamores. These were often expedient but not a tribute to the art of horsemanship. It is interesting to note that an increasing number of steer wrestlers are now using less severe snaffle bits. By the 2003 National Finals Rodeo, a *majority* of the steer wrestling contestants were riding horses in snaffles and, impressively, half of them stood tensed in the box, ready to explode out after their steer, on a *loose* rein. Natural horsemanship has even influenced the fiercely competitive sport of rodeo.

A few years ago, all barrel racers spurred wildly, and many whipped their horses ahead of the drive line, often in an uncoordinated way. Perhaps inspired by jockeys who cannot spur their racehorses and who, when they use the whip, coordinate it with their horse's stride *behind* the drive line, many of today's top professional barrel racers do better. Some are using snaffle bits and some have eliminated the tie-down. These changes must, in part, be the result of the revolution in horsemanship.

Rodeo has to some extent influenced the popularity of Western horse size. Team ropers, single steer ropers, and pickup men need big horses. But most Western riders today are trail riders who don't really need big horses. A very high percentage of today's stock horse breeds reside in suburban stables and carry children or lightweight women. Why do they need horses big enough to rope bulls? Many cowboys prefer a smaller, lithe, and agile horse. It is significant that the most popular cutting and reining horse bloodlines are mostly *smaller* horses. From a veterinarian's standpoint, smaller horses tend to stay sound better than heavier horses do. Wild horses rarely exceed 800 pounds in weight and often mature at far less. Lightweight breeds such as Welsh ponies and other pony breeds, Morgans, the smaller Arabians, and mustangs suffer fewer lower-leg lamenesses than do heavy breeds. It is the horse's own weight, not just the rider's weight, that contributes to breakdowns.

Despite the cited negative influences of the rodeo sport on Western horsemanship, there have been profound benefits.

For one thing, the extreme competitiveness of rodeo, where a fraction of a second often determines a winner in a timed event, has been a great stimulus to the breeding of better horses.

The American Quarter Horse breed, and those breeds with a lot of Quarter Horse blood such as the Appaloosa and the American Paint Horse, have been greatly influenced by the sport of Quarter Horse racing. The infusion of Thoroughbred blood goes back even before the establishment of the American Quarter Horse registry in 1940, but was thereafter accelerated by the racing sport. However, rodeo too has been a strong influence. Steer wrestling and roping require horses with tremendous sprinting ability, able to burst out after the quarry, reaching top speed within a few seconds. Calf-roping horses also need a spectacular sudden stop, and steer-roping horses need to be able to turn at high speed, as do barrel-racing horses. All this has encouraged selective breeding for these attributes so that today's stock horse breeds are the ultimate sprinters, stoppers, and turners of all horses ever bred.

Today, at Mexico's Charro Finals, nearly all contestants are mounted on American stock horse breeds—Quarter Horses, Paints, and Appaloosas—whereas thirty years ago most would have been on Andalusian or other Spanish breeds. The timed events have forced the selection.

Until well after World War II, dally roping as a timed rodeo event was a largely West Coast thing. Dally roping is the traditional Mexican style of roping where, after the bovine is caught in a thrown loop, the rope is wrapped around the saddle horn to stop the animal. Mexicans made this style of roping traditional in colonial California and in the Hawaiian Islands. In Texas, however, during the great trail-driving era, the early cowboys, not knowing how to "dally," simply tied the end of the rope to the saddle horn. This became known as "hard-and-fast" roping. Both styles had their devotees and they strongly touted the pros of their favored style and the cons of the other style.

The hard-and-fast ropers pointed out that careless dally ropers often lost a thumb which got caught in the wraps, and occasionally some fingers or a whole hand.

The dally ropers responded by noting that a wreck when tied hard and fast could easily lead to a disaster—even a sharp knife to cut the rope might not be employed fast enough to save an animal or a cowboy. They also gloated that dally roping was a more skillful art that hard-and-fast ropers simply hadn't mastered.

Even though some rodeo roping events are performed hard and fast (calf roping, and also single-steer roping, which is seen only in a few Western states), the immensely popular sport of team roping is an exclusively dally event. Both the header who ropes the steer's head and the heeler, who ropes the hind legs, must dally.

For most of the twentieth century, a very popular sport in the state of Arizona was a team roping event called "team tying." A header, tied hard and fast, roped a steer's head; then the heeler, tied hard and fast, roped the hind legs. The header then dismounted, ran to the steer, and tied a square knot around its hind legs with a separate length of rope, for time. The popular sport was indulged in not only by ranchers and working cowboys for which it was an everyday working ranch technique, but also by high school and college students, businessmen, and professionals. The team tyers were disdainful of the team roping sport, which employed dally roping and was largely a California thing.

But, by the last third of the century, a great change had occurred. Not only had Arizona converted to the dally roping sport of team roping California style, but the event had spread to every part of the nation and to Canada as well. Today, team roping, dally style, is an immensely popular sport everywhere. Since dismounting is not required, even overweight, out-of-shape older men can compete, and an ever-increasing number of women are active in the sport as well. Since the Quarter Horse excels in the necessary attributes of quick starts, acceleration, fast turns, hard stops, and sheer strength, the breed is an integral part of the sport, another example of how rodeo has influenced Western horses and horsemanship.

WEST TEXAS RANCH COWBOYS

We have seen how men who were rodeo cowboys made a dramatic life change and became pioneers and crusaders in the revolution in horsemanship. However, rodeo cowboys are not necessarily working ranch cowboys. Most of the clinicians we have cited were both at various times, and during the first half century of the rodeo sport, most participants had come, in fact, off the ranch.

That is no longer true. A large percentage of contestants today have never earned a living as a ranch cowboy. They are simply athletes who found their sports. To be truthful, many excellent ranch cowboys could not compete with these professional athletes in the arena, a reason why "ranch rodeos" are now becoming increasingly popular. They are designed for working cowboys and conducted with rules designed to duplicate realistic ranch work.

The real American icon is not the rodeo star, nor the Hollywood cowboy, nor the Marlboro Man. It is the man who earns his daily living mounted on a horse, working for a cattle ranch.

Earlier in this book, we observed that wherever a horse culture exists, that society glorifies its horses and horsemen. The style of horsemanship that evolved there is regarded as the epitome of fine horsemanship. The truth is that regardless of the culture, be it in Australia, in Argentina, in Mexico, in Mongolia, in the Arab societies, or in the North American West, we'll find great riders but examination of the horsemanship employed reveals the use of unnecessary coercion.

Surely no region on Earth is equated more fully with horses and horsemen than the American Southwest. This was frontier not so long ago, and the American cowboy has become an icon synonymous with the vast and spectacular region we know as the West.

In most of the northwestern American states and the western provinces of Canada huge ranches still exist and horses are essential to their operation. In these northern climes, cattle must be fed hay during the winter months and it is during the warm months, when cattle graze, that horses are primarily used.

However, in the southwestern United States, a milder climate means cowboys can be horseback throughout the year. Much of this land is arid, necessitating immense pastures. The cattle are often wild in such an environment, and the terrain can be ferocious.

West Texas is a classic example of such country where great ranches employ cowboys who work on horseback throughout the year, often living out on the range. Many of these big West Texas ranches still run chuck wagons and, although high tech may prevail back at the ranch headquarters, the cowboy's life hasn't changed too much from what it was a century or more ago.

In such an environment it is inevitable that strong traditions evolve and that the people involved take great pride in those traditions. Certainly the horsemanship methods that evolved in West Texas are powerfully traditional and virtually symbolic of the Southwestern cowboy culture.

It is, therefore, absolutely remarkable that the revolution in horsemanship has penetrated the traditional methods in that region. A change has occurred and is occurring, and it is a great tribute to those proud ranches that, having seen a better way, they were willing to make that change. It was no easy thing, because using time-tested traditional methods they produced many, many truly great horses and many gifted horsemen.

Buster McLaury, working cowboy, clinician, photographer, and writer. *(Buster McLaury Collection)*

Buster McLaury

Buster McLaury, of Paducah, Texas, is pure Texas cowboy. He has spent most of his life working cattle on the Great Plains, in Nevada buckaroo country, and in the Big Bend area of Texas, but mostly on the big ranches in the rugged brushlands of West Texas. In pastures that are from 5 to 20,000 acres in size, the cattle rarely see people and are out on the range all year, fending for themselves. They are essentially wild animals.

A top hand and also a talented photographer and writer, McLaury admits that when he first heard of natural horsemanship, he reacted as one would expect. He scoffed at it. But then he attended a Ray Hunt clinic in 1983 at the 6666 Ranch in Guthrie, Texas, and immediately became a convert. At the time, Hunt started colts there every year and did clinics, and Buster McLaury learned. In 1996, he began doing clinics himself because people asked him to. He never planned to become a clinician, but he now does them full time. When we spoke to him in May 2004 prior to the publication of this book, he was on his way to New York City to do a clinic at a dressage stable. Is this or is this not a revolution? Can one imagine, three decades ago, a West Texas cowboy teaching at a New York dressage stable? And would the riders at that stable have listened?

Buster McLaury has a lot of insight. "I've made my living riding horses all my life," he says. "As a working cowboy I liked riding good horses and I had a reputation for being able to handle them. Now I make a better hand. I'm not kept busy trying to stay in the middle of a horse. I have more time for the cattle, which is my job."

He points out that the ranches are changing in regard to horsemanship and that more of them will change in years ahead because of money.

"Ranch horse sales have become a big thing, and the people buying these horses want them to be safe and gentle. Horses are worth a lot these days. And, a lot of it is insurance driven. Liability and lawsuits and workman's comp premiums drive the move to safer horses."

Years ago, a common expression on the cattle ranches was, "He's a good horse, but it takes a cowboy to ride him."

What did that mean? It meant that the horse wasn't trustworthy. That is no longer acceptable.

Pitchfork Land and Cattle Company

The great Pitchfork Land and Cattle Company near Guthrie, Texas, is managed by Bob Moorhouse, a native Texan raised in the cattle ranching business. In the outstanding 1997 book, *The Texas Cowboy*, Thomas "Peeler" Saunders IV, one of the Pitchfork's top hands, says:

> These days, big ranches are adopting a new philosophy on starting their young horses. They bring in outside horsemen to help the cowboys start their colts and develop good horsemanship. The introduction of natural horsemanship through Tom Dorrance's disciples Ray Hunt, Pat Parelli, and Craig Cameron has given hands like myself an opportunity to offer big outfits a service their horses and their hands have responded to.

It is significant that the Pitchfork calls it "starting" horses. Some other ranches still refer to the process as "bronc breaking."

In 1997, the 6666 Ranch or the "Sixes," as it is known, hired a California cowboy full-time to start their colts using the methods he learned from Ray Hunt. Of course, not all of the big ranches in West Texas (or anywhere else for that matter), have converted to natural horsemanship. Many are still doing things the old way: bronc busting, tying up a hind leg, blindfolding and hobbling them, saddling them and then bucking them out.

King Ranch and Lester Buckley

Texas is a big state, and cattle ranching is an important industry throughout. The revolution is by no means confined to the western half. Down toward the Gulf Coast is the largest cattle ranch in the United States, the King Ranch, in existence since 1860. It is famous for its Santa Gertrudis cattle, its *vaqueros*, many of whom have worked there for generations, and its wonderful horses.

Lester Buckley grew up in the ranching country around Graham, Texas. He started training horses to finance his college education at Sul Ross University. In 1981, he met Ray Hunt and was overwhelmed with Hunt's methods, which were so different from those he was brought up with. He says, "From that moment I knew what I was meant for."

Buckley saw the light and became a disciple of Ray Hunt but says that he also learned important things from Bill Dorrance and John Lyons. After college he trained for some big ranches in Texas and in Canada. Then, for seven years, he trained cutting horses.

Traditionally, the King Ranch *vaqueros* started their own colts, using typical cowboy methods. But then the ranch began to hire freelance colt starters, and Buckley and his partner, Jimmy Scudda, would contract to work from November to February, starting around thirty colts. Afterwards, Buckley would go to the Parker Ranch in Hawaii, the largest ranch in the U.S. owned by a single individual, the late Richard Smart. For five years, he did this work for these two huge and famous ranches before becoming foreman on the Parker Ranch, full-time, for three years. He then returned to Texas and resumed training cutting horses and doing clinics for the public. In 2003, he moved to Hawaii permanently, taking his beloved old champion stallion, Colonel Win, with him.

Texas-bred cowboy Lester Buckley has used natural horsemanship techniques on the largest cattle ranches in the United States. *(Lester Buckley Collection)*

This Texas cowboy also goes to Germany to study dressage and classical horsemanship and is an instructor there in colt starting and ground training. Intelligent, sincere, humble and talented, he says that he learned from many people and many sources, but he learned the most from horses when alone with them. His motto is *"Think."*

Kokernot 06 Ranch

The Kokernot 06 Ranch is one of Texas's old historic cattle outfits. Part of each year, owners Diane and Chris Lacy, and their son, Lance, run a chuck wagon and camp-out while tending their cattle in the traditional fashion.

The horsemanship practiced on the Kokernot 06 is anything but traditional, however. Says Diane Lacy, "When we learned this kind of horsemanship from Ray Hunt years ago, the cowboys thought it was stupid and wimpy. Some refused to try it, and it created a lot of conflict. But we overcame that, and today we have a team spirit that includes the cowboys, the horses, and even the cattle. There is a whole philosophy here that is in effect with the horses, the cattle, other people, and our children. We used this approach exclusively with our kids, rewarding the slightest try and recognizing any effort."

"Driving 'em Down to HQ" at the Kokernot 06 Ranch in Texas. *(Diane Lacy, www.dianelacy.com)*

R. A. Brown Ranch

Founded in 1895, the R. A. Brown Ranch in Throckmorton, Texas, is one of the oldest and biggest cattle ranches in the state, often running more than 7,000 head of cattle. Owner R. A. Brown also has a very successful Quarter Horse breeding operation and is a member of the AQHA Hall of Fame. Brown tells how the revolution has affected him.

"Let's Go to Work" is an award-winning photograph that depicts life on the Kokernot 06 Ranch. *(Diane Lacy, www.dianelacy.com)*

"I grew up on a working ranch with Quarter Horses. My father helped organize AQHA. I learned how to break colts when I was in high school. They were three years old or older, and we roped 'em and choked 'em down and tied up a leg and bucked them out. The good hands could hit them with a quirt every jump. These old bloodlines were high tempered and most had buck in them. They were great horses but we had to fix them. Today they are relaxed and learn better. One of Ray Hunt's students came down here and showed us his methods which we'd never seen. We saw outlaw studs made gentle. All of my cowboys now use these methods. My son has his own method using what two or three of these clinicians have shown him. We won't use any other method now. It makes so much difference. We were doing everything wrong and we didn't know it. We were doing things just the opposite of the way we should have been doing them."

Moorhouse Ranch

At sixty-seven, Tom Moorhouse, of the Moorhouse Ranch in Benjamin, Texas, is an enthusiastic and vocal supporter of natural horsemanship.

"I was raised in the old school in ranch country and learned to break colts from men who were good hands for that day. But if I went down by my colt pens and saw horses being handled that way, I wouldn't like it. Today's methods don't use brute force, and things changed here in the '70s. Ray Hunt gets the credit. At first I thought his method might be okay for horses meant for women and kids, but after seeing his clinics I realized that it took years for a horse to overcome the way we started them. Today's broncs come out ready to learn. We try to treat colts here like we should treat our fellow man. We have better horses and better horsemen on the ranches. Today we wouldn't tolerate treating horses the way we did thirty years ago. My old dad liked what he saw when we changed. I'm glad I lived to see it."

Some traditions die hard, especially when they feed the egos of the male of our species. Not every great cattle ranch has adopted these methods, nor have all rodeo contestants. The simple fact is that some people *like* doing battle with a horse. But those who are serious about the most efficient ways to handle horses, who want the horses and cowboys to emerge uninjured and ready to tackle their jobs with gusto, have seen the light.

The most dramatic changes in human attitudes may have come from the rodeo and ranch worlds. But the most dramatic changes in horses have come from the purest bastion of equine behavior, the wild horse. We examine that next.

CHAPTER 9

WILD HORSES—
THE ULTIMATE TEST

WILD HORSES—or, more properly, *feral* horses because these are usually domestic horses gone wild, often centuries ago—exist in many parts of the world.

In western North America, they are known as mustangs (from the Spanish *mesteño*) and in Australia as brumbies.

In the early 1970s, The U.S. Bureau of Land Management discovered a herd of twenty-seven mustangs in a remote area of southeast Oregon. Believed to be pure-blooded descendants of the original Spanish horses brought to America centuries ago, the Kiger Mustang is now a recognized breed with its own registry. *(KMR/Rick Littleton)*

New Zealand has wild horses. Wild pony herds are found in the southeastern United States, and in the Dartmoor, Exmoor, and Dales National Parks in England.

There are wild horses in South America, in the Marquesas Islands in the South Pacific, and scattered elsewhere in the world. Until recently, Mauna Kea mustangs ran high in the mountains of the island of Hawaii.

Well into the twentieth century, "mustanging" was legal in the United States. Regular citizens captured mustangs by trapping them, by roping them from fleet horses, and even by "creasing," or disabling them by firing a rifle shot through the upper part of the neck, an injury from which some recovered and some did not.

After the century's midpoint, political activists obtained protective legislation to outlaw mustanging, and today roundups that cull the oversized herds on federal land are conducted and supervised exclusively by the government. The only way to get a mustang born wild in federal land today is to buy one at government auctions that are held regularly across the country by the Bureau of Land Management (BLM).

Breaking mustangs to saddle has traditionally been a rough, dangerous, and violent affair. It was illustrated in a 1961 movie, *The Misfits*, starring silver screen legends Clark Gable and Marilyn Monroe in the final film role for each of them. About the same time that Hollywood producers were presenting the traditional view in *The Misfits*, an alternative approach was being offered to the public by another Californian, veterinarian and future polo Hall of Famer, Dr. Billy Linfoot. In public demonstrations all over the United States, Linfoot would take a BLM mustang he had never seen before, work it in a round pen for 30 minutes, then ride it quietly about the ring. The remarkable speed with which Linfoot was able to consistently accomplish this work was aided by dispensing with a few steps that were unnecessary to get his point across. For example, he did not accustom the horse to either bridle or saddle. He simply roped the mustang, worked it in the round pen at the

Donner, a Kiger Mustang, was the model for Dreamworks' animated feature film *Spirit: Stallion of Cimarron. (KMR/Rick Littleton)*

end of the rope, carefully desensitized its head, rigged the lariat into a halter or "war bridle," then progressively desensitized the near side of its body, gradually jumping up and down until it would accept his weight upon its back. Finally, in less than half an hour, he was able to take an uneventful bareback ride about the corral. This round pen technique pioneered by Dr. Billy Linfoot is used on unbroken horses by most of today's clinicians. In fact, they have taken Linfoot's work even further, proving that mature, wild horses can be taught to accept saddle and rider, and turned into safe mounts in remarkably short time without using violence. Linfoot was an important early influence on horsemen such as Pat Parelli.

Another horseman well before his time was Australian Kell Jeffery, who worked with brumbies early in the twentieth century. Although he often demonstrated his method and has been recorded on motion picture film, the time was not historically correct. He failed to convince the majority of his countrymen, who were steeped in the frontier traditions.

However, one of Jeffery's disciples, a rancher named Maurice Wright, was an ardent convert, who produced a book and videotape explaining the method in detail. Both are titled *The Jeffery Method of Horse Handling,* and the videotape was popular enough and made late enough to become part of the revolution in horsemanship.

Maurice Wright visited the United States, and one of the people he influenced was a young man named Dave Dohnel, who operates a pack outfit out of The Frontier Pack Station in Bishop, California. Dohnel started buying mustangs at Bureau of Land Management government auctions, and using the Jeffery Method, combined with aspects of Monty Roberts's Join-Up method, he quickly produced mustangs that were safe and gentle enough for tourists to ride on his pack trips into California's Sierra Nevada and White Mountains.

In 1998, the popular television show *20/20,* hosted by Hugh Downs, featured Dave Dohnel and one of his pack trips. It also showed him starting a three-year-old wild mustang purchased at government auction. Edited down to about ten minutes, the training segment demonstrated the essence of the colt-starting technique used by most natural horsemanship practitioners, beginning with the frightened colt entering the round corral and ending with Dohnel riding the horse around, safely and gently, three hours later.

The next year, Dohnel led pack trips on this horse, named Keno, riding him much of the time with only a halter on his head. No bridle. No bit. See the sequence of photographs documenting this remarkable transformation.

From the 1998 TV program *20/20*, Dave Dohnel works a mustang colt in the round pen until the colt accepts him as a herd leader. They "join up." *(Debby Miller)*

An hour is spent quietly rubbing and stroking the colt, desensitizing him, picking up his feet, and occasionally reminding him to follow Dohnel. *(Debby Miller)*

Dohnel spends another half hour getting the mustang used to weight on his back. *(Debby Miller)*

The moment of truth: Dave Dohnel quietly and smoothly mounts. No problem. He is soon riding, using the halter to turn the colt. *(Debby Miller)*

Next, he introduces the colt, named Keno, to a bridle, a snaffle bit, and a saddle pad held in place with a surcingle. He works Keno around the pen, and they "join up" again. *(Debby Miller)*

Keno is then introduced to the saddle and it is quietly cinched in place. *(Debby Miller)*

But, when turned loose, Keno bucks violently, after which he anxiously returns to Dohnel for security. *(Debby Miller)*

From the ground, using the halter rope, Dohnel teaches the mustang colt to flex and yield laterally in each direction. *(Debby Miller)*

Demonstrating Join-Up once more, Keno follows Dohnel before he mounts up again, this time into the saddle. *(Debby Miller)*

Finally, the young mustang is mounted while saddled. *(Debby Miller)*

Keno, saddled and in the snaffle bit. CREDIT: *(Debby Miller)*

With Dave Dohnel's coaching from the sidelines, Hugh Downs creates a relationship with Keno. The colt accepts Downs's leadership and allows his feet to be picked up. Just three hours earlier, Keno had been a terrified wild animal. *(Debby Miller)*

Here is Dave Dohnel, the Frontier Pack Train outfitter, leading on Keno, one year after the mustang was started. On this day he rode him in a halter. Note the BLM freeze brand. *(Debby Miller)*

1999. Dohnel with Keno, this time in a snaffle. *(Debby Miller)*

In the year 2000, another TV documentary, "America's Lost Mustangs," was shown on National Geographic's Explorer series. In this show, a band of mustangs in northern New Mexico was rounded up and corralled in order for scientists to take blood samples for DNA testing. The goal was to determine whether these wild horses were direct descendants of the horses introduced centuries earlier by the Spanish Conquistadors. Pat Parelli and his crew were hired to capture the horses and then to gentle them enough that they could be blood-tested. Selecting one of the wilder mares in the group, Parelli used his natural horsemanship techniques to get her to bond and trust him. Forty minutes later, the relationship had progressed to the point that Parelli was able to *stand* on her back for the cameras. The veterinarian then drew blood from her jugular vein without using any form of restraint. The rest of the band was similarly gentled.

California clinician, Bryan Neubert, produced a video showing the entire process, in which he is introduced to a wild horse and, at the end, is riding it and reining it. No bucking, no choking it down, no battle.

Clinton Anderson has also made a series of six mustang-starting videotapes, showing the process from introduction to man to a compliant riding horse, the transformation taking but a few hours.

Monty Roberts is marketing a three-hour videotape series. In it, a mature mustang is seen from its first learning session to the end where it is quietly and responsively carrying a rider. At no point was the horse traumatized or brutalized in any way.

Richard Shrake has made a videotape demonstrating the system he calls Resistance Free™ Training applied to a wild horse, a captured and adopted BLM mustang. This tape, *Resistance Free™ Training the Wild Mustang*, like those mentioned above, demonstrates that even a mature horse born and grown up in the wild can be started and made a safe mount using quiet, gentle, and natural communication methods. Shrake says that properly started mustangs make fine riding horses. They are also excellent for driving and packing, are intelligent, have good feet, and are just generally tough. He has seen many make excellent show horses for children.

The National Wild Horse Show, held in Reno every summer, is limited to mustangs. Shrake, a very experienced judge of traditional horse shows, has also assisted in judging this event.

MUSTANGS AND INMATES

In 1985, the BLM hired Richard Shrake to start a mustang training program for inmates at the state prison in Cañon City, Colorado, under the auspices of the Secretary of the Interior, the Governor of Colorado, and the prison warden.

The prison had been using "bronc busting" techniques, and inmates and horses had been injured. Shrake worked for two weeks to set up a training program using his Resistance Free™ method. The program continues today.

According to Shrake, many ranchers who had previously regarded mustangs as pests changed their attitudes when they saw the good

An inmate goes bridle-less as supervisor Hank Curry looks on. Warm Springs Correctional Center, Carson City, Nevada.

using horses that were resulting from mustangs started in this non-traumatic way.

In 2000, another program using Shrake's methods was started at The Warm Springs Correctional Center, a state prison in Carson City, Nevada. Two years later, Hank Curry, a team roper and convert to natural horsemanship, was put in charge of the program, which used BLM mustangs and stray feral horses from state lands. After being trained by the inmates, these horses are sold in an annual auction. In 2003, the average price paid for mustangs at this auction was $1,150 per head, and one horse brought $4,700. One hundred percent of the horses in their program have been successfully adopted. Most of the horses are two- or three-year-olds, but older ones up to eleven years of age, are occasionally available.

Curry states that one of the most moving parts of the program has been the effect on the involved inmates. They develop great pride in their horses, and he believes some have developed a work ethic and sense of value they lacked before. Working with these wild colts has turned some lives around.

A few decades ago, a handful of American prisons had mustang-breaking programs for inmates. Brutal men were given frightened, wild horses and allowed, sadistically, to fight it out until one or the other was subdued. Thanks to the revolution in horsemanship, all that has changed. Men who have relied upon violence as a way of life are now learning that gentleness, kindness, and persuasion are a more effective way.

No stronger proof exists of the efficacy and logic in natural horsemanship than what can be done, and is being done, with the mustangs—animals born and grown up as wild animals, but tamed in hours and started on their way to becoming reliable saddle horses.

CHAPTER 10

IT'S NOT JUST ABOUT HORSES

IN ORDER TO UNDERSTAND THE BEHAVIOR of any domestic animal, we must first understand the behavior of its wild ancestors. The reason is evident in the light of modern scientific knowledge, but this wasn't true until relatively recent times. We now know that each species adapts to its habitat in three ways: anatomically, physiologically, and behaviorally. Natural selection establishes these three qualities. Reproduction in wild species occurs naturally.

In a domestic environment, however, reproduction is controlled artificially, by the intent and the whim of the humans who control the animals' lives. The criteria that suit us may be quite different from those that best adapt the animal to its natural environment. We humans, therefore, have bred various domestic species for such qualities as color, size, conformation, and specific attributes such as scent tracing or herding talents in dogs, aggressiveness in fighting cocks, marbled muscle in beef cattle, long soft wool in some breeds of sheep, and lack of horns in some breeds of cattle.

In the horse we have bred for extremes in size, color, speed, extreme animation, smooth gaits, extremes in conformation, and docility. These qualities usually do not enhance the wild horse's chance for survival in a predator-filled natural environment. That is why, when horses become feral, as in the case of America's mustangs, they soon begin to revert to resemble their primitive ancestors. They become hardier, smaller, and more alert. They also tend toward bland coloration like dun, buckskin, or roan.

Although it may profoundly *alter* the natural behavior of the ancestral wild horse, domestication does not *eliminate* the basic characteristics of the species. Why? Because they are genetically fixed! Flightiness, perceptiveness, speed of learning, phenomenal memory, herd instinct, desire to follow a leader, precocity of its young, and method of establishing dominance hierarchy with its peers are retained in the domestic descendant.

Only genetic engineering can completely eradicate these qualities, and with modern technology there is little doubt that some people can and will do just that.

Humans too are a domestic species, if you will. Certainly we do not live as our primitive ancestors did, and even the earliest human cultures departed from the reproductive criteria natural to our species and substituted artificial selection for natural selection. Reproduction in *Homo sapiens* from early times has been artificially determined by parental selection of mates, family ties, the size of dowries, enslavement and other forms of force, and placing value upon physical characteristics that would have little value in ensuring the survival of prehistoric man.

Diseases that would have culled the population of early man because afflicted individuals would not have survived to reproduce are controlled today via the science of modern medicine. Thus people with such potentially inheritable afflictions as diabetes mellitus, severe allergies, certain renal and cardiac diseases, or simply a weak immune system, can survive and reproduce. Such physical problems are therefore increasing in the human population. Indeed, the simple athletic ability necessary for very early man to hunt and survive is no longer an essential criteria. Civilization prioritizes other qualities, such as handsomeness, personality, articulateness, and intelligence.

The point is to make it clear that we humans are still encumbered with animal instincts and congenitally predetermined behaviors that are detrimental in a civilized society.[1] In some ways we have not evolved very much at all. The evidence is all around us: graffiti, gang warfare, spousal and child abuse, felony, and the quickness to use force and inflict pain upon domestic animals to obtain their compliance.

---

[1]Yet, until the late twentieth century, it was widely believed, even by many distinguished academic behavioral scientists, that behavior in man was all learned behavior, and that we lacked the instinctive behavior that exists in all other mammals.

The great religions teach the brotherhood of man and decry our baser human emotions, but behavior is so firmly entrenched in the DNA of our species that mankind has repeatedly corrupted the teachings of the great religious leaders and has repeatedly reverted to its animal instincts.

That people *can* put aside their differences and get along quite well has, of course, been demonstrated many times. As a single current example, the state of Hawaii is populated by an incredibly diverse population of many different racial, ethnic, and social origins. They get along remarkably well, most them regarding themselves primarily as Hawaiians and as Americans, serving as a notable example to the rest of a troubled world.

The revolution in horsemanship has proven that we humans can use our *power of reason* to displace our animal instincts, and to have an amicable relationship with another individual, no matter how different that individual is from us. We *can* avoid the use of force, eliminate conflict, and establish a mutually beneficial relationship *if we know how.*

Why can we make this statement? Haven't we had a strong relationship with dogs since long before we domesticated the horse? Yes, but our relationship with dogs has been facilitated by our similarities. Both the human and the canine species are omnivorous pack hunters. Each has qualities that are superior to the other's: the dog has speed, endurance, and exceptional sense of smell; the human has the power of reason and the use of tools. Both species defer to the alpha male. Both are strongly bonded to the group. They are highly compatible species.

The horse, on the other hand, is the antithesis of man. One is the ultimate prey, the other the ultimate predator.

The horse, unlike most herbivorous grazers, lacks horns as a last-ditch means of defense. Its primary survival behavior is flight, and its entire anatomy and physiology are designed for flight. It *is* the ultimate prey creature.

Man, on the other hand, because of his unique brain and because he is a tool user, became the ultimate predator. Bipedal, with an opposable thumb, and binocular stereoscopic vision that gave him excellent depth perception, primitive man, when armed with a spear or a sling, became an incredibly effective hunter. He remains the ultimate predator and today he outnumbers any large mammal that has ever existed on this planet, past or present, and completely dominates every habitat in which he resides.

If these two extremes in life forms can get along well without one controlling the other simply by the use of force, that is indeed a significant

Assertive body language has replaced physical violence in training horses. Clinician Linda Parelli demonstrates how she would ask a horse to back up. *(Photos by Coco)*

accomplishment and the reason why the success of the revolution in horsemanship has implications far beyond the simple domination of a domestic animal that is now largely archaic and relegated to the role of a recreational object.

Most traditional forms of horsemanship may be compared to human slavery. Both were a part of every past culture. Both were widely accepted morally. Both were effective and had an important role in human culture. Although often tempered with kindness and consideration, both were based upon involuntary servitude and backed by force. Both justified the use of violence if the subject rebelled. Both had enlightened critics who knew there was a better way, a more just and moral way, and a *more effective* way, but their voices were ignored throughout history.

Natural horsemanship, by contrast, utilizes persuasive methods, natural to the horse, spurning forceful methods, to obtain the willing cooperation of the horse. It emphasizes partnership, not enslavement.

The clinicians who pioneered this movement use phrases to explain their philosophy like "nonconfrontational," "resistance free," "natural," "make your idea his idea," and "make the wrong thing difficult and the right thing easy."

We need these skills in our human relationships. We have not, as a species, learned yet to adequately control our animal instincts. Our divorce rate, our crime rate, the percentage of our population that is incarcerated, and the prosperity of the legal profession all attest to our inability to get along with others. So do labor disputes, and so does a glance at any major newspaper.

Human history is a chronicle of warfare. Any differences create conflict. Why? Witness the Balkan nations. Observe the animosity in Northern Ireland between Protestant and Catholic, each professing to be Christian.

Observe Africa. The common enemy, the European white man, has been diminished or ousted. In his place tribe has turned on tribe, committing unspeakable acts.

Observe the Middle East. Who benefits by the unending horror? Why does it occur?

Racial, ethnic, or religious differences precipitate conflict. Even language differences pit us against one another. What possible gain is it to either side if Canada splits into English- and French-speaking territories?

The most minor differences are an excuse for human conflict. Consider soccer riots. How do we explain the blind fanaticism so many of us show for sports teams? Isn't this just another version of primitive tribalism?

Look at regional conflicts, even where other differences do not exist. Upstate New York derides New York City. Northern California denounces Southern California. "Yankees" and "Rebels." Scots and English. Bavarians and Northern Germans. Basques and the rest of Spain.

Are we wrong to draw an analogy between such human conflicts and our traditional relationship with the horse? Is it fallacious to state that the principles of natural horsemanship can be utilized to overcome so many of our human conflicts?

Every one of the leading clinicians with whom we have spoken has told us that the skills he acquired to improve his relationships with horses have also improved relationships with fellow humans. Our lives are filled with potential conflicts, with our spouses, with our children, between teacher and student, between employer and employee, between merchant and customer, between professional and client, between voter and legislator, between citizen and law enforcer.

Consider this revolution and those who launched it. They were just a bunch of cowboys. Most of them grew up with some form of hardship. Many were traumatized by a less than ideal parental relationship. Half of them have confessed to paternal abuse, not sexual but verbal or physical abuse by a father. Several of the clinicians have described this publicly in their books or in public clinics or in conversation.

We discussed this phenomenon with a psychotherapist who worked with prison inmates incarcerated for felonious abuse. She explained that boys, abused by their fathers, usually either became abusers themselves after they were grown, or conversely, became very empathetic, kind, and solicitous.

All the founding clinicians were originally schooled in traditional Western horsemanship: Rope 'em, blindfold 'em, hobble 'em, sack 'em out, and then buck 'em out. These methods grew out of a harsh frontier when men and horses were wild and cheap. It was expedient. It worked well enough for that time and place.

But the world has changed. These clinicians rose above their crude teachings and saw the horse for what it is: a timid prey creature that wants only to survive, preferably by running away. Using kinder, calmer, less intimidating, and less traumatic methods that they either conceived or learned from an inspiring mentor, they perfected their horsemanship. Then, driven to share this revelation, and imbued with an evangelical spirit, they went public with it, determined to convince as many people as possible that a better way exists—a more civilized way—a more moral way.

They have proven the validity of natural horsemanship. For millennia most of the human race treated horses as slaves. These men have shown us a better way. Their contributions deserve to be recognized.

Numerous men and women have joined the campaign, as clinicians or simply as horse people who revel in having found a better way.

This book was written to celebrate the accomplishments of the horsemen who launched a revolution, to recognize their contributions, to encourage people everywhere, whether or not they work with horses, to adopt the Golden Rule: to treat other individuals as they themselves would like to be treated.

PART II

CHAPTER 11

EARLY NATURAL HORSEMEN

THE OLD TESTAMENT TELLS US "there is nothing new under the sun" (Ecclesiastes 1:9) and when it comes to horse training, there is a great deal of truth to that simple maxim. Much of the philosophy and many of the training methods embraced by natural horsemanship today can be traced to earlier horsemen.

SIMON OF ATHENS (ca. 400 B.C.)

"What a horse does under compulsion he does blindly, and his performance is no more beautiful than would be that of a ballet-dancer taught by whip and goad" (H. G. Dakyns translation). This statement is attributed to Simon of Athens, the earliest known writer on humane horse training.

Little is known for certain about Simon. The Greek general and writer Xenophon called him a "great expert on horsemanship" and referred to him repeatedly in his own writings. Simon also wrote a book on horsemanship, but aside from a few fragments, only one chapter, dealing with selection and conformation, has survived. The manuscript resides at Emmanuel College in Cambridge, England.

Clearly Simon was already famous at the time Xenophon wrote of him. As a way of identifying him to the reader, Xenophon referred to a bronze statue of a horse near the Eleusinion sanctuary, an important ceremonial site in Athens. Simon's exploits were represented in carved relief on its pedestal.

History remembers an odd little story about Simon. It seems he offered some criticism of a painting by Micon, a Greek artist of the mid-400s B.C. known for his paintings of battles, including the battle of Marathon. "The famous rider Simon" was said to have stated that he had never before seen a horse with eyelashes on the lower lids. It was the only defect anyone could find in the painting.

This is all we know for sure about Simon. There are several other interesting possibilities, however.

Simon was reputed to have been an excellent rider who developed his humane system of horsemanship when assigned to resurrect a cavalry unit in Athens.

Simon's horses may have been the models for the horses depicted in the frieze of the Parthenon, generally considered representative of the Greek ideal in equine conformation.

Gaius Plinuis Secundus (Pliny the Elder) wrote in his book *Natural History* circa A.D. 50 that the sculptor Demetrius had made a statue of Simon dressed as a knight. Modern scholars believe, however, that old Pliny was mistaken on this point.

In the nineteenth century, German archeologist and vase expert Friedrich William Eduard Gerhard (1795–1867) felt he had found Simon represented as a charioteer with his name inscribed on a vase.

Archaeologist Wolfgang Helbig (1839–1915) speculated that he was the Simon mentioned in Aristophanes' comedy *The Knights* and that he was Hipparch, or cavalry general, in 424 B.C.

As an historical figure, Simon is a bit of a mystery man. What is indisputable, however, is his influence on the venerable Xenophon, who included the "dancer" quote in his writing. This quote deserves closer examination.

Simon surely felt that the use of force and pain in training horses was wrong. By invoking the image of a human dancer being treated in this manner, he ensured a certain moral indignation on the part of the reader. But in this one sentence, Simon also revealed that he was a pragmatist. Whether applied to dancer or horse, physical coercion does not produce pleasing results. From a purely practical standpoint, both horse and dancer will deliver better performances if they want to do the jobs they are being asked to do.

The modern natural horseman would undoubtedly agree. The ideal today is the relaxed yet attentive horse that is eager to tackle the next job given to him but that will wait quietly until the rider's wishes are made known. That is simply not attainable when the horse is in constant fear of being hurt.

One writer on horsemanship known to predate Simon focused almost entirely on the physical conditioning of horses for war and chariot racing. He was Kikkuli, a respected horse trainer in the country of Mitanni, near modern-day Syria. Around 1345 B.C., Kikkuli defected to the service of the Hittite king, Suppiliiuma, and wrote a horse-training regimen in cuneiform on four clay tablets. These were later found in the royal archives at the Hittite capitol of Hattusas and are known today as "The Kikkuli Text."

Kikkuli's seven-month training plan began with a culling process that subjected the prospects to severe tests of endurance and near-starvation diets. He also confined the horses for ten days in stables with minimal ventilation to identify any that were prone to chronic respiratory disease. Horses that made the cut faced months of intense workouts—sometimes three a day, in what we would call Interval Training—with carefully timed rest periods, precise feeding, and regular bathing and grooming.

The Kikkuli Method was duplicated in 1991 at the University of New England in Australia and the test horses remained sound while becoming extremely fit. Kikkuli clearly excelled at the physical side of training, but his writings gave no indication at all that he worked with the horse's mind. The earliest known writings on that approach to training came ten centuries later.

XENOPHON (430–355 B.C.)

Xenophon was a Greek general, statesman, philosopher, writer, and horseman. A Renaissance man 1,800 years before the Renaissance and a contemporary of Socrates, Plato, and Aristotle, he is still celebrated today for his forward-thinking views on horsemanship.

Several complete Xenophon treatises on a variety of subjects have survived intact, including *Peri Hippikes* or *The Art of Horsemanship*, written in 360 B.C. This short and unpretentious book is required reading for any serious horseman (it is easily found in book form and may be read online in its entirety). At least three different translations from the original Greek are available. The M. H. Morgan translation is quoted here.

Early in *The Art of Horsemanship*, Xenophon stated that his intent was to educate his younger friends, the rank and file soldiers or "privates," in matters of horsemanship. In a separate treatise, Xenophon discussed the duties of the cavalry commander.

Whether Xenophon was a nonconformist in his views on horsemanship or simply reflected the prevailing thought of his time is impossible to say with certainty. We know that he was in general agreement with Simon, and the fact that both argued for the humane and psychological training of horses suggests that it was not practiced as widely as they would have liked. The period in which they lived, which produced some of the greatest thinkers mankind has known, is also known for behavior that is barbaric by modern standards. Presumably some of that barbarism was directed at horses.

Xenophon was born into a family of knights and had a great deal of experience on the battlefield before writing *The Art of Horsemanship*. He was, first and foremost, a soldier, and as such he could not afford to be an idealist, an ivory-tower dreamer. His philosophy and methods of horsemanship were undoubtedly founded, as were Simon's, on the practical concerns of getting maximum performance and obedience from the horses they took into battle. "A disobedient horse is not only useless," he wrote, "but he often plays the part of a very traitor."

The genius of Xenophon was that he obtained obedience from the horse without resorting to violence. Like the great natural horsemen who would follow him, he tried his best to see the world through the horse's eyes. He also understood, better than most, man's foibles. His suggestions, written more than 2,300 years ago, are timeless and universally respected.

Let's take a look at a few of them.

1. "The one great precept and practice in using a horse is this—never deal with him when you are in a fit of passion." Anger, impatience, fear, virtually any human emotion undermines a horseman's ability to effectively handle his horse. It's best to just walk away from the situation if you are losing your self-control.

2. "Smooth bits are more suitable for such [high-mettled horses] than rough, but if a rough one is put in, it must be made as easy as the smooth by lightness of hand." Any bit may be made gentle by the technique of the rider.

3. "The groom should also be directed to lead him through crowds, and to make him familiar with all sorts of sights and all sorts of noises. Whenever the colt is frightened at any of them, he should be taught, not by irritating him but by soothing him, that there is nothing to fear." This is progressive desensitization, the backbone of modern problem solving with horses.

4. ". . . it is the best of lessons if the horse gets a season of repose whenever he has behaved to his rider's satisfaction." Often, the

greatest reward one can give a horse is to let him rest and think about the lesson.

5. "Neither horse nor man likes anything in the world that is excessive." Xenophon seemed to favor moderation as did Aristotle, who felt it was the key to happiness and the path to virtue. However, this quote is noteworthy for another subtler reason. As Dr. Eve Browning (University of Minnesota Duluth) puts it in her essay *Xenophon on the Minds of Horses*, ". . . the emphasis of the training advice is upon what is pleasing to the horse. Thus the horse is conceived as a partner, rather than an object . . . a partner whose willing and appreciative participation in the project is essential to its success." Xenophon repeatedly advised making training enjoyable for the horse.

6. "Anything forced and misunderstood can never be beautiful." This is the most frequently quoted of Xenophon's ideas, and its truth is self-evident.

Throughout his writing, Xenophon promoted the idea of psychological harmony between horse and rider. To him, the good horseman had empathy for his horse. He genuinely cared about the quality of his horse's life, from one moment to the next. He cared not only because it was the morally correct thing to do, but also because ultimately, it produced the most reliable partner and the greatest chance of survival in battle.

ALEXANDER THE GREAT (356–323 B.C.)

Just how great Alexander the Great was is a question still open to debate. Some consider him the most charismatic and heroic king of all times; others accuse him of unbridled ambition and vanity. He was probably all of that and more. He was certainly a military genius, and in his short life—he died in his thirty-third year—he changed the world forever.

The tale of the precocious boy Alexander taming the fiery stallion Bucephalus has been told and retold, embellished and analyzed. It is here as translated from the account written by Plutarch.

Philonicus the Thessalian brought the horse Bucephalus to Philip, offering to sell him for thirteen talents; but when they went into the field to try him, they found him so very vicious and unmanageable, that he reared up when they endeavoured to mount him, and would not so much as endure the voice of any of Philip's attendants. Upon which, as they were leading him away as wholly useless and untractable, Alexander, who stood by, said, "What an excellent horse do they lose for want of address and boldness to manage him!" Philip at first took no notice of what he said; but when he heard him repeat the same thing several times, and saw he was much vexed to see the horse sent away, "Do you reproach," said he to him, "those who are older than yourself, as if you knew more, and were better able to manage him than they?" "I could manage this horse," replied he, "better than others do." "And if you do not," said Philip, "what will you forfeit for your rashness?" "I will pay," answered Alexander, "the whole price of the horse." At this the whole company fell a-laughing; and as soon as the wager was settled amongst them, he immediately ran to the horse, and taking hold of the bridle, turned him directly towards the sun, having, it seems, observed that he was disturbed at and afraid of the motion of his own shadow; then letting him go forward a little, still keeping the reins in his hands, and stroking him gently when he found him begin to grow eager and fiery, he let fall his upper garment softly, and with one nimble leap securely mounted him, and when he was seated, by little and little drew in the bridle, and curbed him without either striking or spurring him. Presently, when he found him free from all rebelliousness, and only impatient for the course, he let him go at full speed, inciting him now with a commanding voice, and urging him also with his heel. Philip and his friends looked on at first in silence and anxiety for the result, till seeing him turn at the end of his career, and come back rejoicing and triumphing for what he had performed, they all burst out into acclamations of applause; and his father shedding tears, it is said, for joy, kissed him as he came down from his horse, and in his transport said, "O my son, look thee out a kingdom equal to and worthy of thyself, for Macedonia is too little for thee."

This story is a textbook example of natural horsemanship at work:

First, young Alexander did not see force as the way to get what he wanted from Bucephalus. He looked for another way.

Second, he had empathy; he was able to imagine himself in the horse's position. When he saw the world through the horse's eyes, he realized that Bucephalus was acting from fear.

Third, he used his powers of observation to find the source of the fear. In this case, it was the horse's shadow. (Scholars speculate that Bucephalus was handled roughly prior to this incident and that the shadow only exacerbated his fear.)

Fourth, Alexander demonstrated confidence, leadership, and sensitivity when he addressed the horse. He didn't coddle Bucephalus, but he did comfort him and give him adequate time to process what was going on. When he saw signs that Bucephalus understood and accepted his new master, Alexander put him immediately to work.

This remarkable exhibition was recorded as the first portent of the greatness Alexander would achieve.

Alexander and Bucephalus were both twelve years old at the time, according to most accounts. Over the next eighteen years, they developed a deep bond. It is said that Bucephalus never allowed another rider to mount him and, although he was not a particularly large horse, he would lower his body to help the rather slight Alexander climb on. At the time, horses were ridden with only bridles and cloths over their backs; leather saddles and stirrups were not yet in use. Still, Alexander and Bucephalus rode thousands of miles together and fought valiantly in many battles. Bucephalus died in 326 B.C. at the ripe old age of thirty. Some accounts claim it was from battle wounds suffered during Alexander's invasion of India. Others attribute the stallion's death to fatigue and old age. For his beloved horse, Alexander led a grand funeral and, in memoriam, built a city by the name of Bucephala near the site of his death and burial. Archaeologists still search the area near modern Jhelum, in Pakistan, for traces of Bucephalus' tomb.

As for Alexander the Great of Macedonia, he died under mysterious circumstances just three years later. It is likely that he was deliberately poisoned.

The stallion's name, Bucephalus, meant "ox-head." The horse had a rather large head with huge eyes, set well on the side of his head, a wide poll and broad forehead, wide cheekbones, and a crisply defined muzzle with sensitive nostrils and lips. These were traits favored in well-bred cattle— quite different from the look of the Arabian horse—and were typical of locally bred horses of the time. Equine phrenologists might say that Bucephalus' head suggested intelligence and tractability. Thus, far from being an insult, "ox-head" was a highly complimentary descriptor, and could probably be correctly applied to many of today's finest American Quarter Horses.

Bucephalus was brown in color and was said to have carried on his forehead (or his haunch, according to some), a white mark in the shape of an ox's head, a rather remarkable coincidence. Some historians claim that Bucephalus had three toes on each leg, with the middle toe bearing all the weight; if so, he was a throwback to a primeval form.

The tale of Alexander and Bucephalus is natural horsemanship's first success story. It has a romantic, timeless appeal to it, and likely inspired Walter Farley's acclaimed 1941 novel *The Black Stallion*, the story of another fiery stallion that could be ridden by no one except a young boy named, fittingly, Alec.

THE UNKNOWN PERIOD (ca. 355 B.C.–1434 A.D.)

After Xenophon came a gap of nearly 1,800 years—spanning the decline of the Greeks, the rise and fall of the Roman Empire, the Middle Ages, and well into the Renaissance—before we find more writing on horse-training techniques.

It was during the Middle Ages that feudalism came and went. Knights in heavy armor riding massive chargers used severe curb bits with shanks up to 20 inches long, spiked nosebands, and spurs with razor-sharp points to control the massive horses they rode in battle and in jousting competition. It was a dark age for horsemanship as it was for human behavior in general.

Stirrups and horseshoes came into use during this period, but these inventions were more for making riders more efficient at killing their enemies than for pure horsemanship.

The picture changed during the Renaissance (circa 1350–1550 A.D.), a period of revived intellectual and artistic activity in Europe. As early as 1381, books on equitation may have been in Portugal, but the long literary silence was officially broken with the 1434 book by Dom Duarte I (King Eduard of Portugal), *Livro de Ensynanca de Bem Cavalgar toda a Sela*. Duarte wrote about jousting on the lighter Iberian (modern-day Lusitano) horses.

In the waning years of the Renaissance, the tools of warfare changed. Lances, broadswords, and heavy armor went out, as did the heavy horses needed to carry them. Crossbows and firearms came in and smaller, nimbler horses became popular once again. The forgotten works of Xenophon were rediscovered and writing on horsemanship commenced in Italy, with the focus on arena riding. The words painted a disturbing picture. Widely admired horsemen such as Grisone and Pignatelli quoted Xenophon, but advocated an almost psychotic blend of kindness and extreme cruelty[1] to subdue what they claimed was a naturally vicious creature. It would be several more generations before a French classical master changed that mindset.

ANTOINE DE LA BAUME PLUVINEL (1556–1620)

The Frenchman Antoine de Pluvinel was repulsed by the violent training methods used by his teacher, Battista Giovanni Pignatelli of the Neapolitan Riding School, and Federico Grisone, the founder of the *haute école* (French for "high school") type of arena riding. He rejected the corporal punishment and torture these men recommended to achieve total obedience from a horse. He was the first known riding master after Xenophon to take the horse's mind into account in his teaching and training.

Antoine de la Baume Pluvinel.

Pluvinel was a riding arena academic who considered the art of riding a worthy end in itself, a common view held well into the 1700s. "He insisted on and promoted the combined development of the rider's mind and body," writes Paul Belasik in *Dressage for the 21st Century.* "Pluvinel taught dancing, fencing, art, mathematics and philosophy to his students . . . (and) instilled in the young nobleman such ideals as honor, courage, pride and virtue—the qualities of classical humanism." Pluvinel clearly saw riding as part of a broader program to make better human beings. Nothing could be more in tune with the revolution in horsemanship of the late twentieth century.

At a time when others viewed the horse as a dressage object without a soul, Pluvinel considered it a sensitive creature and treated it as such. He encouraged a horse to perform for him of its own free will rather than by forced subjugation. In his words, "We must take care not to discourage the horse and suffocate its natural grace, which is like the flowery scent of fruit that will never return if it is lost!"

---

[1]According to Gill Stuart, in his *Dressage* magazine series "The Classical Masters," Grisone's recommendation for a horse that was difficult to mount was to hit it between the eyes and about the body with a stick. "He also advocated letting a cat tied by its back to a pole crawl over the horse's belly and between its hind legs," Stuart writes. "When a horse did not want to go forwards, Grisone's treatment was to hold burning straw under its tail or a live hedgehog and also had human helpers armed with sharpened spikes to strengthen his dominance. All of these actions were accompanied by loud verbal threats."

Pluvinel conducts a training session in the pillars as young King Louis XIII looks on. *(Crispin de Pas)*

It is believed that Pluvinel invented the pillars, a training tool used to teach horses the leaping movements known as "airs above the ground." The horse, with or without a rider, was tied to a single immovable pillar, or tied between two such pillars, and urged into attempting these difficult and dangerous airborne maneuvers. The pillars are still used by some *haute école* trainers today.

Curiously, Pluvinel saw the whip and spur as a "confession of failure," yet both are present in the scenes that illustrate his book. Pluvinel's whip, or *chambriere,* was a 4-foot cane with a 6-foot, loosely braided leather thong attached. It is the forefather of the "stick and string" devices used by today's natural horsemen.

Pluvinel also advocated the use of the voice as a riding aid, calling it "the spur of the mind."

As Simon and Xenophon did a thousand years earlier, Pluvinel believed there was a practical connection between the horse's state of mind and the outcome desired by the rider. ". . . the horse should enjoy himself in his work," he said, "otherwise neither the horse nor the rider would be able to give an elegant performance."

Said to have been a perfect rider by the age of seventeen, Pluvinel was admired throughout his life for his riding skills and is remembered as the greatest French rider of his time.

Pluvinel was a highly educated man and became both riding teacher and advisor to King Louis XIII, spending part of his time serving as a diplomat in foreign countries.

His book, *Le Manege Royal par Antoine de Pluvinel*, was his crowning achievement. It was composed as a dialogue with the king and was illustrated with stunning copperplate engravings. Unfortunately, Pluvinel died before it was completed. The book was finished by a friend and presented to the king in 1623.

WILLIAM CAVENDISH, DUKE OF NEWCASTLE (1592–1676)

Englishman William Cavendish, the first Duke of Newcastle, was a vain and arrogant man who was absolutely convinced that his riding and training methods were the best ever conceived. He considered those around him to be fools with no appreciation of the art of classical dressage. In the conclusion of his first book, *A General System of Horsemanship*, published in 1658, he wrote, "If this work pleases you, I shall be thoroughly well satisfied; if not, I shall be content in my own mind, because I know certainly that it is very good, and better than anything that you have had before of the kind."

His work *was* very good, at least some of it, and the high esteem in which he would later be held by Guérinière is reason enough to look past his personality quirks to consider his actual horsemanship.

Cavendish (pronounced "Candish" at the time) was born to the English aristocracy. He learned to ride as a ten-year-old boy and studied under some of the best riding masters in Europe before developing his own training methods. His formal education was at St. John's College, Cambridge. He fought as a cavalry officer on the side of King Charles I in the English Civil War. After his side's defeat by Oliver Cromwell, he went into exile in France where he was exposed to the French theories of arena horsemanship. Later he joined the dead king's son, the future Charles II, in Antwerp, Belgium, where Cavendish started his famous riding school and wrote his first book. Upon

William Cavendish, the first Duke of Newcastle.

restoration of the English monarchy in 1660, he returned to England, regained most of his land, and was elevated to dukedom in 1665.

In 1667 he published his second book, *A New Method and Extraordinary Invention to Dress Horses and Work Them According to Nature.* At a time when coercion was still the rule in *haute école*, Cavendish urged employing patience and understanding of the horse's nature. He wrote, "I work on the horse's memory, imagination and judgment, which is why my horses go so well. Forgive him his faults that in the morning he may well know you have mercy as well as justice."

He used soft, narrow leather in his bridles and cavessons ". . . for I would not hurt his mouth nor his nose nor anything about him if I could help it."

But, like the *haute école* trainers he disdained, Cavendish seemed to many to be inconsistent and unnecessarily cruel. Gill Stuart, in his *Dressage* magazine series "The Classical Masters," explained.

Cavendish apparently did believe in reward and affection. Two examples of his practice, however, could lead one to think otherwise. Firstly, he says that the horse should be made to fear the rider, a sentiment echoed by quite a few of the masters. In Cavendish's case, he said it was necessary "to make the horse follow my ways and obey them. If he fears you, he loves you for his own sake." Secondly is his recommended use of the spurs, which were made out of silver so that they would not rust: "The shanks of the spurs should be long, the rowels should have six sharp points. When they are used, the blood should flow freely." He also says "I seldom beat them, or punish them with either rod or spur but when I meet with great resistance, and that rarely."

Cavendish disapproved of using the pillars, saying the practice is "against the natural order and mortifies all horses," yet he had a penchant for using draw reins and driving the horse with whip and spur into an unnatural, overbent posture. By his own admission, he ruined many horses in his learning process.

His faults notwithstanding, Cavendish did advance the idea of training horses using psychological techniques, and his contribution to the study of dressage, especially the airs, is undeniable. The shoulder-in movement, invented for dressage and performed along the arena wall by Guérinière, was first a training exercise performed on a circle by Cavendish.

Cavendish believed that the whole object of dressage schooling is to "get the horse upon the haunches," that is, to get him to shift his weight back and get his hind legs more underneath him. This is necessary not only for the advanced high school maneuvers known as the airs, but is also desirable in every other form of riding as well, for the hind end is the source of a horse's power and forward thrust, and he has best use of it when it is more underneath him rather than strung out behind him.

FRANÇOIS ROBICHON DE LA GUÉRINIÈRE (1688–1751)

Called "the Father of Classical Equitation" and "the Patron Saint of Dressage," François Robichon de la Guérinière marked a true turning point in the history of horsemanship in Europe. The Spanish Riding School in Vienna, Austria, still adheres closely to his methods today.

It is believed that Guérinière based his teachings on the work of fellow Frenchman Antoine de Pluvinel, but his timeless 1729 book *École de Cava-lerie* ("School of Horsemanship") mentions Pluvinel only once, giving more ink to Pluvinel's colleague, Salomon de la Broue and to the Duke of Newcastle. Guérinière seemed particularly concerned that these men received credit for inspiring his most famous invention, the shoulder-in movement.

What is so special about the shoulder-in? Modern dressage master Paul Belasik explains, "The shoulder-in, in one exercise, marries these two great lines of technical study: lateral balance and longitudinal balance. Guérinière goes on to plait in a third strand of humanity—compassion—to come up with a beautiful braid, the art of dressage."

The Portuguese master Nuno Olivera said of the shoulder-in, "It's the aspirin of horseback riding; it cures everything."

Besides the shoulder-in, Guérinière is also credited with inventing the half-halt, the counter canter, and the flying lead change.

Guérinière is remembered as a thoughtful, intelligent man of high ideals, a skilled

F. R. de la Guérinière demonstrates the shoulder-in exercise in an engraving from his book *École de Cavalerie*.

teacher who cared more about the art of riding than making money. He attracted riding students from all over Europe, but the riding academy he opened in Paris in 1716 still operated at a loss.

Guérinière believed that basic training should be the same for every horse, regardless of its intended use, and stressed the importance of *understanding* the horse: "The knowledge of the nature of the horse is one of the first foundations of the art of riding it, and every horseman must make it his principal study."

Concern with preserving the horse's physical and mental well-being runs strongly through Guérinière's work. He writes, "Neither should . . . the lessons be for too long a period; they fatigue and bore a horse, and it should be returned to the stable with the same good spirits it had upon leaving it." He well understood the value of pacing training correctly.

Guérinière rejected the type of saddle popular at the time and introduced a light, flat saddle that in principle is still used. He was instrumental in the development of the modern seat, which utilizes both the seat bones and the crotch, and in changing the leg position from outstretched to softly hanging down on the horse's sides.

Although he didn't refer to it by its modern name, Guérinière also preached the value of developing an *independent seat.* He spoke of "grace of posture," taking a deep seat and letting the upper body act as a counterbalance. Not only did this affect how well a horse moved, it also determined to what extent the rider had control over the horse's hindquarters.

As a way of achieving this sort of balance, Guérinière had his students ride at the trot, *without stirrups,* for at least six months. Many riding instructors still use this exercise to develop the student's seat.

Like Xenophon, Guérinière cautioned against being emotional in handling horses. He said, "Above all, a horse should never be chastised out of foul mood or anger, but always with complete dispassion." This recognizes that horses do need to be "chastised" or reprimanded for undesirable behavior, but that it should be done with a dispassionate or business-like attitude.

Of course, this is exactly how horses interact among themselves. A display of dominance, even if expressed in an act of aggression, is treated afterwards as if it never happened. The horses often resume grazing side-by-side with complete nonchalance. There is no residual anger or fear. It was just a business decision. Both horses understand that. That Guérinière recognized and taught this further cements his position as a forefather of the revolution in horsemanship.

CHAPTER 12

WHISPERERS, TAMERS, AND PROFESSORS

EQUITATION AS AN ART FORM practiced in indoor arenas was fine and dandy for the European upper crust, but the common man needed help with his horses too, and for him it was a matter of survival. Thus came the era of the equine problem solver.

Some of these men worked their magic on rogue horses in private, collected their fees, and moved on. Others liked to demonstrate their training expertise in public, and some even attempted to teach the public these techniques. Then, as now, the quality of the horsemanship varied. And then, as now, we can learn something from each of them.

Like Xenophon and other early horsemen we have already met, these are forefathers of the revolution. When we compare their methods to those of modern natural horsemen, we begin to see an even stronger family resemblance.

To really know these men is perhaps impossible, for all we have to go on is what they wrote or what was written about them, and in so many cases there was more at work in such writings than the desire to share knowledge. As men who worked with horses for a living, they had a vested interest in presenting their work in the most favorable, if not always most accurate, light. When you factor in the journalistic license taken by the press and the friendships and feuds that are known to have existed, you begin to have a new appreciation for the task faced by the historian.

Still, this journey into the past is a worthwhile one, for we will meet not only some colorful characters but also the ideas that they championed, many of which are as valid today as they were back then.

DAN SULLIVAN (?–1810)

In eighteenth-century Ireland, horses were indispensable to life, as they were most places. Anyone who could tame a vicious horse became a bit of a celebrity. A man named Dan Sullivan, from Mallow in County Cork, was one such person.

It was said that Sullivan could transform any horse into a model of good behavior simply by whispering a few words into its ear. Thus he became known simply as "The Whisperer."

Sullivan was reportedly an awkward, illiterate alcoholic of the lowest class, but he did have a way with horses. He supposedly learned his secret method, for the price of a meal, from a penniless soldier in a public house. It was believed to be an Indian charm, leading to speculation that the soldier learned it either from a mystic while serving in India, or from plains Indians while serving in America. In any case, the soldier swore Sullivan to secrecy and Sullivan kept his word. The secret was never revealed, not even to Sullivan's own son who tried unsuccessfully to follow in his father's footsteps, or to the parish priest.

When he worked on a horse, Sullivan insisted on complete privacy ostensibly to honor his oath, but probably also to eliminate any threat to his livelihood.

A typical taming session began with Sullivan leading the unruly horse into a completely enclosed space, probably a barn or large stall, where no one could see what he was doing. In a relatively short amount of time, maybe 30 minutes and occasionally overnight, he would signal for the doors to be opened. As one observer wrote,

> . . . the horse was found lying down, and the man by his side playing familiarly with him like a child with a puppy dog. From that time he was found perfectly willing to submit to any discipline, however repugnant to his nature before.

No commotion had been heard, no angry yelling, no defiant whinnying, no pawing, no whip cracking, kicking, or scuffling about. Some bystanders had heard nothing at all. Others thought they had heard quiet talking, which further cemented his title as the first "horse whisperer."

The nature of Sullivan's secret technique has been the subject of speculation for nearly two centuries. In her 1983 book *The Horsemasters: The Secret of Understanding Horses*, Josephine Haworth describes one intriguing possibility.

> Could it have been that Sullivan had stumbled on to some primitive form of brainwashing? Under pretext of keeping his secret safe from prying eyes, he may well have blacked out the barn in which he was working, or he may have blindfolded the animal as soon as they were alone. Sullivan was never seen to be carrying any special equipment, but a blindfold would have been easy to improvise. Once deprived of its sight, the horse was ready for the next step in the treatment—the introduction of some sound which would further disorientate the animal. It did not need to be loud, but insistent and meaningless so that it blotted out everything else and replaced all that was normal and familiar with a nightmarish state of total confusion. Blind and deaf to anything but this unnatural noise, the horse would be entirely at the mercy of the man who had induced this terror and who alone could release it from its torment.

Haworth also points out that horses have very acute hearing; their skulls are built like sound boxes, so they are naturally sensitive to sound. Whispering, with its breathiness and sibilance, could well be disorienting to a horse robbed of its sight. Still, it is hard to imagine such a horse, especially the savage sort that Sullivan worked with, standing quietly in such a state.

Using what we know today about horse psychology and the gentling techniques that have proven themselves over and over both before and after the time of Sullivan, we can paint our own, very different picture of what Sullivan probably did—and didn't do—behind those closed doors.

It is most likely that he used *control of movement* to create a submissive attitude in the horse. As he was in a confined space and no commotion was heard, it's not likely that he *caused* the horse to move, at least to the degree required to produce submission. That leaves only one conclusion. Dan

HOBBLES

Hobbles come in several varieties. The most common is the two-leg grazing hobble, which links the front legs of a horse together and, in theory, prevents the horse from running off while grazing unattended. In reality, however, many horses learn a peculiar hopping gait and can travel a surprising distance in two-leg hobbles. Two-leg training hobbles in a "figure 8" configuration decrease movement greatly. Four-leg hobbles provide the ultimate restraining effect.

A one-leg hobble serves a different purpose altogether. It holds one front leg in a flexed position such that the horse can't use it at all. Although he can still move around on three legs, the horse tires quickly and with his number-one defense mechanism—flight—taken from him, he submits. The one-leg hobble is used only in the handler's presence, and only for the purpose of controlling a difficult horse. It is a very old tool, dating to at least 600 B.C. A silver vase from that time has been found showing in carved relief a Scythian warrior using such a device in preparing a horse to ride.

Variations on the one- and two-leg hobble are occasionally used to accomplish specific training goals. Sideline hobbles, which link front and hind legs on the same side of a horse, are used for teaching the horse to pace. Scotch hobbles tie one hind leg to a loop around the horse's neck and teach him to relax when his feet are handled. Diagonal hobbles, above-the-knee hobbles from Australia, and hind-leg hobbles from Argentina have also been used.

Sullivan, the horse whisperer, *inhibited* the movement of the horse in order to create an attitude of submission.

Sullivan's secret weapon was probably a one-leg hobble, a simple and ancient restraining device that American John Rarey would share with the world a half century later.

Although it was said that Sullivan took no special equipment in with the horse, some observers noted that he had a length of soft rope, so we can surmise that the rope was used in the hobbling (Rarey would use a soft leather strap, but rope or leather, the principle remains the same).

Before applying the hobble, Sullivan probably desensitized the horse to the touch of his hands. The whispering some people thought they heard was probably a steady, comforting banter designed to let the horse know where

Sullivan was at all times, to reassure it during the desensitization process and to keep Sullivan's own emotions in check.

Once the hobble was applied, we can imagine Sullivan sitting back, perhaps on a milking stool, lighting his pipe, and casually noting the time on his pocket watch. In ten minutes or so, he released the hobble, proving to the horse that it was not a permanent condition and that he had the power to both take and give the horse its movement. Then the hobble went back on. A few minutes, perhaps another pipeful later, the procedure was repeated with the horse growing calmer at each turn.

A one-leg hobble is a means of controlling a horse's movement and creating a submissive attitude.

The final step was apparently laying the horse down, which is relatively easy to do when one leg has been restrained. Sullivan's treatment of the horse once he was down was final proof that in this most vulnerable of positions, the horse still had nothing to fear from the human.

Sullivan's reputation was built upon producing a docile and submissive horse out of a dangerous one, but some reports added another, rather troubling descriptor. Although there was no evidence of physical abuse, Sullivan's subject was described as being *terrified* when Sullivan looked at or spoke to it after their tête-à-tête. Furthermore, the horse was inclined to return to its former ways once Sullivan was gone. The latter is not so surprising. A horse reads every human with which it comes in contact and adjusts its attitude accordingly. Sullivan failed to generalize the horse's learning enough to make the desired behavior transferable to other handlers. But what about the terror? Was this simply the fearless Sullivan's "instinctive power of inspiring awe" or the result of something more sinister happening in private? We'll never know for certain.

Whatever his secret method, Sullivan obviously worked on the horse's mind rather than working over the horse's body. Thus, he represents an improvement over the physical brutality so often inflicted on horses back then and deserves a place here among other forefathers of the revolution.

Although Sullivan was not burned at the stake (he drank himself to death), local clergymen repeatedly accused him of being an agent of Satan. His failure to reveal his methods made him a suspicious character and a bit of a thorn in the side to village priests who liked to keep their parishioners well under thumb. One story has it that Sullivan finally had enough of such silliness and, when confronted yet again on a country road, placed the offending priest's horse under a spell. Whether he was having a little fun at the priest's expense or actually believed he could cast spells is not known. The priest was so upset that he agreed to leave Sullivan alone.

DENTON OFFUTT (ca. 1790–1861)

Denton Offutt was born around 1790 in Montgomery County, Maryland. For a time, in the mid-nineteenth century, he was said to be America's most famous horse trainer.

His 1843 book, *Best & Cheapest Book on the Management of Horses, Mules, &c.* contained both horse-training instruction and remedies for various equine diseases. It came with glowing endorsements by nine of his customers, all "men of high standing," including the following:

> For humanity and justice to the animal, his practice surpasses every other and is a salutary lesson to those who treat the creature of his power with so much cruelty. The horse is expressly created for the use of man, and when treated with humanity and upon correct principles can be brought into complete submission with the most perfect ease; this controlling power upon natural principles, Denton Offutt certainly does possess, and can impart it to others.
>
> THOMAS CRAIGE
> At the Philadelphia Riding School

Other endorsements described the results Offutt could obtain often in less than an hour with any manner of wild or difficult horse. Unfortunately, nothing specific was revealed about his methods in these testimonials, and the book itself is no longer available. His customers did note, however, that Offutt employed gentle techniques and common sense to accomplish his goals.

Offutt also published *A Method of Gentling Horses, their Selection, and Curing their Diseases, A New and Complete System of Teaching the Horse on Phrenological Principles* and *The Educated Horse.* Phrenology is the study of the shape of a horse's head with the purpose of gaining insight into the nature and character of the horse's mind. Horsemen have long recognized this connection, but phrenology remains a controversial, nonscientific field of study.

Offutt clearly wanted to put his methods before the public, but he also wanted to be sure he was paid for it: Those who studied with him had to promise not to reveal his methods to anyone else. Rarey, Pratt, and others would try this approach in later years with limited success.

In spite of his skill as a horse tamer, Denton Offutt is better remembered for an earlier period in his life when, as a rather inept merchant, he gave twenty-two-year-old Abraham Lincoln his start in business.

It was March of 1831 and Offutt, then a prosperous trader and sawmill owner in New Salem, Illinois, needed help getting goods from Springfield to New Orleans via flatboat. Abe Lincoln, his stepbrother, John D. Johnston,

Denton Offutt meets Abe Lincoln at the Buck Horn Tavern. *(Artwork by the late Lloyd Osterdorf from the Phil Wagner Collection, www.abelincoln.com. Used by permission.)*

and second cousin, John Hanks, heard about the job and met with Offutt at Andrew Elliott's Buck Horn Tavern, in Springfield, to talk about it. All three were hired, for generous wages, to build the flatboat at Sangamontown, not far from Springfield.

Lincoln then piloted the heavily laden boat to New Orleans, with Offutt making purchases along the way. Low water and other logistical challenges repeatedly hampered their progress, but Lincoln's ingenuity always prevailed. The strapping, charismatic young man made a big impression on his new boss and when they got back to Illinois, he was hired to run Offutt's new general store in New Salem.

Offutt, who became a mentor and friend to young Abe Lincoln, was probably the first to appreciate the magnitude of Lincoln's potential.

Denton Offutt himself was nothing very special at the time. Some town-folk remembered him as polite, but scatter-brained and overly talkative. Others were less kind, calling him "bustling and none too scrupulous." Lincoln's biographer, Carl Sandburg, labeled him "a liar and a cheat." Whatever the truth, Offutt lost his business during the following year, putting him and Lincoln out of work. This has been cited incorrectly as an early failure on the part of Lincoln.

Needing to reinvent himself, Offutt left New Salem to help his brother raise horses near Lexington, Kentucky. It was there that he found his true calling.

At the time Offutt's first book was published, a young man from Ohio, sixteen-year-old John Solomon Rarey, was already busy taming horses. Seven years later, in 1850, the two met at Ohio's first state fair in Cincinnati. Rarey was intrigued by the "unique mind and powerful personality" of Denton Offutt. Rarey purchased Offutt's 1846 book and, hoping to learn more, crossed the Ohio River to take lessons at Offutt's farm in Covington, Kentucky. It has been claimed that Rarey learned from Offutt a method of laying down a vicious horse that would one day be known as "Rareyfying." In 1856, Rarey published his first work. When Offutt sued him in 1859 for stealing his technique, Offutt won, but a higher court subsequently reversed the decision. In spite of some obvious similarities, there was no word-for-word duplication.

Documents from later in Offutt's life refer to him as Dr. Denton Offutt, but it is unknown how or where he earned that title.

Among the Lincoln presidential papers is one final letter from Offutt, dated 1861 and sent from Baton Rouge, Louisiana. Apparently in failing health, Offutt asked his old friend for a government job. It is believed that Denton Offutt died later that year.

JOHN SOLOMON RAREY (1827–1866)

Like Alexander the Great, John Rarey is said to have tamed a horse at the age of twelve. Like Alexander, he is remembered for his work with one particularly difficult horse, a vicious Thoroughbred stallion named Cruiser. Also like Alexander, Rarey died young, felled by a stroke at the height of his fame and dying a few months later at the age of thirty-eight.

Irishman Dan Sullivan may have been the first horse whisperer of record, but it was American John Rarey who was introduced to modern readers in the book by that title, *The Horse Whisperer* by Nicholas Evans.

There was a man from Groveport, Ohio, called John Solomon Rarey, who tamed his first horse at the age of twelve. Word of his gift spread and in 1858 he was summoned to Windsor Castle in England to calm a horse of Queen Victoria. The queen and her entourage watched astonished as Rarey put his hands on the animal and laid it down on the ground before them. Then he lay down beside it and rested his head on its hooves. The queen chuckled with delight and gave Rarey a hundred dollars.

He was a modest, quiet man, but now he was famous and the press wanted more. The call went out to find the most ferocious horse in all England.

It was duly found.

He was a stallion by the name of Cruiser, once the fastest racehorse in the land. Now though, according to the account Annie read, he was a "fiend incarnate" and wore an eight-pound iron muzzle to stop him killing too many stableboys. His owners only kept him alive because they wanted to breed from him and to make him safe enough to do this, they planned to blind him.

Against all advice, Rarey let himself into the stable where no one else dared venture and shut the door. He emerged three hours later leading Cruiser, without his muzzle and gentle as a lamb. The owners were so impressed they gave him the horse.

John Solomon Rarey. *(Groveport Historical Museum)*

Rarey brought him back to Ohio, where Cruiser died on July 6, 1875, outliving his new master by a full nine years.

An interesting fact omitted by Evans is that Cruiser reverted to being an unmanageable, dangerous beast after Rarey's death, contradicting Rarey's own beliefs on the permanence of the behavior modification he produced. We understand this better today. Training the horse does little good if you don't devote equal attention to training the handler and generalizing learned behavior.

In the years that followed his royal performance, Rarey became a rich man, demonstrating his methods before packed houses in England, France, Sweden, Germany, Russia, Norway, Egypt, Turkey, and the Arab Countries. On several occasions, he donated the proceeds of his appearance to charity—most often a Widows and Orphans Fund or a local soup kitchen—but he still accumulated enough wealth to build an opulent mansion on the site of his father's original brick tavern in Groveport.

A typical Rarey performance would include a lecture, the introduction of Cruiser with the exciting story of his taming, and then the display of Rarey's tiny Shetland ponies, Gyp and Prince, true novelties for the time. The highlight, however, was always Rarey's attempt to tame one or more vicious local horses. Everywhere he went, he invited the public to bring out their worst offenders. There were kickers and strikers, biters, rearers, and screamers. Rarey often completed the transformation in minutes, but in

Cruiser before and after being tamed by John Rarey, as depicted in the *London News,* April 1858.

some cases, the taming became an hours-long endurance contest between man and beast, with Rarey suffering a fair amount of physical abuse by the horse in the process.

John Rarey was not a large man—he stood 5 feet 9 inches and weighed 167 pounds—but he was wiry and strong, with tremendous determination and self-control. He relished every opportunity to prove that his system worked. Beginning the evening in formal attire, Rarey was often drenched in sweat and covered head to toe with sawdust by the end. Even when it took hours to accomplish, he always completed his task. The accolades he received were well deserved. He did it all without hurting the horse or losing his temper.

Rarey's foreleg strap, fetlock strap, surcingle, and rope in place.

Just how did Rarey tame a horse? He started with the horse in a snaffle bit and strapped up the horse's near foreleg with a one-leg hobble. Next, he placed a strap around the fetlock on the other foreleg and a surcingle around the horse's belly. Then he attached a rope to the fetlock strap and ran it through the surcingle. Once all of this had been accomplished, the horse was his, for what remained *always* worked.

Standing at the horse's left shoulder, Rarey took hold of the bit with his left hand and pulled the horse's head toward him while also pushing against its shoulder. Off-balance, the horse would eventually have to take a hopping step to reposition the one front leg still on the ground. At that moment, Rarey would pull on the rope with his right hand, causing the horse's one good leg to fold and bringing the horse to its knees. At this point some horses would become incensed, and would lurch and thrash about. Some even managed to get their hind legs under them enough to rear up. Rarey made no attempt to resist and simply followed the horse wherever it went, remaining at its shoulder, holding the rein and rope until the horse gave up and laid down on its side. Rarey immediately began stroking and petting the horse, speaking quietly, reassuring it and lavishing attention upon it. No matter how much the horse may have resisted prior to this point, once it was on its side being soothed, it calmed down. This change didn't mean its spirit was broken; indeed, some horses were fiery as ever, but they still lay quietly and remained so when he urged them to their feet. In some cases, the process was repeated several times to get the degree of calmness desired. If the lesson were repeated often enough, the horse would reportedly lay itself down upon cue, with no rope or straps necessary.

Why did being laid down (or "thrown") in this manner change a horse's attitude in such a dramatic way? We can offer one logical explanation: as discussed earlier, we know that a horse yields leadership when its movement is controlled by another creature, either a horse or a human. Being completely immobilized in a vulnerable position *with no hope of escape*—as in lying trussed with ropes upon the ground—would be an extreme example of controlling a horse's movement. The horse may simply respond with an extreme form of submission. Zebras, for instance, cease all resistance when downed by a lion. They just give up, mentally disconnecting with the reality of their predicament, a way of perhaps minimizing the horror of imminent death. The horse, being a prey animal and not knowing that the human isn't about to eat it, may go through a similar mental process.

It is difficult to imagine the international popularity that John Rarey enjoyed in the early 1860s. At a time when the United States was on the brink of its great civil war, seething with passion and discontent over slavery and states' rights, Rarey was still front-page news wherever he went, sharing headlines with Abraham Lincoln. Writers arguing against war sometimes appealed to Rarey's philosophy of using kindness, firmness, and patience instead of brute force in dealing with an adversary. The poet, Ralph Waldo Emerson said of Rarey that he "turned a new leaf in civilization." With tongue in cheek, the English magazine *Punch* suggested that the Rarey method be practiced on obnoxious politicians, and *Harper's Weekly* recommended it as a cure for wayward husbands. For a while, the verb "to Rareyfy" appeared in English language dictionaries.

The United States Army taught soldiers to "Rareyfy" their cavalry horses and take cover behind them. During World War I, a soldier shows a local schoolmarm how it is done. *(Robert Miller Collection)*

It is also difficult to imagine today the degree of brutality with which all horses, but especially working horses were often treated in John Rarey's time. It was not unusual for horses to be literally worked to death in harness or beaten senseless by indifferent handlers who did not know or care about a better way. Rarey championed a very different approach where kindness, firmness, and patience were mixed in equal measure. Even though the horse was put through considerable exertion during Rarey's taming, and may have had a few scrapes or bruises to show for it, there was no violence, no anger, no injustice.

John Rarey's methods, effective though they were for him, are far too difficult and dangerous for most modern horsemen to use. Rarey was a superb athlete, fearless, persistent, and patient. He also had the benefit of experience, having applied his methods to hundreds of difficult horses over the years.

The methods of Rarey are also largely unnecessary today, as few of us own truly savage horses and virtually no one must rely on such a horse for transportation or work. Horses as incorrigible as those tamed by Rarey were often one step away from being sold for slaughter.

Without an appreciation for the context or subtlety of Rarey's work, one could easily conclude that he was excessively rough or forceful with horses. Throwing a horse was generally reserved for the toughest equine customers and could therefore be considered the most drastic of the immobilization techniques. Still, on most horses, it was a rather anticlimactic procedure. The horse came to no physical harm and the psychological transformation could be remarkable.

When it was filmed for the movie *The Horse Whisperer*, the procedure was deemed so dull to watch that it required a whole arsenal of special effects to make it work on-screen. According to Buck Brannaman, the horse-training consultant for the film, the actor horse was wetted down to appear sweaty and bushels of fine powder were used to simulate flying dust. Multiple camera angles, slow-motion photography, dramatic music, and creative sound effects gave the procedure a completely different feeling and made it finally worthy of being the climax of one of the story lines. That cinematic magic misrepresented this classic gentling technique did not escape Brannaman, but it was a minor battle lost, and the movie was a major victory in the promotion of natural horsemanship.

In spite of his international celebrity—or perhaps because of it—John Rarey made an easy target for criticism. Throughout his life, he claimed to have conceived and developed his system of training himself. Not only did

Denton Offutt sue him for stealing his ideas, Rarey's originality was publicly challenged by horse breaker James Telfer of Northumberland, England, author of *Telfer's System of Horse Taming*. Rarey's friend, Charles Dickens, the novelist and magazine editor, had his staff search equestrian, veterinary, and military literature of the past 200 years for evidence of a system like Rarey's. They claimed to find nothing.

Today we know that the tying up of the foreleg and the throwing of a horse, primary components of Rarey's and other systems of gentling, have been practiced for centuries.

Regardless of who initially conceived the techniques he used, John Solomon Rarey's contribution to the revolution in horsemanship can hardly be overstated. Were he alive today, he would undoubtedly be on the front line fighting for everything it stands for. As he wrote, "The only science that has ever existed in the world relative to the breaking of horses, that has been of any value, is that method which, taking them in their native state, improves their intelligence . . . for everything that we get him to do of his own accord, without force, must be accomplished by conveying our ideas to his mind."

PROFESSOR O. S. PRATT (1835–1875?)

In the 1800s and on both sides of the Atlantic, the title "professor" did not always imply a university affiliation or any particular level of education. It just meant teacher. Numerous horse trainers of this era adopted the title.

One was New York–born Professor O. S. Pratt, who taught his horsemanship system in giant classes to thousands of city-dwellers. He also wrote two books, *The Horse Educator* and *The Horse's Friend*. The former, published in 1870, introduced "A Practical System of Educating Horses and Dogs to Perform Different Tricks" while the latter, published in Buffalo in 1876, confidently proclaimed its contents to be "The *Only* Practical Method of Educating the Horse and Eradicating Vicious Habits" (emphasis added).

Pratt's ego fairly screamed from the pages of his books, which at times seemed more like advertising copy than instruction in horse training. The first thirteen pages of *The Horse Educator* featured accounts of honors bestowed upon him by his students, and an eight-stanza poem entitled "Pratt the Great Horse Trainer." Stanza six was typical:

> *This PRATT will take your full-blood, fierce and wild,*
> *And forty minutes find him like a child;*
> *Your blooded charger, full of trick and balk,*

Is taught to do most ev'rything but talk.

He'll nod for "yes," and shake his head for "no,"

Lie down, go lame, back, stop, or forward go;

He'll pick up kerchiefs, kiss you, and he'll seem

Some human friend with intellect supreme.

A plaque he claimed was given to him by his Washington, D.C., class dubbed him "The Horse Educator of the World" and stated, ". . . we are convinced that your method of educating the horse and reforming his vicious habits *by kind and gentle treatment,* is the only TRUE SYSTEM" (emphasis original).

O. S. Pratt was born in Genesee County, New York, in 1835. As a youngster, he worked on the family farm and at the family saw mill instead of going to school. It was the way his father wanted it.

Pratt showed an early aptitude for controlling animals of all kinds. He also showed an early entrepreneurial streak, starting his first business at the age of twenty in the town of Batavia. Later, he started a horse-training academy 100 miles to the east in Geneva, taking it eventually to Penn Yan, Watkins Glen, Ithaca, Elmira, and Scranton, Pennsylvania.

By the age of thirty-four, Pratt was a hot commodity. Between 1869 and 1871, he conducted three Horse Education courses in "tent-schools" in Philadelphia, Baltimore, and Washington, D.C. The Philadelphia class was said to number 2,523 students. Baltimore had 3,504, and Washington 2,503. In two months at each location, Pratt supposedly personally educated a total of 8,503 students in his system, and with such good results that prominent townspeople were falling over themselves to publicly thank him and present gifts to him.

It is said that even President Grant requested private lessons from Pratt, who provided them on a daily basis for the president and his special friends.

Most of what we know about Pratt came from the writings left by the man himself. There were two important exceptions. One was Captain M. Horace Hayes, the eminent British veterinarian and horseman who referred to some of Pratt's tools and techniques in his book, *Illustrated Horse Training.* Hayes's tone was neutral, neither praising nor condemning.

The other was Dennis Magner, another celebrated horseman and author of the time, who was clearly not enamored with Pratt. Magner claimed publicly that he had worked with a horse that Pratt had ruined, and he pronounced Pratt to be an "ignorant pretender." He further stated that Pratt resorted to the "boldest methods of charlatanism, such as buying articles and arranging to have them presented to him as if voluntary gifts from his classes."

The animosity apparently stemmed initially from a transaction in which Magner sold Pratt a matched pair of trick horses and a pony after a week of intensive training in how to handle them. Shortly after, Pratt started advertising himself as "The greatest horse tamer in the world" and began writing a book on his new system of training. Magner may have felt that Pratt plagiarized his work.

To his thousands of students, however, Professor O. S. Pratt could do no wrong. Like today's most successful clinicians, Pratt put his efforts into teaching people to train their own horses, rather than doing the training himself. The system that Pratt taught for a price was so perfect and easy, he claimed, that "a boy ten years of age can, with its assistance, manage the most ugly and vicious of horses with ease and safety, throwing them from ten to twenty times a minute, with his hands in his pockets."

A recurring theme in Pratt's work was convincing (or reminding) the horse that the handler was the one in control. He suggested various ways of doing so, depending on the problem being addressed: "throwing" the horse (laying him down), applying a one-leg hobble, tying head and tail together and spinning him, and various bitting and harnessing combinations that made the wrong behavior unpleasant or outright painful, and the right behavior pain free.

Pratt had no problem with making the horse uncomfortable, but he did not advocate cruelty. In fact, he urged self-restraint, pointing out that when the handler acts in anger or impatience, the horse nearly always learns the wrong lesson.

Egotistical though he was, Pratt's writing paints the picture of a kind and compassionate horseman who was quick to reward a correct response with a kind word, a gentle caress, a cube of sugar, or a chunk of apple.

Little, if anything, in Pratt's system of training was original, but he was clever in his application of the tools and techniques available to him and had great respect for the horse's mind. "I do believe them to be reasoning creatures," he said, "possessing a keen sense of right and wrong."

It is unlikely that even Pratt would ascribe human-like brain function to horses. More likely, he meant that horses could be taught to make choices based on past experience, which is nothing more or less than operant conditioning that is at the heart of all animal training. Many of the solutions Pratt

Pratt recommended this sort of arrangement for curing a horse of bucking.

Pratt called this "a new method of breaking a kicker."

suggested for specific problems consisted of making the right thing easy and the wrong thing difficult, a concept that goes to the very heart of natural horsemanship.

Pratt was particularly progressive in one area. He advocated training foals from a very early age, teaching them to accept handling, to lead calmly, and to move away from pressure when they were still babies. He also recommended getting them used to the saddle as yearlings, but waiting two years longer than normal to start riding them. At the time, it was customary to break horses for riding at three-and-a-half to four years of age. Pratt recommended waiting until they were *six years old*, a practice unheard of today. Pratt claimed, "Two years lost in early life will generally add six or eight years to a horse's working time." Although good for the horse, this idea could not have been very popular with the public. That he persisted with it is a mark in Pratt's favor.

We don't know when Professor O. S. Pratt died, but there is one interesting possibility. The Fowlerville Review in Livingston County, Michigan, ran the following obituary on Friday, November 12, 1875:

> Tuesday night of last week O. S. PRATT and a little 5-year-old daughter of John BOTSFORD were burned to death. The parties lived at King & Rust's mill, between Saginaw City and St. Louis. BOTSFORD and wife put two children to bed, and went to PRATT'S to spend the evening. During their absence BOTSFORD'S house took fire, and, in attempting to save the children, PRATT was burned to death. The little boy escaped.

If this was Professor O. S. Pratt, the self-styled Horse Educator of the World, he died a hero at about forty years of age.

DENNIS MAGNER (1833–?)

The "skilled and astute horse tamer" Dennis Magner was born in Ireland. He came to the United States at the age of fourteen and apprenticed initially with a carriage builder in New York. Young Magner learned the trade well and later became partner in a carriage manufacturing business in Myersville, Pennsylvania. The business sometimes took in a difficult horse as partial payment on a carriage, which gave Magner the opportunity to develop his horse-taming skills.

Focusing first on breaking in carriage horses, he developed the Magner Breaking Rig in the late 1860s but didn't obtain a U.S. patent on it until 1880. The rig was a cart-like contraption that was attached to and traveled around a center post. Poles and harness confined the horse in the rig and got him used to how it would feel to pull a real carriage, without endangering horse, human, or property.

Dennis Magner.

The rig was very similar to a breaking rig shown in London around 1860 by an inventor named Dr. Bunting, but it is not clear whether one man copied the other or it was simply a remarkable coincidence.

Magner called his horse-training system "the art of direct subjugation," and he offered three methods of "subjection." The first one was throwing the horse, or causing it to lie down. The second method was spinning the horse until it became dizzy, and the third method was exerting pressure just behind the ear where the neck joins the head, by using a war bridle.

At one of his first demonstrations in a small New York town, Magner was given a vicious biting mare to tame. She attacked him immediately, and he was forced to dive out of the ring. Gathering his wits, Magner reentered the ring and successfully subdued the mare by drawing upon all three of

his methods of subjection. Using a variation on the well-known Head and Tail
Method, he took hold of the mare's halter
with one hand, her tail with the other, and
spun her around five or six times in each
direction. Following this, he threw her, and
lastly he applied his "war bridle." Used
singly or in combination, his three methods of subjection apparently produced outstanding results on any sort of problem
horse.

The Magner Breaking Rig, patented in 1880.

The press loved Magner. *Turf, Field
and Farm* said of him, "At last we have one man who professes horse taming,
and who at the same time rises above the vulgar tricks of the charlatan." *The
New York Sunday Democrat* compared Magner favorably with the most celebrated trainer of the time, John Rarey: "Rarey taught us our ABC, but Magner teaches us how to put the letters together." Robert Bonner, a publisher
and owner of trotting horses, said Magner was "the most scientific and successful educator or tamer of vicious horses that I have ever met."

Magner boldly advertised that he could "take any colt that had never
been haltered and, within twenty minutes, make him perfectly gentle to lead,
ride and handle." The comparison to modern natural horseman Monty
Roberts, who has publicly started many hundreds of colts in 30 minutes or
less, and veterinarian and polo legend Dr. Billy Linfoot, who did the same
sort of fast-starting demonstration with wild mustangs decades ago, is inevitable.

Problem horses were another matter, and the most vicious and dangerous horses were generally fixed within a matter of a few hours. One was
nicknamed "the Allegan man-eater, the Cruiser of America," a reference to
Rarey's famed British equine challenger. *The Michigan Gazette* said of this
horse that he

   . . . had previously killed one man, and crippled several for
   life. When brought in to the ring his eyes became bloodshot and
   gleamed like balls of fire, he sprang at his trainer like a wild beast,
   biting, striking and kicking in the most determined manner,
   breaking the ropes and stakes, springing upon the seats and
   throwing them down, tearing pieces from the centre pole with his

THE HEAD AND TAIL METHOD

The Head and Tail Method is a way of gentling a wild or difficult horse. With a rope, the trainer ties the horse's headstall to his tail in such a way that his head is bent around to one side. The trainer then drives the horse away. Because of the way the horse is tied, he can only go about in a circle, in effect, spinning. If he wishes, the trainer may take advantage of this opportunity to expose the horse to various sensory stimuli (sounds, sights, touches) to which he would like the horse to become desensitized. When it is clear that the horse is becoming dizzy, the trainer stops him and unties him. The horse stands quietly and submissively, with a completely transformed attitude. As a bonus, he is desensitized to any stimuli that had been correctly presented during the spinning. A more dangerous variation on this method dispenses with the rope and has the trainer holding the headstall and tail for the spinning. Unfortunately, this also makes the trainer dizzy.

teeth, lunging at any person who met his eye, actually screaming with rage when foiled in his attempts to seize his intended victims. Nearly every person was driven from the tent, some in their haste tearing holes in the canvas and escaping through the roof.

Magner tamed this killer beast in three hours and the following day it could be driven by strangers in the street.

The Head and Tail Method of gentling a horse.

One problem many tamers faced was recidivism; the horses didn't always stay fixed when returned to their original situations, and that could be a publicity nightmare. Magner's training apparently had more staying power than most others. One horse owned by the Buffalo Omnibus Company had so mangled one man's arm as to have nearly killed him. After Magner's taming, the horse became "one of our best horses, docile as a lamb, and all the drivers like him," according to the company's agent, Mr. M. Ford.

According to Clive Richardson in *The Horse Breakers*, "Another horse was subdued to quiet obedience so effectively that when one day in the street a passing street car struck and demolished the rear wheels of the buggy it was harnessed to with a splintering crash, the horse was not alarmed and stood patiently as the wrecked buggy was moved."

Magner's method of "throwing" or laying down a horse.

Magner may not have been a charlatan, but he was not above a little showmanship in his presentations. After breaking a horse, Magner liked to demonstrate just how submissive it was. Sometimes he would pick up the horse's hind legs as if he were a rickshaw driver. Other times, he would grab its tail and place a foot on each of its hocks, as if he were skiing. Most dramatic of all, he would sometimes harness the horse to a stripped-down cart consisting of only an axle and a pair of wheels. Standing on the axle and holding onto the tail of the newly tamed horse, he would drive the horse around the arena to the delight of his audience.

Many of the horses brought to Magner for training were driving horses, partly because of his known expertise with them, but also because of the times in which he lived. People depended on driving horses for everything from tilling fields to delivering goods to taking families to church on Sunday. The danger posed by a difficult horse was magnified when he was placed in harness and attached to a carriage, wagon or cart. It is still true today. Unlike a riding incident, where the horse's panic usually subsides quickly once the rider is off his back, a simple driving incident can escalate to an all-out disaster. No matter how hard he runs, the horse cannot escape the scary thing following him, the careening, often broken and fallen-over carriage.

Dennis Magner wrote several books, including *The Art of Taming and Educating the Horse.* Published in 1884, it is considered one of the best of the gaggle of horse-training books published in the nineteenth century.

After breaking a horse, Magner liked to demonstrate just how submissive it was.

PROFESSOR SILAS SAMPLE (ca. early 1800s–late 1800s)

The American horseman "Professor" Silas Sample is remembered for advocating an unusual way of gentling a horse: spinning him until he became dizzy. This approach is not without merit—it had already been used to good effect by Dennis Magner—and Sample was taken seriously in his day, at least at the beginning.

For instance, in his 1889 book, *Illustrated Horse Training*, Captain M. Horace Hayes, the eminent British army veterinarian and horseman, called Sample a "clever horse-tamer" and quoted his simple, if somewhat arrogant, decree: "Make the animal rideable and driveable before he is ridden or driven."

According to Hayes, Sample deserved credit for introducing one particular American horse-gentling method, the Head and Tail Method used by Magner and others, into England and Australasia.

Flamboyant and self-possessed, Sample was certain no one on Earth could teach him anything about horses. If anyone suggested such a thing, he would fly into a rage. Still, Hayes remained friendly with him, undoubtedly finding him a unique and interesting character.

Sample *was* a very good horseman and he also deserves credit for originality at a time when most horse tamers seemed to be doing pretty much the same thing. He took the idea of spinning a horse to dizziness one creative step further, patenting in 1891 a "Horse-Taming Machine," by which he proposed to gentle up to four wild horses per hour.

Captain Hayes wrote, "it consisted of a box, which was supposed to hold the horse, and which he [Sample] rotated either by hand or steam at a speed sufficient to render the enclosed animal so giddy that, on being taken out, it would be perfectly quiet to handle for the time being, no matter how wild it had previously been."

Both the Head and Tail Method and Sample's Horse-Taming Machine aimed to produce a horse that was calm, submissive, and oblivious to the usual distractions. The principle behind these unusual methods is sound, and it is applied occasionally today, sometimes spinning the horse until he lies down, taking care, of course, that he does not hurt himself in the process.

Today we understand that it is not the physical sensation of being dizzy that produces submission; the horse recovers from that in a matter of seconds. It is the psychological effect of having his movement under external control that causes the horse to reconsider his situation. Again we see the central principle of natural horsemanship: control of movement is the key to producing a submissive, compliant horse.

Unfortunately for Sample, exhibitions of his Horse-Taming Machine in London received a lukewarm reception, due mostly to the "Professor" himself. The old showman, in his excitement about his new technology, had forgotten about entertaining the audience. "If only Sample had not been so infatuated with his infernal machine," Hayes lamented, "he might have extracted a few jokes out of it, but he *would* treat it seriously at a time when his audience were pining to be made to laugh." The English audience, mostly foxhunters and park riders who had little experience with wild or outlaw horses, didn't appreciate Sample's breakthrough. They came to have a good time.

Still, the loyal Captain Hayes believed in the legitimacy of Sample's invention. "I feel certain," he said, "that it would be a valuable means for saving labour in rendering quiet freshly-caught horses which have been brought up under uncivilized conditions."

"Professor" Sample never quite achieved the status he sought and, to make matters worse, he was repeatedly distracted by ex-students presenting his methods as their own. An Australian rough rider named Frank was one example. Another was "Professor Leon, the Celebrated Mexican Horse-Tamer," who appeared decked out in cowboy boots and sombrero. Leon, also known by the names Franklin and Sexton, was an ex-printer's clerk and brother-in-law of Sample's most famous student, the future Professor Galvayne.

In what seems a rather desperate move, Sample cajoled the colorful Leon into participating in a rigged horse-taming contest between the two of them, staged by *Sporting Life* journal every evening for two weeks at the Imperial Theatre in London. With his beloved machine in pawn and no money in his pockets, Sample convinced Captain and Mrs. Hayes to put up his entry fee and help him get his machine back.

The first evening of the contest, the slope of the stage caused Sample's steam engine to fail. The ill-prepared professor had only one assistant, an ex-sailor named Joe, available to turn his machine by hand. As poor Joe struggled to move the heavy, awkward contraption, the audience howled with laughter. "Professor" Leon, with his Mexican Horse-Tamer act, was clearly the audience favorite in round one.

The next evening, Sample was forced to abandon his machine altogether. Fortunately, the horse he was to face was a true outlaw, a savage "man-eater," and just the sort of horse that Sample excelled at handling, even without his machine. As John Richard Young writes in *The Schooling of the Western Horse,*

> Sample, harassed by worry, debts, poor health, and public ridicule, looked frail and old in his shabby evening clothes as he calmly announced that he would have the savage stallion turned loose on the stage. "Merely with a buggy whip, ladies and gentlemen," he told the audience, "I shall, without hurting him, make this horse so quiet that he will walk up to me to be petted."
>
> An assistant swung open the gate of a horse crate in the wings. Onto the stage, as into an arena, charged a big bay stallion. Jaws gaping, ears flattened, the stud rushed at the old man. Sample, popping the whiplash, diverted the charge.
>
> As though the whip were a magic wand, the old tamer controlled the stud, at once preventing him from attacking, from rushing into the wings, from leaping over the footlights into the audience. Each time the horse whirled to kick, Sample goaded him into facing around with inescapable flicks of the whiplash on the hindquarters.
>
> Finally, powerlessness to do anything else forced the stallion to stand still. Then step by step under the dreaded whip's exacting guidance the horse master forced the animal to approach to within arm's length.
>
> In less than fifteen minutes Sample fulfilled his promise to the audience. The horse stood motionless under his hand, unmoved even by the spectators' thunderous applause.

The experts judging the event declared that, in spite of his earlier problems with the machine, Sample was winning the contest.

Later that night, while celebrating over dinner with Captain and Mrs. Hayes, Sample casually admitted that the whole contest had been rigged. He and Leon had agreed ahead of time to split the prize money.

"Do you suppose that faker would actually challenge *me* to a fair fight?" he laughed. Sample had orchestrated the contest purely to gain publicity for his machine. It had failed him two nights in a row, but he still believed he could make it work.

Hayes erupted in a fit of Irish temper, "Then you're fleecing the public! I'll have nothing to do with such a scheme!"

Deeply offended by the deception, Hayes withdrew his support. The contest was declared invalid, and the rest was canceled. Not long afterward, disgraced and swamped in debt but unshaken in the belief that he had given the world something important, "Professor" Silas Sample died.

Ironically, Sample's final performance proved to everyone that he was a real horseman. One can only imagine what he might have accomplished had he not been obsessed with showing the world that horses could be tamed by machines.

PROFESSOR SYDNEY GALVAYNE (1846–1913)

Fame came in far greater measure to another of "Professor" Sample's students, Frederick Henry Attride[1]—better known as Professor Sydney Frederick Galvayne, Scientific Horse Breaker and Tamer, of Kilmarnock, Ayrshire, Scotland. Although he did not discover it as he claimed, Galvayne did popularize a method of determining a horse's age by looking at its teeth, a method that is still used today.

Professor Sydney Galvayne. *(Ronda Foster)*

Galvayne traveled Europe in the 1880s, aging horses at sales and selling his secret to others. His 1885 book, *Horse Dentition: Showing How to Tell Exactly the Age of a Horse up to Thirty Years,* described Galvayne's Groove, a dental feature of the horse that would make Galvayne's name familiar to horsemen for generations to come.

Galvayne's name also attached itself to a method of breaking a young or difficult horse. In the 1911 Encyclopedia Britannica, "Galvayning" was described in some detail and was essentially identical to the Head and Tail Method used by Galvayne's teacher, "Professor" Sample. It was said to be a gentler method than others used at the time.

Galvayne was a competent horseman, but certainly not a great one. Even his descendants consider him to have been a charlatan, a master of self-promotion who regularly stretched the truth. According to his great-grandson, Jonathan Jones, Galvayne lived with gypsies and other travelers during his travels around Europe, and learned the way of aging horses from

---

[1]Notes for the historians: Several sources have it that Galvayne's given name was Sydney Osborne (or Osburn) and that he was an Australian. According to his great-grandson, Jonathan Jones, that is not true. Galvayne was born Frederick Henry Attride in 1846 in the United Kingdom. Wanting to "create a unique name that had never been heard of before," he called himself Sydney Frederick Galvayne in the U.K. from 1884 on, but did not officially change his name until he went to Australia, for the second time, in 1901. The name change was done by deed poll in Liverpool, Australia, on September 30, 1902. He died in the U.K. on October 6, 1913.

these people. He brought the method back to the United Kingdom and stated that he invented it.

Galvayne wrote at least three additional books on horses and horse training: *The Horse: its Taming, Training and General Management: with Anecdotes &c. Relating to Horses and Horsemen*, *War Horses Present and Future, or, Remount Life in South Africa*, and *The Twentieth Century Book of the Horse*. The second edition of Galvayne's final book contained a polo supplement, with nineteen photographs attributed to Fred Galvayne, one of Galvayne's two sons by his first wife, Emily Westley, who died prior to 1891.

GALVAYNE'S GROOVE

Galvayne's Groove is a darkened longitudinal indentation that begins to appear at the gum line of the horse's upper corner incisors at nine to ten years of age. As the teeth erupt, the groove is exposed at a measured and predictable pace, extending the full length of the tooth by age twenty, and disappearing entirely at about thirty years of age. This, coupled with other indications of tooth wear, gives a very accurate way of aging a horse. However, it has long been recognized that the method is not infallible.

Galvayne's Groove is still used to estimate a horse's age. This horse would be about fifteen years old. *(Ronda Foster)*

CAPTAIN MATTHEW HORACE HAYES, F.R.C.V.S. (1842–1904)

"While writing for practical men, I have kept in view the fact that by working on the principles of equine psychology and equine locomotion, we can make horse-breaking a science as well as an art." With these words, Captain M. H. Hayes prefaced the second edition of his most important book on horsemanship and proved without a doubt that he was a horseman ahead of his time.

Irish-born army Captain Matthew Horace Hayes, a British soldier, veterinarian, horseman, and author, is the most enduring of all nineteenth century horsemen. His book *Veterinary Notes for Horse Owners* has been a standard work on equine health care for nearly 125 years. The book is amended and updated periodically by modern-day equine veterinarians and, at this writing, is in its eighteenth edition.

Other books by Hayes included *Points of the Horse, Training and Horse Management in India, Stable Management and Exercise,* and *Riding and Hunting.* He also edited a book written by his wife, Alice Hayes, *The Horse-woman: A Practical Guide to Side-Saddle Riding.* It is possible that Hayes had a sense of the pivotal role women would later play in revolutionizing horsemanship.

The most important contribution by Hayes, however, was *Illustrated Horse Training,* for many years the definitive book on the subject. In it, he cited the required attributes of the ideal horseman: knowledge, patience, readiness of resource, sympathy, skill, coolness, and pluck. It is noteworthy that these are the very qualities that best describe the horsemen who launched the late-twentieth-century revolution in horsemanship.

Captain Hayes was more willing than most to acknowledge the work of other horsemen. His writing is peppered with such references, a comparison here, a casual point of interest there. Some names he mentions are familiar to the modern student of horsemanship and some aren't. In some cases, he goes to the trouble of illustrating a particular tool or technique, particularly those involving ropes and knots. Hayes was clearly interested in passing on useful information, regardless of the source.

In Captain Hayes's writing, as in that of many great horsemen, we see a strong reminder of the importance of maintaining control of our emotions when dealing with horses:

> All such indispensable knowledge will, however, be in vain, unless the breaker has patience to apply it in an exact manner, and without allowing himself to be influenced in any way by feelings of impatience, anger, or resentment. . . . the exhibition of his annoyance will assuredly frighten out of the timid ones whatever sense may have been in their heads, and will provoke the sullen ones to resistance, if not to retaliation. To be successful, he should adopt the maxim of patience, patience and still more patience.

It is the nature of the horse that it responds best to infinite patience, quiet persistence, and soft kindness, yet, when appropriate, commanding assertiveness. Hayes understood this. Too often, those who have worked with horses have lacked these qualities, being impatient, intolerant, aggressive, emotional, and lacking in understanding of the creature with which they were working.

Captain Matthew Horace Hayes, one of the nineteenth century's most important horsemen.

Hayes lived in an era when "throwing the horse," or laying him down, was a common way of gentling horses on both sides of the Atlantic, made popular earlier in the century by American John Rarey as "Rareyfying." Although Hayes himself used the technique upon occasion, he grew to condemn it as too dangerous for the horse. "It is liable to injure him by causing him to fall violently on the ground," he wrote. This attitude probably stemmed from an incident in South Africa when Hayes allegedly broke a young horse's back during a demonstration.

Captain Hayes was a world traveler and twice had the opportunity to test his abilities on a more exotic equine, the zebra. Rarey had done so to great acclaim earlier in the century and it was considered the ultimate test of skill. On both occasions, in less than an hour, the zebra was calmly carrying a rider, in one case, Mrs. Hayes. Hayes commented, "In doing this, I did not throw the animal down, nor did I resort to any of the usual heroic horse-taming methods." In fact, it went so smoothly that Hayes recommended using the Burchell's zebra for saddle and harness work in South Africa because of its ease of breaking and its immunity from the Tsetse fly bite.

Faded photographs show Hayes with a large white mustache, wearing a bowler hat and suit, demonstrating many of the techniques about which he wrote. He was a proper British gentleman as well as a highly competent, hands-on horseman.

Captain Matthew Horace Hayes is alive today in the hearts and minds of horsemen around the world, whether they know him by name or not. The intelligent, humane, and reasonable approach to horsemanship that this man championed is at the heart of the revolution.

PROFESSOR JESSE BEERY (1861–mid-1900s)

Another of the nineteenth-century American horse-training "professors" was Jesse Beery. He is best known for having developed *Prof. Beery's Illustrated*

Course in Horse Training, a correspondence course used all over the world. More than 300,000 of these courses were sold, beginning in 1908.

The course came in eight small blue booklets, each dedicated to one or more specific topics: Colt Training, Disposition and Subjection, Kicking and Balking, Shying and Running Away, Bad to Shoe and Halter Pulling, Miscellaneous Habits, Pony Training and Special Fears, and Teaching Tricks to Horses and Dogs.

In addition to his correspondence course, Beery wrote several books on horse training and is said to have made a film of his work around 1911 in Dayton, Ohio. The Beery School of Horsemanship continued publishing correspondence courses in horse training and animal breeding until at least the mid-1990s.

Professor Jesse Beery as he appeared on the seal for his correspondence school of horsemanship.

Jesse Beery was born in Pleasant Hill, Ohio, in 1861, amid the early rumblings of America's Civil War. At the time, another Ohio horseman, John Rarey, was bringing glory to their state, touring stateside and abroad, lecturing on horse taming and showing off his reformed killer stallion, Cruiser. Beery helped his father care for the animals on the family farm, and it was there that young Jesse's special gift for training horses became clear. At twenty-eight he married and began traveling to perform demonstrations at fairs and expositions all over the country.

Everywhere Beery went, people not only admired his abilities but also wanted to learn his methods. He had more business than he could handle, and in 1905, after his father died, he returned to the family farm in Pleasant Hill and established his School of Correspondence in Horsemanship, later renamed the Beery School of Horsemanship.

As a teacher, Beery wanted his students to understand from the beginning that horses are very different from humans. "The horse cannot reason like a human," he said. "The horse recognizes only objects and actions—what he gets immediately through his keen senses—while man goes beyond and back of that to the cause and effect." According to Beery, this fact is proven, not only by observation of the horse's behavior, but also by examination of its brain. Compared to that of a human, the horse's brain is very small relative to its body size, and its cerebrum shows minimal wrinkling and convolution on its surface.

Beery also stressed the individuality of each horse and that training must be adapted to the individual's disposition. He identified four types of horses:

1.   The teachable, kind horse
2.   The stubborn, willful horse
3.   The nervous, ambitious, determined horse
4.   The treacherous, ill-tempered, resentful horse

He believed that you can identify which type or combination of types a horse falls into by simply looking at, and sometimes feeling, its head. (This is known as phrenology and has been practiced for centuries.) Training was then tailored to the type of horse you had.

Horses of type 2, 3, and 4 have some bad tendencies; why bother with that kind of horse at all? Beery said, "If he is properly trained, these bad tendencies are kept in the background and allowed to perish unused, while the weaker tendencies are brought to the front and strengthened by use."

Beery's own horse, Charley, was offered as a prime example. A type 2–3 combination, Charley was deemed by head shape to have no "horse sense." Beery said of Charley, "These natural qualities were so overcome by patient training, that he has been considered one of the greatest trick horses in the world, and the crowds that saw him perform often expressed the opinion that he had more sense than any horse living."

"Subjection" was Beery's word for the process of convincing the horse that the human had absolute control over him, no matter how much he may resist. This was done, as you might expect, by controlling the horse's movement.

To do this, Beery made maximum use of the surcingle, a piece of harness that encircles the horse's midsection where the front girth—or front

A surcingle has many uses, from preparing the horse for the feel of the saddle to laying the horse down. *(Charles Hilton)*

and rear girths—of a saddle would go. The surcingle has several rings fixed to it for attaching lines or running lines through.

For the complete subjection treatment, Beery, like so many before him, laid the horse down. He did so by first strapping up one foreleg to the surcingle, effectively forming a one-leg hobble. He then used a single cotton rope attached at the surcingle, passing through the halter on the side opposite the strapped up leg, back to the surcingle, and finally to his hands. With gentle pressure on the rope from a safe distance, Beery could pull the horse's head around enough to place him off balance and bring him to one knee, then down on his side, where he would learn that the human was truly in charge and would not hurt him. His technique is identical to one shown in Captain Hayes's 1889 book, *Illustrated Horse Training*.

In other instances, especially to teach the all-important "whoa" command to a difficult horse, Beery recommended his "Double Safety Rope." Using the surcingle rings again, he connected a single 18-foot rope to padded foot straps on both of the horse's front pasterns. The way the rope went from the trainer's hands to the surcingle, to one foot, back to the surcingle, and attached to the other foot, it looked like the letter W, hence its nickname the "running W." Beery also held a pair of long reins that ran through the surcingle to the bit. To protect the horse from injury, knee pads were used.

Standing safely behind the horse, Beery would drive him in a circle, then utter "whoa" and pull on his Double Safety Rope, forcing the horse quietly to its knees. The horse quickly learned the command.

In this rig, a horse could also be desensitized to the usual array of stimuli used at the time: feed sacks, newspapers, jangling cans, umbrellas, pistol shots, and so on. Later, using the Safety Rope on just one leg was usually sufficient to remind the horse of his lessons.

Professor Beery used the "running W" to control the horse while desensitizing it to various stimuli.

THE RUNNING W

The "running W" was adapted by Yakima Canutt, the legendary movie stuntman, to allow horses to be toppled to the ground from a dead run. He used it extensively in 1930s westerns and claimed never an injury to horse or rider. Although former rodeo champion Canutt was renowned for his dedication to the safety of both human and equine, and later won an Academy Award for his contributions to the industry, animal welfare activists still objected to the use of the running W, and Canutt eventually abandoned the technique.

Professor Beery's course is fascinating from a number of standpoints. It was pure information with virtually none of the hype sometimes seen in such writing. Although he described his surcingle and other tack, there was very little in the way of a sales pitch. Indeed, he seemed to invite homemade copies. He offered very practical advice, aimed at the real problems people had with their driving and riding horses. His system was carefully organized and progressed logically from beginning to end. And it was humane without coddling the horse.

Beery promoted his own version of the Head and Tail Method used by Magner, Pratt, Sample, Galvayne, and others.

Modern horse lovers may still cringe at some of Beery's techniques, but although he certainly believed in punishing the horse as a way of discouraging unwanted behavior, his Pulley Breaking Bridle, Guy Line, First Form War Bridle, and Second Form War Bridle were all designed to release quickly after exerting punishing pressure on sensitive parts of the horse's head.

It is clear that Beery did not intend to be cruel or unnecessarily harsh with horses, but he was a pragmatist. He was determined to get the end results he sought and did whatever he had to do to get them. He took this modern dictum very much to heart: Be as gentle as possible but as firm as necessary. His little booklets were an early influence on a teenaged Bill Dorrance, who went on to become one of the twentieth century's greatest horsemen.

The Beery family produced more than its share of achievers. The Academy Award–winning American actor, Wallace Beery (1885–1949), was said to have been Professor Jesse Beery's cousin.

KELL B. JEFFERY (ca. 1878–1958)

There is no more unlikely candidate for the Horseman's Hall of Fame than Australian Kell B. Jeffery.

Jeffery did not plan to be a horseman. He was a law student at Melbourne University when he fell ill and his doctors sent him to the country to recuperate. At the time, he could not ride and had no prior experience with horses. As the story goes, Kell Jeffery ended up with relatives on a big cattle ranch at Chandler's Peak in northern New South Wales. Every day, the frail young man watched the stockmen mount up and go out to work cattle. Sometimes they were gone for days at a time.

As he regained his strength, Jeffery began looking for things to do to relieve his boredom. There were many horses on the property, and he discovered that he had a genuine interest in this animal. One mare was particularly intriguing to him and he noticed that she was not being worked with the others. When he asked why, he was told that she had proven too difficult to break.

Early one day, after the other men headed out, Jeffery decided to see what he could do with the mare. He managed to get her into a small yard, then went in with her, carrying the only thing he could find, a plaited greenhide rope with a ring on the end. He had no idea what he was going to do, but felt that gaining the mare's confidence was the place to start.

He formed a loop with the rope and somehow got it over her head. Exactly what happened next is anyone's guess, but when the crew returned at the end of the day, they found the delicate young man riding the "wild" mare bareback around the big yard with nothing but a rope around her neck.

During those few short hours, the seeds of a training method were planted. It was a method unprejudiced by what had come before and created from equal parts intuition, creativity, and compassion.

Kell Jeffery's horse-training career spanned more than forty years. What came to be known as the Jeffery Method was very effective, but unconventional for its time and place. Jeffery was not a very good or patient teacher of people, and so, to his great disappointment, the method never really caught on with the public during his lifetime.

Maurice Wright establishes a bond with a horse after performing Kell Jeffery's "magic longe." Note the plaited greenhide rope still on the horse's neck.

Jeffery wrote a book, *A New Deal for Horses*, which has been lost to history. In fact, we might not know anything about the Jeffery Method today were it not for another Australian horseman, Maurice Wright.

Wright, a rancher, read articles Jeffery had written about his method and attended several demonstrations Jeffery gave as an old man, the latest in 1953. He persisted in learning the system and wrote the book *The Jeffery Method of Horse Handling*. This book presented both the Jeffery Method and Wright's own minor deviations from it.

A video of the same name was released later, followed by a second video by Wright titled *The Thinking Horseman*.

The torch passed next to Australian Des Kirk (1916–1999), whose booklets *Horse Breaking Made Easy with Des Kirk* (self-published in 1977 and revised in 1978) and *The Gentle Art of Horsebreaking* (published by his wife, Phyllis Kirk, after his death) kept the Jeffery method alive and attempted to "modernize" it.

Today, few trainers practice the Jeffery Method in its original form, but elements of the method have become firmly entrenched in natural horsemanship. Australian-born clinician Clinton Anderson is the strongest advocate and he refers to Kell Jeffery by name as he demonstrates the techniques.

Clinton Anderson demonstrates fellow Aussie Kell Jeffery's way of desensitizing a previously unhandled horse to human touch in less than an hour. *(Charles Hilton)*

To gain a horse's confidence, Kell Jeffery used what we now call Approach and Retreat, the method of progressive desensitization used by John Rarey and others. Once the horse accepted the human's touch, Jeffery liked to give him a healthy dose of it. A rare film clip shows Kell Jeffery in his late seventies, slithering on his belly all over the horse's bare back, and rubbing and reassuring the horse all the while. Jeffery seemed to believe, as did John Rarey, that maximizing body contact with the horse enhanced the bonding and gentling process. Today, several natural horsemanship clinicians utilize this technique, sometimes nicknamed the "human curry comb" technique, in colt-starting demonstrations.

More unique to the Jeffery Method is the "magic longe" (or "lunge"). It is also sometimes called the "Jeffery hold." At first glance, the magic longe may seem cruel, as it involves tightening a noose around the horse's neck and pulling when he looks away from the handler or prepares to strike or kick. In reality, this momentary choking action is only mildly uncomfortable to the horse. It serves not as a punishment, but as a means of redirecting the horse's attention when he becomes distracted or chooses to ignore the handler. Jeffery understood that a horse can think of only one thing at a time. When a noose tightens on his neck, interfering with his breathing, he gives his full attention, and both eyes, to the person holding the rope. He then is rewarded with rest and comfort.

The control pulls of the Jeffery Method are usually made at an angle to the horse's direction of movement, but they still require a certain amount of strength to execute. In his later years, Jeffery would wrap the loose end of the rope around a post when he performed this procedure.

The Jeffery rope is 20 to 25 feet in length, with a 2-inch ring on one end. By passing the tail of the rope through the ring, a noose, called the "control loop," is formed. The composition of the rope and size of the ring make it possible for the handler to tighten and loosen the loop instantly.

The Jeffery Method calls for the loop to be carefully placed over the horse's head by using a wooden pole. Alternatively, Jeffery himself would sometimes sidle up to his subject on a saddle horse and simply drop the loop over its head by hand. In either case, his concern seemed to lie in not startling the horse. Good ranch ropers today could no doubt accomplish the same effect with an easy toss from a safe distance.

On a tour of Australia in 1988, Pat Parelli and co-author Miller received instruction in the Jeffery Method from Maurice Wright. Today, the 22-foot line used in Parelli Natural Horse-Man-Ship is, for all practical purposes, a Jeffery rope, and its use in the PNH curriculum would likely please the old man.

One subject on which Kell Jeffery would probably differ with the modern natural horseman is round pen training. Although he personally preferred a small, pear-shaped pen with outward-sloping, slatted sides for his work, the shape of the working area mattered little to him because he never drove the horse away from him. In fact, he did not believe in long-lining horses before riding them because that, too, required driving the horse away from the handler. It matters not, because both methods control movement and therefore obtain respect.

MONTE FOREMAN (1915–1987)

A horseman, inventor, and artist, Monte Foreman focused on producing excellence in performance, rather than gentling wild horses or solving problems. He might even object, with his usual irreverence, to being characterized as a "natural" horseman. Whether he fit the definition is open to debate, but Foreman was an original thinker who cared about the welfare of the horse, and his influence on riding and saddlery is still felt today.

Monte Burdette Foreman was born in 1915 in Alabama, where his father was mayor of Garden City for many years. He graduated from high school in New Orleans, and during his teen years rode a racehorse owned by Al Capone, the infamous Chicago gangster. On one occasion, he received a $100 tip from "Scarface" himself. A polo scholarship from Auburn University took him next to Atlanta, but he stayed only a year before heading west to be a cowboy.

Monte Foreman claimed that by the age of twenty-nine, he had professionally ridden more than 25,000 horses in a wide variety of situations: on cattle ranches, jump courses, polo fields, and race tracks.

Foreman also rode with the United States Cavalry and even on film. It was while working in the visual aids department of the Horse Cavalry School at Fort Riley, Kansas, that he developed his appreciation of the value of film in improving horsemanship. He went on to become the first person to use motion pictures in the research and teaching of high-level riding.

By using slow motion, Foreman was able to analyze how the horse used his body and how the rider's actions could positively or negatively affect the horse's reaction time. He was an excellent artist and illustrated the articles on his work that appeared in *The Cattleman* magazine from 1948 to 1956, and in *Western Horseman* from 1953 to 1956. For more than thirty years, he conducted his film research, developing from it a complete training method that he taught in clinics attended by more than 75,000 students.

Ray Smith, first president of the National Cutting Horse Association (1946–1947), quoted Monte,

Monte Foreman. *(Gary Foreman Collection)*

As I rode more horses and met other professionals, I became convinced that most training techniques were steeped in tradition and ignorance, with little concern over how efficiently or humanely they motivated a horse to perform. This led me to try approaches which seemed to place less restriction on the animal's working ability. In those days, for example, the accepted method for stopping a horse was to lean way back in the saddle, stick your legs out in front, and haul back on that poor old pony's mouth. Then I discovered that getting

Monte Foreman's training method came from analyzing slow-motion film of horses and riders. *(Gary Foreman Collection)*

off their backs and checking them in time with the motion of the front legs produced the balanced stops all my horses are famous for. But I never would have made the discovery if I had accepted tradition.

Monte Foreman saw himself as a "research scientist for horsemen" and taught the elements of a "basic handle" that guaranteed better performance on virtually any horse. Stories are told of Monte climbing on horses of only average ability and conducting impromptu riding demonstrations that left observers with their mouths gaping open. Today, Foreman's best student, Patrick Wyse, carries on this work.

Monte Foreman is remembered as much for his innovations in saddle design as for his riding and training expertise. The Monte Foreman Balanced Ride Saddle is still being made today, more than half a century after its introduction (it is discussed in more detail later).

Three videos, which contain much of Foreman's film work, are available at this writing, as is *Monte Foreman's Horse-Training Science*, a book comprised mostly

Monte Foreman demonstrating his "balanced stop." *(Gary Foreman Collection)*

of his magazine articles. It also contains more than 300 of his photos and drawings.

Monte Foreman blazed a number of trails during his life. In the early fifties he designed the first insulated aluminum camper body for pickups. In 1958 he began conducting the first clinics for riders who wanted to train and show their own horses. In the mid-sixties, he was the first to build a large indoor riding arena in his backyard.

Monte Foreman was ahead of his time in many ways and suffered what many revolutionaries suffer: being misunderstood and underappreciated in his lifetime. Couple that with an absolute conviction that he was right and a nonchalance about who he might offend, and it is no wonder that he had as many critics as converts. The feeling was mutual. Before he died, blinded by diabetes, in a Veterans Hospital in Denver, Foreman made it clear that he wanted to be buried face-down, so the world could "kiss my ass."

CHAPTER 13

REVOLUTIONS IN BRIDLING AND SADDLING

THE REVOLUTION IN HORSEMANSHIP has been characterized by a willingness to consider nontraditional methods of horse training, and to use one's own creativity, coupled with an understanding of the true nature of the horse, to devise one's own techniques. A similar questioning of tradition and outside-the-box thinking have been seen where tack is concerned, especially in bits and saddles, which have gone through a bit of a revolution themselves.

But before examining today's innovations, let's review how we got here.

EARLY RIDERS

Horses and riding are so linked in our minds today that we can hardly think of one without the other, but there was a time when the horse was, to man, simply another meal on the hoof. Domestication was a gradual process and most likely was motivated initially by the desire of man to ensure a supply of meat. Eventually, however, someone thought of putting the horse to work, probably first as a pack animal, then for riding, and later for driving.

Of course, the practical problem remained: how do you mount and ride this wild and wonderful beast and live to tell the tale? History leaves us no account of how the first horses were caught, subdued, and mounted or how many would-be riders were hurt or killed in the process, but we can assume that it was a spectacle to rival the most exciting of today's rodeos.

It was worth every scrape, cut, and broken bone. On the horse's back, man had speed, visibility, and stamina he'd never imagined possible. He had the ability to move himself and his things over great distances like never before. From day one, riding a horse changed his world.

BRIDLES AND BITS

It didn't take man long to realize that he needed a means of controlling the horse and that this could be done most easily by controlling the head. He tried a number of methods.

The Standard of Ur, more than 4,400 years old, shows equines being controlled by nose rings.

Ancient art such as the Standard of Ur, a Sumerian artifact dating to at least 2400 B.C., depicts equines being controlled with nose rings, the way some cattle are controlled even today. Lip rings may also have been tried, but quickly abandoned.

The first bits were presumably of organic materials such as rope, sinew, or rawhide. Evidence of their use has been found on horse teeth dating to 4000 B.C. Metal bits and sophisticated bridles were in use by 1600 B.C. in Egypt.

Illustrations of Syrian horsemen from 1400 B.C. show the use of bitless bridles, predecessors of today's hackamores.

TYPES OF BITS

There are two primary categories of bits, the snaffle bit and the curb bit. The snaffle bit transmits the rider's signals without magnifying them. It is designed for two-handed riding, and, because the mouthpiece is usually jointed in the middle ("broken"), the rider may influence each side of the horse's mouth independently of the other. A snaffle bit has a ring attached to either end of its mouthpiece and reins attach directly to these rings.

The curb bit magnifies the rider's signals through the use of leverage. The mouthpiece of a curb bit is usually not jointed or broken, thus one-handed riding is possible. A curb bit has a cheek piece attached to either side of its mouthpiece. The reins attach at the end of the lower portion ("the shank"), the length of which determines the amount of leverage afforded. A curb strap or chain is also used to apply pressure at the chin groove area of the lower jaw.

The double bridle is a system whereby separate snaffle and curb bits are used at the same time on a horse. The Pelham bit approximates this same effect in a single bit by offering separate places to attach the reins to get either the snaffle or curb action. Both the double bridle and the Pelham require the rider to operate two sets of reins.

As humans became more dependent upon horses, they began feeding them better and controlling their breeding. The result was larger and stronger animals. Bridling evolved, too, always with the purpose of allowing one to exert enough pressure on sensitive parts of the horse's head to control him.

Sculptures from the sixth century B.C. depict the horses of the Persians, then considered the world's top horsemen, being ridden with over-bent head carriage and extreme collection, a posture made possible by large-cheeked snaffle bits, nosebands containing knobs or spikes, and tie-down straps connecting head to breast collar.

Not everyone was obsessed with forceful control of the horse, however. The light cavalry of the Numidians of Northern Africa, who fought alongside Hannibal against Rome in the third century B.C., rode their small horses with no bridles at all, keeping their hands free to throw javelins. They controlled the horse's speed and direction with their seat and legs and when they needed additional steering guided the horse's head with a stick or crop. Students of natural horsemanship today sometimes use a similar technique to develop their riding skills.

The curb or leverage bit was introduced by the Celts of Gaul around 300 B.C. The armored knights of the Middle Ages used curb bits of monstrous proportions, due to the sheer size and strength of the horses they rode and the load, often up to several hundred pounds in rider, tack, and armor, that the horses carried. It was believed that this was the only way to control such horses, and just as important, the only way to put them in balance for battle maneuvers.

The Renaissance was slow to bring enlightenment to the training of horses. As the weapons of warfare changed, lighter, nimbler horses became more desirable, and by 1532 early dressage master Federico Grisone founded in Italy the school of riding known as *haute école*, or high school. The enigmatic Grisone produced completely obedient but broken-spirited horses. Many of the bridles and bits he used were torturous devices of his own design, with spikes on both the mouthpieces and nosebands. Grisone believed that horses were vicious creatures and passed on his recommendations for completely subjugating them in his 1555 book *Textbook on Riding*.

One of Grisone's emulators was Count Cesar Fiaschi of Ferrera, whose pupil, Battista Giovanni Pignatelli, later became director of the famous riding academy at Naples. Pignatelli was a progressive thinker who advocated the use of the snaffle bit in early training and reasoned that the bit should be used to signal the rider's intentions rather than restrain the horse. Still, he did not completely abandon the cruel methods of his teachers. Pignatelli's name was associated for more than a century with a particularly harsh type of bit, whose mere presence in the horse's mouth was said to be painful even before it was activated through the reins.

It was during this period that the double bridle first appeared. A thin bradoon, a type of light snaffle bit, was added to the curb bit. Separate reins controlled each bit. The bradoon was used in turning the horse, and the curb bit was used to encourage the horse to relax his jaw, poll, and neck.

Still, the curb bit by itself with cheek pieces as long as 20 inches remained the bit of choice for jaw-crushing, coercive horsemanship until the 1600s, when later classical masters like Pignatelli's rebellious student, Antoine de Pluvinel, advocated a gentler and more patient approach to training. By the following century, largely due to the influence of François Robichon de la Guérinière and his colleague, Gaspard de Saunier, the curb bit, though still used, was no longer seen as an instrument of coercion.

In the 1800s and early 1900s, bits of every conceivable design were produced, each claiming to solve this or that equine problem. Mechanization reduced the demand, however, and today there are relatively few styles of bits in use.

A byproduct of the revolution in horsemanship is a new appreciation for the principle that a bit, any bit, is only as good or bad as the hands holding the reins. Heavy hands can make any bit a severe bit, and light hands can make any bit a mild bit.

New Respect for the Snaffle

The snaffle bit, for centuries considered a training bit only and not appropriate for serious pursuits such as hunting or battle, has in recent years

The snaffle bit has become emblematic of the natural horseman. *(Peter Campbell Collection)*

enjoyed a strong resurgence in popularity for a wide range of applications. Certainly it remains the bit of choice for training young horses and for teaching beginning riders, for unlike a curb bit, the snaffle will not intensify the effect of a misstated cue. But even in prestigious competitions such as the National Finals Rodeo in Las Vegas, Nevada, expert horsemen are increasingly seen using snaffles rather than curb bits with their elite cow horses. The revolution in horsemanship, which emphasizes communication of a rider's request rather than enforcement of a rider's demand, has elevated the status of the snaffle to a bit appropriate for the most demanding types of riding. Leverage and the infliction of pain are simply not needed.

The revolution has also had an impact on the way horses are expected to carry their bits. Traditionally, a headstall was always adjusted so that the bit created two or three wrinkles in the skin at the corner of the horse's mouth. Many natural horsemen today prefer no wrinkles at all and make the bit loose enough that the horse can find his own comfortable way of carrying it.

The Hackamore

The revolution has also revived interest in bitless bridles.

The best known of the bitless bridling systems is the hackamore (from the Spanish *jaquima*). The traditional hackamore consists of a rawhide nosepiece weighted with a knot under the jaw and called a *bosal*; heavy rope or horsehair reins called *mecate* reins; a throatlatch, usually of cotton cord, called a *fiador*; and a light latigo (leather) headstall. The bosal is connected at the knot to the fiador and to the mecate reins. One end of the mecate often leaves the knot again to serve as a lead rope.

THE *VAQUERO* AND THE CALIFORNIA TRADITION

California horsemen who chased cattle, or *vaca*, were known as *vaqueros*.
(*Ernest Morris*)

The California tradition began with the Portuguese and Spanish explorers who brought the horsemanship of their homelands to Mexico and southern

continued on next page

California when they came to the New World in the 1500s. Horsemen of the Iberian Peninsula (Spain and Portugal) had a great deal of experience herding cattle and bulls from the backs of horses. The cattle-oriented horsemanship that developed in the New World had its own flavor, however, especially with regard to time. Time was a friend, not an enemy. The *vaquero* (literally "cow-man") did not rush a horse's training. There was always tomorrow, *mañana*. Without the pressure of deadlines, there was less tension in the training, less urgency, less predatory behavior on the part of the trainer.

The *vaquero* made his own horse gear, and he didn't rush that either. With countless *mañanas* stretching out before him, ropes, hackamores, bosals, quirts, reins, and other leather and rawhide items could become works of art.

Likewise, the bridle bits (leverage or curb bits with solid mouthpieces) used by the *vaqueros* were often stunning displays of craftsmanship, each hand-made and each different from the last, with its own way of signaling the horse. To the novice horseman of today, the bits of the *vaqueros* might look extreme, harsh, even ghoulish. But in the hands of a master horseman, they were as gentle and humane as any snaffle.

Interestingly, the snaffle bit was not part of the original California *vaquero* training system. In fact, the Californios never saw or heard of a snaffle until the white men came in from Canada and the northeastern United States. The *vaquero* started the horse in a hackamore with a heavy bosal, then graduated to a lighter bosal under the bridle and finally into a full bridle alone, with a half-breed or spade bit.

The system was so prevalent that a horse's mane at his withers was clipped to indicate his level of training. It was called the Training Mark of Distinction and it is still practiced by some horsemen today. When the horse was in the hackamore stage, his mane was roached (clipped short) for about eight inches starting at the withers and going up the neck. The next stage, the double-reined horse (hackamore and bridle together), was represented by two tufts of hair an inch high and half an inch wide, spaced an inch apart in the middle of the roached area. The distinguishing mark for a "straight-up bridle horse" was a single tuft. With this system, the training level of every horse in a herd could be determined by just looking at it.

The *vaquero* is an important link in the history of horsemanship. He came about as a result of adapting the pure riding-as-art horsemanship of the dressage arena to a specific task, herding cattle. In the hands of the gringo cowboys of America, it would evolve further into what we now call Western horsemanship. Today, several teachers of horsemanship specialize in keeping this *vaquero* tradition alive. Some teach a modified version that starts with the snaffle, before "going California."

While the bit operates on the horse's mouth, the hackamore affects the horse's nose. The beauty of the hackamore is that when adjusted correctly—and when the horse is carrying himself correctly—it hangs freely, with the bosal scarcely touching the nose.

It is in a hackamore that these horses learn to move correctly on a loose rein. The impact of the revolution on horsemanship can be seen in a new view of the hackamore. Like the snaffle, it is no longer seen only as a training tool. It is now a viable option for the highest levels of performance, while remaining an integral part of the process of creating a "bridle horse" in the California tradition.

The *mechanical* hackamore is not really a hackamore at all, but simply another form of bitless bridle. A noseband, with or without padding, connects to cheekpieces on each side. These cheekpieces have shanks, similar to those on curb bits, for attaching reins. The length of the shank determines the amount of leverage afforded the rider. A back strap, similar to a curb strap but riding a bit higher, completes the device.

Pressure is exerted primarily on the nose and secondarily on the jaw and poll. A mechanical hackamore may seem to be milder and more humane than a bitted bridle, but it isn't. Mechanical hackamores have the same potential for abuse as bridles with curb bits. They differ only in that they have no mouthpieces. Again, the hands of the rider determine the mildness or severity of the headgear.

The Sidepull

If you removed the shanks from a mechanical hackamore and replaced them with rings, you would have the essence of the sidepull. It is also very similar to a simple halter with rings on the sides for attachment of reins. A sidepull is intended for schooling a horse only. Monty Roberts's Dually Halter is a good example of a sidepull. A sidepull is sometimes fitted with a rope snaffle, i.e., a rope bit instead of a metal one.

The Bitless Bridle™

Another form of bitless bridle is the Bitless Bridle devised by Robert Cook, Ph.D., veterinarian and Professor of Surgery *Emeritus* at Tufts University in Massachusetts. This device controls the horse's head in yet a different way.

At first glance, the Bitless Bridle appears to be an ordinary headstall and reins, with a ring on each side where the bit would normally attach. There is a major difference, however, in the way the reins work.

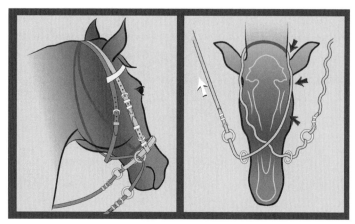

The Bitless Bridle™ works differently than a traditional bridle. *(Dr. Robert Cook)*

It pushes the head instead of pulling it. *(Dr. Robert Cook)*

Instead of attaching to the headstall ring on its own side, the rein
passes *through* the ring, then under the horse's jaw, up the far cheek, and
over the poll, where it follows a similar path down the near cheek, under the
jaw, through the far ring and becomes the other rein. Pressure on the right
rein causes a pushing action on the *left* side of the horse's head. Pressure on
the left rein causes a pushing action on the *right* side of the head. Dr. Cook
contends that horses steer better and their heads remain straighter when
the head is pushed rather than pulled.

To stop the horse, pressure is used on both reins together, or in quick
alternating pulls. The squeezing action on the horse's entire head is said to
trigger a submit response and a desire to stop.

The Bitless Bridle was invented after Dr. Cook conducted an in-depth
study of airflow factors in racehorses. This study led him to the conclusion
that the bit interferes with a horse's breathing because it encourages lip and
tongue activity, salivation, and swallowing—eating types of responses—
which are physically and psychologically at odds with flight, and thus performance.

A horse can breathe only through its nose; it cannot breathe through
its mouth. For maximum performance, a horse must have maximum intake
of air, and that happens only when the mouth is closed and quiet, and the
nostrils are flared. Horses with bits in their mouths always have mouth
movement, some more than others, and that compromises the ability to
breathe. Dr. Cook predicts that someday bits will be abandoned entirely, not
only for humane reasons, but also for performance reasons.

The Rope Halter and Reins

Finally comes the rope halter and reins. As the name implies, it is the joining of two items, each made from a single length of rope.

The rope halter is made of 1/4-inch nylon climbing cord thin enough to communicate clearly and convincingly to the horse and cleverly knotted to form a bridle. It is reminiscent of the old Johnson rope halter. However, there is no hardware on this halter; the handler ties it on with a special knot (known as a "sheet-bend") at the left cheek of the horse. A small loop hangs at the halter's lowest point, behind and below the horse's chin. A lead rope may be clipped or tied to the loop when doing groundwork.

Many clinicians today use reins made of braided marine poly rope. *(Emily Kitching)*

When it will be used for riding, however, the rope halter comes pre-tied to a length of hefty 5/8-inch braided marine poly rope that serves as both reins and lead rope. This rope is tied above the loop in the halter. The resulting knot adds weight and is loosely reminiscent of the knot on a bosal.

In his twenties, Robert Miller, coauthor of this book, privately developed his own humane way of starting colts. In this 1955 photo, he poses on a four-year-old filly he has just started. Note that she has only a Johnson rope halter on her head. *(Robert Miller Collection)*

The reins are continuous, California style, and have the safety advantage that all continuous reins have: if you loose your grip on them, you can just pick them up again off the horse's neck. If you drop split reins, not only are they difficult to pick up without dismounting, but the horse may step on the reins, break them, scare himself, run off, or all of the above. (Note: Working cowboys often prefer the split reins when gathering cattle because they won't snag on dense undergrowth and yank on a horse's mouth.)

Rather than terminating at the knot on the halter, one end of the rope takes a wrap or two and goes on to form a lead rope, again similar to the way mecate reins work with a bosal.

The rope halter and rein combination is sometimes called a rope hackamore, and while there are obvious similarities, it is not designed to hang freely on the horse's head when he is in the desired head carriage, as a true hackamore does. Regardless, the rope halter and rein is proving valuable in teaching the beginning rider, or the experienced rider wishing to relearn from a more natural perspective, that he can effectively control his horse without pulling on its mouth.

Through the mid-twentieth century, there was a saying among hunting men that "there are three kinds of fools: the fool, the damn fool, and the fool that hunts in a snaffle." It was considered the height of folly to take onto the hunting field a horse one could not forcibly restrain through the bit.

Today, thanks to the revolution in horsemanship, we see the function of headgear differently. It is no longer to impose our will on an unwilling servant. It is now to communicate the wishes of a benevolent leader to an eager and willing follower. There are many ways to accomplish that.

SADDLES

As rugged and athletic as early riders undoubtedly were, they found out quickly enough that sitting directly on a horse's sweaty, bony back for extended periods of time was no fun. It is believed that around 2000 B.C. the first crude pads were used, most likely made of animal skins. A strap to hold the skin in place couldn't have been far behind. Voilà! The early ancestor of the saddle.

By the eighth century B.C. in the Middle East, Assyrian horsemen were using decorative saddle cloths, and three centuries later in the area now known as Siberia the Scythians had taken the art of the saddle to another level. One frozen Scythian tomb yielded a saddle cover decorated with

THE STIRRUP AND FEUDALISM

Before stirrups, most riders used mounting blocks or simply leapt onto their horses' backs. In *The Art of Horsemanship*, Xenophon described how to use one's spear to vault gracefully onboard.

Occasionally, leaping backfired. One day in 522 B.C. Persian king Cambyses II, fully armed, attempted to mount his horse in this fashion. The cap came off his sheathed sword and he stabbed himself in the thigh. He died from the injury.

It is believed that as early as the second century B.C. in India, a leather toe loop was being used to help the barefooted rider mount. Before long a second loop was added—on the other side of the horse—to steady the rider while riding. By the fourth century, the Chinese had developed full-sized iron stirrups that could accommodate booted feet in colder, more rugged areas, and by the eighth century the stirrup had found its way to Western Europe. This was about the time that feudalism was started in northern France by the Frankish king, Charles Martel[1] (676–741 A.D.). Coincidence?

Twentieth-century historian Lynn White, Jr. didn't think so. In his 1962 book *Medieval Technology and Social Change*, he proposed a *causal* relationship between the introduction of the stirrup and the rise of feudalism. It was a fascinating and controversial hypothesis, and it went approximately as follows:

Before the stirrup, cavalrymen could not fully engage their enemies while mounted for fear of being knocked off their horses. They were limited to tossing spears and shooting arrows while riding by. When stirrups (and saddles with higher pommels and cantles) were introduced, "shock warfare" became possible. With his feet braced in stirrups and his war lance couched (held under the arm), a mounted warrior could charge the enemy and deliver a blow that had the full power of the horse behind it, without being unhorsed in the process. This gave stirrup-users tremendous tactical advantage over foot soldiers or regular cavalry. Charles Martel was one of the first leaders to embrace the new technology, and shock warfare dominated the Middle Ages from then on.

But the king had a problem. Mounted shock warriors (knights), with all their horses and saddles and lances and armor and training, were very expen-

---

[1]Martel was not Charles's last name. It was a title, a nickname, he had been given for repeatedly attacking the Moslems. It was from the French word *marteler*, meaning "hammer."

continued on next page

sive to support as a standing force. Martel's solution was to use land that he had already appropriated from the Church to buy himself an *on-call* mounted military. In exchange for receiving land from Martel, noblemen agreed to maintain a certain number of knights and make them available at the king's request to do battle. The idea caught on through much of Europe. Thus a new class of landowners was created and the system known as feudalism was born, with its fiefdoms, noblemen, knights, serfs, and yes, damsels in distress.

White's theory sparked furious debate in academic circles, and by 1970 his basic argument had been refuted. Feudalism, it seems, was just too complex and varied too widely throughout Europe to have had a single, simple cause like the arrival of the stirrup, no matter how much it changed riding.

intricate animal motifs made from leather, felt, hair, and gold. The saddle itself was padded for comfort.

Being mounted made the nomadic life of early riders a lot easier and gave them a competitive edge in fighting, although this was mainly in the logistics of getting to and from the field of battle. Hand-to-hand combat on the ground was still considered the manly way to meet your enemy. To try to do so from horseback meant you were likely to lose your balance, which could be deadly.

Several centuries later, however, the American Indian would prove that it could be done. According to Lakota Sioux historian and horsewoman, Linda Little Wolf, the Plains Indian hunter and warrior used his weapons while riding, often at full speed, and tucked his foot in the girth strap to gain stability, presumably hoping all the while that he didn't become unseated and dragged to death by his horse, a rather ignominious way for a brave to go.

The stirrup changed everything. It gave the rider greatly improved stability on the horse's back and transformed an average rider into a formidable hunter and fighter. Few inventions are as significant to the history of mankind as the stirrup. It has been argued that the stirrup actually *caused* feudalism, the political and economic system based on vassalage that characterized the Middle Ages in Europe. But we are getting ahead of ourselves.

SADDLE FIT

By the fourth century A.D., the saddle had evolved from a flexible pad on the horse's back to a rigid structure that bridged his spinal column. Getting the rider off the spinal column was as much for the comfort and stamina of the horse as for the rider. What made it possible was the saddle tree.

The basic concept of the saddle tree was simple, yet brilliant. Imagine taking two thin slabs of wood and placing them on either side of the horse's spine and parallel to it. These bars rest on the large muscles of the horse's back. Now we'll use an additional piece of wood to arch over the spinal column and connect the bars at the back—we'll call this the cantle—and also at the front—we'll call it the pommel. The 1859 McClellan saddle shown on page 238 displays these components clearly. Functionally, this is the construction of a saddle tree, even today. Trees designed for different types of saddles vary in appearance, sometimes dramatically, but each still contains these original elements.

From the beginning, the saddle tree was refined in shape to fit the curve of the horse's back and to provide a reasonably comfortable place for the rider to sit. Padding was placed between the bars and the horse's skin. As time went on, leather became an integral part of saddle design, protecting the wooden and metal parts, enhancing the beauty of the saddle, and adding to the rider's comfort. But there was a problem with having the tree buried under layers of leather and oftentimes fabric: it became harder to see how the tree fit the unique contours of a particular horse. This remains a challenge today, especially with the proliferation of mass-produced saddles designed to fit the "generic" horse.

Why do we care how well a saddle fits a horse? Because it affects his comfort, his health, his performance, and his behavior.

When a saddle fits poorly, it causes *pressure points*. Instead of the rider's weight spreading evenly over the entire surface of the bars as originally intended, it becomes concentrated in certain areas. In effect, the bars dig into the horse's back instead of sitting atop it.

Evidence of pressure points can be seen in the sweat pattern on a horse's coat after exercise. Sweat should uniformly cover the area under the saddle. Dry patches indicate pressure points, places where the blood flow to sweat glands has been inhibited and the glands have been unable to function. Eventually, hairs in the affected areas may turn white, leaving permanent evidence that at one time that horse had been subjected to a saddle that didn't fit.

A horse may carry himself in an unnatural way in an effort to escape the discomfort of an ill-fitting saddle. Over time, this leads to uneven muscular development and in extreme cases may affect the underlying skeletal structures. Ill-fitting saddles may lead to medical problems, including "sitfasts,"

Champion and Wilton's gauge for the withers.

fistula of the withers, scar tissue in the girth area or under the saddle, and even chronic back pain.

Obviously, such horses cannot perform at their maximum potential. What's worse—and this is the most disturbing of all ramifications of poor saddle fit—the horse may manifest his displeasure by bucking, rearing, bolting, biting, or engaging in other behaviors that are dangerous to the rider. Who can really blame him? He is in pain.

If our goal is to build a saddle that really fits a horse—or a mule, which has a very different back from a horse—the first task is to capture in a meaningful way the shape of that animal's back. The saddle tree can then be made to fit.

This is easier said than done because we are dealing with a three-dimensional object. One tried and proven—though admittedly low-tech—way is to bend a coat hanger to fit the horse's back, then trace it onto a sheet of paper. Saddle makers who use this method usually request that a longitudinal tracing (spine from withers toward the tail) and multiple lateral tracings be provided. The lateral tracings typically start at the withers and are made every 4 inches through the saddle area.

In his 1901 book *Riding and Hunting*, Captain M. H. Hayes illustrated a more sophisticated use of wire for replicating the curvature of a horse's back and withers: the wire gauges developed by Champion and Wilton. Similar in principle to head measuring gauges used by hat makers, these gauges have hundreds of wire pins, like the teeth of a comb, in a wooden carrier. The pins move freely in the carrier and when pressed against the horse's back conform to its exact curve. The pins can then be locked in place and traced to paper.

In recent years, molds have been used to convey to a saddle maker the three-dimensional shape of a horse's back. One system, the Silhouette, utilized strips of gauze dipped in fast-drying plaster and spread across the horse's back with the hope that the horse would stand still enough long enough for the plaster to dry and the true shape of his back to be recorded. That particular product failed in the marketplace.

One that seems destined to survive is the EQUImeasure, a rigid plastic sheet that can be warmed in a conventional oven to become pliable, then placed on a horse's back to harden relatively

Champion and Wilton's gauge for the back.

quickly into the proper shape. Its packaging also serves as an insulated carrying case, allowing up to 40 minutes' travel time between oven and horse. The hardened mold must then be packed carefully into a large box and sent to the saddle maker. Heated again and flattened out, a single EQUImeasure may be used up to five times.

A more complicated approach is the Saddletech Gauge created by eclectic inventor and horse enthusiast, Robert Ferrand. According to its maker, it captures the shape of a horse's back by "reducing the polyform shape into a series of angles and arcs." In effect, the horse's back can be represented by a group of numbers, each corresponding to a measurement made by some part of this device. The value of this gauge is intuitively clear to the observer: it is an easier and more reliable way of collecting and re-creating at a later time the coat hanger data.

Ferrand has gone a couple of steps further, however, to develop what he calls "Evidence-Based Saddle Fitting." First, he has devised a mathematical formula to compensate for the effect of the rider's weight, relative to the horse's weight. And second, he has a way of measuring the "interface pressure" that is exerted on the horse's back by the saddle and rider. This provides valuable feedback for adjusting the saddle's fit. Saddletech also offers a custom-fit orthotic that can go a long way toward making a poor-fitting saddle usable.

We can now build a saddle that reflects the exact topography of a particular horse's back. We can adjust it to compensate for the weight of a certain human being on that horse's back. What we have yet to account for, however, is perhaps the most perplexing part of the puzzle: the fact that the horse's back constantly changes shape. Making a saddle fit a horse is rather like trying to hit a moving target.

Researchers in recent years have learned a great deal about the physiology of the horse's back and what happens to it during movement. From this has followed an inescapable conclusion: *perfect* saddle fit is a dream, an ideal, a goal that can never be attained.

It's important to understand the two ways that a horse's back changes, as both bear on saddle fit.

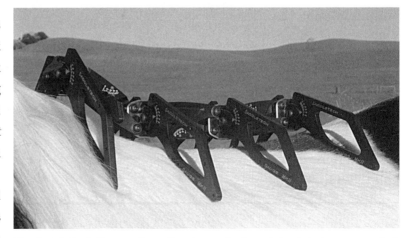

The Saddletech Gauge allows the shape of a horse's back to be represented as a series of angles and arcs. *(Robert Ferrand)*

Gradual change. In as little as a few weeks, modifications to a horse's diet and exercise can alter his muscular development and the shape of his body, including his back. As the horse ages, he is likely to change shape as well. He becomes essentially a different horse.

Instantaneous change. This is the bigger of the two problems because it happens *from moment to moment.* The contour of the back when the horse is in motion is different than when he is standing still, especially if he has learned to move in a collected frame, with his back elevated, his hindquarters more underneath him, and his poll lowered. The weight and balance of a rider affect the way the back is carried. Even from gait to gait and from one stride to the next, the back's shape changes as the muscular and skeletal systems do their jobs. A saddle that fits well one moment may not fit as well the next because of the way the horse's back moves under the saddle.

Logic tells us that when we try to fit two non-identical surfaces together, there will be points where pressure exists. In the case of horses and saddles, it's not exactly a matter of fitting a round peg into a square hole. It's more like fitting a round peg into a round hole that morphs every few moments into an elliptical hole. Occasionally the fit is perfect, but most of the time it isn't.

The rigid saddle tree would seem to be the problem. But saddles are built on rigid trees for very good reasons: the tree affords the rider the greatest possible comfort and stability, and it protects the horse's spinal column. Without rigidity, the saddle offers little advantage over riding bareback.

The rigid tree has thus been the key challenge facing saddle makers in the twentieth century. Let's take a look at some of the revolutionary ways they have faced it.

Adjustable trees. Seen primarily on English- and Australian-style saddles, the adjustable tree allows the spread of the bars to be made wider or narrower to accommodate horses of varying thickness through the withers and back. A special wrench is generally provided to allow the owner to make the adjustment without sending the saddle back to the factory. Wintec, Rembrandt, and Laser Equestrian Products are examples of manufacturers who have taken this approach.

Flexible panels. The flexible panel solution has gone through several generations of evolution, but the basic concept, originally brought to market in the Ortho-Flex saddle, remains unchanged. Rigid wooden bars are replaced with flexible plastic panels that move with the horse's movement. The panels connect to the seat of the saddle by means of mounts that allow the panels to move in all directions and can also elevate the seat on either side by up to an inch to compensate for uneven conformation in the horse.

Treeless saddles. Some saddle makers have dealt with the rigid tree problem by doing away with the tree entirely. The Ansür Saddle, for instance, is constructed by building up many layers of materials that possess different degrees of flexibility to create a saddle with a great deal more rigidity and stability than a bareback pad, but less than a conventional saddle. The Bob Marshall Treeless Sport Saddle takes a different approach, featuring a wooden front tree section and a wooden back tree section with a flexible pad, on which the rider sits, connecting the two. Treeless saddles also tend to be lightweight. The Marshall saddle is advertised at 11 to 20 pounds, as little as a third the weight of a typical Western saddle.

Greater flare and/or wider gullet. Trees are being made with bars that flare out more at the front and back to give greater freedom of movement to the shoulders and hindquar-

The Imus 4 Beat Saddle, with its flexible tree bars, is made specially for gaited horses. *(Brenda Imus Collection)*

ters. Saddlemaker Dave Genadek has campaigned for this design feature. Other saddles, such as the English saddles made by Balance International, have extra-wide gullets, again to allow more freedom of movement in the front.

THE McCLELLAN SADDLE

Originally little more than a saddle tree with stirrups, the McClellan saddle was used by the United States Army for more than 80 years, making it one of the longest-issued pieces of equipment in American military history. Today, nearly a century and a half after its conception, it is still preferred by many mounted police units across the country.

The McClellan design came about in the late 1850s as the result of an ambitious effort by the United States Army to find the most practical, efficient and cost-effective equipment for its mounted soldiers. Captain George Brinton McClellan submitted a saddle design based on a Hungarian model used by the Prussian military, with features from Mexican and Texan saddles, and characteristics of the Hope, Campbell and Grimsley, three saddles already vying for adoption as the official army saddle.

continued on next page

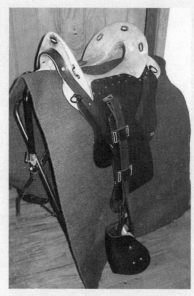

The 1859 McClellan saddle was official issue for the Union Army during the Civil War. Saddlemakers for the Confederacy were copying it as early as 1862. *(Carrico's Leatherworks)*

After extensive field testing, McClellan's design was chosen. It was lightweight but sturdy and durable. It was simpler and perhaps most important, less expensive to make. Nearly half a million of the 1859 McClellan saddle (the "M1859") were made, by hand, before the end of the Civil War.

The saddle featured harness leather saddle skirts and hickory or oak stirrups with leather hoods. The most prominent feature, however, was the saddle's exposed wooden tree. The tree had a large open slot over the horse's spine and a deep gullet over the horse's withers. It came in three sizes, allowing a comfortable fit for most any horse, even if the animal lost considerable weight. The tree was reinforced with metal and covered with rawhide for added strength.

Although comfortable for the horse, the first McClellans were said to be rather uncomfortable for all but the most experienced riders, a problem worsened when the rawhide covering on the seat began to crack from exposure to the elements. Beginning with the M1872, a layer of black collar leather was used over the rawhide, which effectively addressed the problem.

In the M1904, the black leather changed to russet, pre-twisted stirrup leathers were introduced to reduce stress on the rider's legs and sheepskin was added on the under side of the tree for the added comfort of the horse.

But by this time, the basic McClellan design, now 50 years old, was under fire. Cavalry officers considered it old technology that was being surpassed by better designs and changes in riding theory emanating from Europe. The McClellan, with its high cantle and pommel, forced the rider to sit quite vertically, with a deep seat and little movement. Adaptations and modifications were attempted but there could be no significant change in the McClellan until the stockpiles of saddles that amassed during World War I had dwindled. Thus the last major change in the McClellan did not come until the M1928.

The M1928 allowed closer contact between horse and rider and allowed the rider to better follow the horse's movement. It was lighter in weight, had fewer buckles and narrower stirrups without hoods. It borrowed some of its features from English saddles of the time. The McClellan saddle continued its military service until the United States Horse Cavalry was abolished in 1943.

In the history of equitation, the McClellan saddle is perhaps the finest example of function over form. Each and every feature of the saddle and its accompanying accoutrement had a purpose, a practical reason for being. Every ounce of weight and penny in cost had to be justified as aiding in the survival of the rider. Before changes of any kind were adopted on a large scale, extensive field trials were always conducted.

Ironically, the man who started it all, Captain George B. McClellan, never spent a day in the cavalry, and resigned his army commission to take a management position in the private sector before the saddle he designed even went into production. During the Civil War, McClellan rejoined the military and served in the Union army as a major general, then was defeated by Abraham Lincoln in the 1864 presidential election.

Manufacturers of saddle pads have also contributed greatly to mitigating less-than-perfect saddle fit. Today we can purchase anything from a simple felt pad to a cushion constructed of space age rubberized honeycomb material.

Also available are gel-filled pads and pads containing adjustable air bladders filled with foam rubber. These conform to the contours of the horse's back and the underside of the saddle, providing a malleable interface, like a do-it-yourself orthotic, and addressing another, thoroughly practical aspect of saddle fit: Even if we could make a saddle that perfectly fit a horse, what happens when we switch horses? Who can afford to have a different saddle for every horse they ride? And what happens when the horse dies? Do you shoot the saddle?

Another product intended to help aching equine backs and their riders' bank accounts is the CorrecTOR. Inventor Len Brown insists that it is not a saddle pad. Indeed, it resembles nothing familiar. Perhaps best described as a dynamic pressure distribution appliance, the CorrecTOR, according to Brown, works with any horse or mule and any saddle, English or Western, to "evenly distribute excess saddle pressures as your horse moves." At just 3/8-inch thick and less than half the size of a typical saddle pad, it is nearly hidden under most saddles.

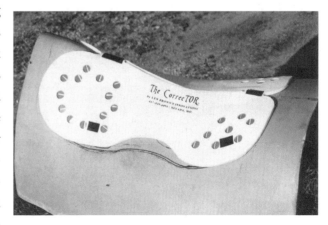

The CorrecTOR is a "dynamic pressure distribution appliance." (Len Brown)

WADE SADDLES

Any discussion of saddles and natural horsemanship would be incomplete if it did not acknowledge the type of saddle used by so many of the industry's working clinicians.

Some call it a Ray Hunt–style saddle because Hunt has probably been riding one the longest. Even Hunt's saddle maker, the legendary Dale Harwood, now calls it by that name. However, a more accurate description is the Wade tree saddle.

The original Wade saddle belonged to the father of Clifford Wade, longtime friend and neighbor of Tom Dorrance. In 1937, Wade took his dad's old saddle to Hamley's saddle shop in Pendleton, Oregon, and they made an agreement with him to use his name for the tree. Dorrance adopted the saddle tree for his own use, and Hunt got it from him.

Wade saddles are distinguished by these features:

1. The deep, hard seat and high cantle, shown here with a small "Cheyenne roll" but just as often seen without the rolled edge on the cantle.

Western saddles built on the Wade tree are popular with clinicians today. This one was built by Jeremiah Johnson of Albany, Oregon. *(Jeremiah Johnson)*

2. The large, but rather squatty mulehide-wrapped, leather-covered wooden post horn. The post horn, sometimes called a Mexican or Guadalajara horn, is part of the saddle tree rather than a bolt-on addition.
3. Pre-twisted stirrup leathers, usually with bell-shaped, metal-covered stirrups.
4. The dropped, flat-plate rigging for the girth.
5. The slick fork design, entirely devoid of the swells so often seen in rodeo-influenced Western saddles.
6. The low-riding pommel, of minimal thickness, with a wide gullet and extra depth from front to back.

Many modern horsemen find the nostalgic, "buckaroo" look of this saddle irresistible. More important, every feature mentioned has a purpose.

The deep seat and high cantle give the rider more security in the saddle, better lower back support, and more comfort on long rides. The hard seat also contributes to the rider's comfort by allowing for maximum ventilation and avoiding the heat buildup produced by padded seats. The leather of the seat may be smooth-side up or rough-side up as shown in the picture. Riding on a rough-out seat, especially with chaps, gives the rider extra purchase for advanced maneuvers.

The post horn is both sturdier and lighter in weight than a bolt-on horn. Its larger diameter means fewer wraps are required when dallying (tying off) after roping a cow. It also allows more controlled slippage of the coils when that is needed. These are hardly concerns for the average recreational rider, but the oversized horn makes a good handhold as well.

The bell stirrup, whether covered in metal or not, serves several purposes. It provides a larger surface on which the foot can rest, lessening the rider's fatigue on long rides. It makes it less likely that the rider's foot will go all the way through the stirrup and allow him to be dragged by the horse if he falls. And it discourages the horse from lying down in the saddle because, whichever way it hangs, the stirrup is very uncomfortable to lie on.

The twisted stirrup leathers make it easier to find the offside stirrup with the foot after mounting, and exert virtually no pressure on the rider's knees while riding.

The dropped, flat-plate rigging allows for minimal bulk from the latigo under the rider's legs.

The absence of swells allows the rider's legs to be in the "rider's groove," that place where the legs hang naturally when riding bareback. As seen on this saddle, bucking rolls are often added to give the rider the security of swells, but with the advantages of being adjustable and removable.

Finally, the most important feature of the Wade tree saddle is the design of the pommel. Because of its extra wide gullet, the front of the saddle sits down lower on the horse's withers. In this respect, the tree has more in common with an English saddle than the typical Western saddle. This, of course, places the horn lower, and as a result less torque is placed on the horse's back when dally-roping or when the rider pulls on the horn during mounting. It is also less in the way when reining.

THE BALANCED RIDE SADDLE

Although historically it preceded the revolution by nearly thirty years, the saddle pioneered by horseman Monte Foreman also deserves mention. In 1948, after twelve years and $17,000 spent on research, Foreman introduced the Monte Foreman Balanced Ride Saddle.

"[On] these old saddles," Foreman said, "the stirrups were hung way behind the cinch. There was too much padding under the legs. I measured and found out it was like riding with a 2-by-4 under each leg. The rider was

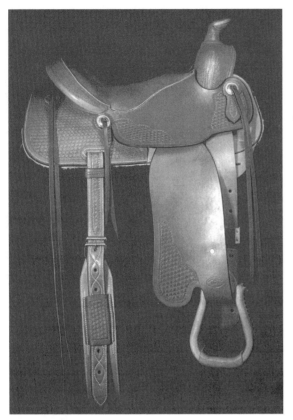

The Monte Foreman Balanced Ride Saddle. *(Gary Foreman Collection)*

always thrown out of the horse's carrying circle, that groove where he should always be. The rider's legs were so far away from the horse that they might as well have not been on him. You couldn't be in touch with the horse and you had no security. That's why you saw so many Western riders grabbing the horn to stay on."

Foreman put the rider in the rider's groove by creating a bulkless rigging that allowed the stirrups to be hung farther forward. Instead of ring rigging or an in-skirt metal rigging plate, his saddles had reinforced rawhide in-skirt rigging to reduce bulk. Foreman also developed ways of attaching and wrapping the latigo that prevented bulky overlapping and reduced the lump under the rider's knees.

Innovative though it was, Monte Foreman's saddle design did not replace traditional Western designs. The forward hang of his stirrups did not suit everyone. But the Monte Foreman Balanced Ride Saddle is still being made and can be ordered from the original Foreman Ranch in Elbert, Colorado, operated by Foreman's son, Gary.

The Fallis Balanced Ride Saddle, introduced in 1954 by Myrlin "Slim" Fallis and built today by his son, John M. Fallis of Wyarno, Wyoming, is similar to Foreman's because of an early saddle-making partnership between Foreman and the Fallis family.

There is a tendency, when one is overwhelmed with information, to be afraid to do anything for fear of making a mistake. Pat Parelli calls it "paralysis of analysis." That can easily happen to the conscientious horseman trying to do right by his horse on the matter of saddle fit. It's important, therefore, to stress that perfect saddle fit isn't necessary. As is so often the case, *striving* for perfection in an imperfect world gets you close enough. A reasonably well-fitting saddle with a good pad is good enough for most applications and is a dramatic improvement over the days when a working cowboy used his one and only saddle on all the horses in his string, no matter how different their backs might be.

CHAPTER 14

OTHER TRAINING CONCEPTS

THROUGHOUT HISTORY, THE AVERAGE HUMAN has been clumsy, crude, and too often, cruel in his interaction with the horse. Still, this remarkably adaptable creature has served us well. He has plowed our fields, herded our cattle, hauled our possessions across uncharted wilderness, and carried us into battles that often cost him his life. He has performed for our amusement and for our survival. He's done what we've asked even when we've asked poorly.

Is it any wonder, then, that the human who asks well gets even better results?

Enter the fine horseman, the horseman who understands the horse's nature, who is willing to work with that nature instead of against it, who provides the leadership the horse so desperately needs and consistent, compassionate communication. The particular tools and the methods the horseman uses become secondary to these personal traits and spectacular results are obtained in many different ways.

We have focused in this book on a general approach to horse training that is widely known as natural horsemanship, not because it is the only effective or morally sound way to train a horse, but because it is at the heart of this historical phenomenon, the revolution in horsemanship, that we have chosen to document. It is time to acknowledge some other approaches that share the spirit, if not the specific techniques of natural horsemanship.

TRADITIONAL HORSEMANSHIP

If there's one disturbing tendency caused by the phenomenal popularity of natural horsemanship, it is the general disdain that new converts feel toward anything that smacks of "tradition." In their zeal, they sometimes alienate other horsemen who have not yet been converted.

This is a normal stage in the process of resetting the mind to see the world from the horse's point of view. But it is a transitional stage. When Pat Parelli advises, "Do the exact opposite of what everyone else tells you," he is making a point in a dramatic way. He wants to wipe the slate clean to free the mind of preconceptions. It is a teaching technique.

Does this mean that everything in the long history of horsemanship prior to the mid-1970s has been wrong? Of course not. Does it mean that you should question everything and accept nothing simply because it is "the way we've always done it"? Absolutely. Traditions—even new ones such as natural horsemanship—must always be considered on their own merits.

The ability to analyze critically, to separate good traditions from bad ones, comes with experience. It is too much to ask the beginning student, who is already struggling with new ideas, to do so. Thus, the message is simplified. "Put on your blinders and disregard everything you thought you knew about horses." The blinders come off after the foundation concepts are learned. Then the student discovers that some aspects of traditional horsemanship are very worthwhile indeed, and entirely consistent with his new mindset.

For instance, natural horsemanship emphasizes riding with loose reins. In the beginning this seems to rule out nearly all traditional non-Western riding styles—dressage, hunting, jumping, endurance, eventing, steeplechasing, flat racing, and gaiting—because these are done with contact, i.e. without slack in the reins.

Yet, once the foundation principles are learned, the student discovers that they apply regardless of the riding style, regardless of the amount of slack in the reins, regardless of whether there is continual contact with the horse's mouth through the bit. Advanced riders in natural horsemanship programs are even taught how to ride cor-

Riding with contact doesn't mean holding the horse's head immovable; it means just a presence that says "I'm here." *(Dennis Reis Collection)*

rectly with contact to achieve finesse. World-class competitors in a number of non-Western riding disciplines are now outspoken ambassadors of natural horsemanship, and have not had to abandon all of the traditional aspects of their disciplines to be so. David and Karen O'Connor, Olympic medalists in three-day eventing, are good examples.

Dressage master Charles de Kunffy, in his 1993 book *The Ethics and Passions of Dressage*, makes a strong plea for nonconfrontational horsemanship, advocating in the process many of the core principles of the revolution in horsemanship. Indeed, horsemen at the highest levels in most traditional equestrian sports, whether they openly support natural horsemanship in so many words or not, use psychology and empathy in their training. It has been so with great horsemen down through history. Why? Because this approach is superior on both moral and practical grounds.

Traditional Western riding gets its share of criticism, too, for its use of curb bits. Natural horsemanship does not *preclude* the use of curb bits. Remember Xenophon's lesson from so many centuries ago: even the harshest bit may be made light by the rider's hands. Any bit can be used cruelly or humanely. The entire California system of bridling is calculated to produce a horse that can be controlled with a very light touch on a curb bit. There is nothing inconsistent there with natural horsemanship.

The traditional Western sports of reining and cutting now have world champion competitors such as Craig Johnson and Leon Harrel, respectively, extolling the virtues of natural horsemanship.

Traditional ranch horsemanship, the ultimate in practical, get-in-and-get-the-job-done horsemanship, is too often stereotyped as harsh and insensitive. But working cowboys like clinician Curt Pate are successfully blending traditional and progressive natural approaches. "I like to take the best of both worlds," he says simply. Curt, for instance, limits the groundwork he does on a trained horse, preferring instead to mount up right away and work out any kinks from the saddle while heading out to ride the fence line or gather cattle.

That Curt doesn't spend a certain amount of time going through ground exercises before riding doesn't make him wrong, nor does it mean that he wouldn't recommend that very thing to a beginning rider who lacks his experience and judgment or to riders who don't have a full day's work in front of them.

Spurs have often been used to cause a horse pain. William Cavendish, Duke of Newcastle, actually recommended that they draw blood. But spurs are capable of being used in a different, entirely humane way. Many top natural horsemanship clinicians use spurs not to punish the horse nor to ask for more forward movement, but to clarify a request for *lateral* movement. Spurs are used for precision of communication, for clarity, for creating pressure with pinpoint accuracy, for making things black and white for the horse. If horses could vote, they would vote for us to use spurs if we used them in this way. They hate not knowing what it is that we want.

In any approach to horsemanship, we must consider both its philosophical basis and its practical application. What has often been missing in traditional horsemanship as practiced by the average rider is a commitment to seeing the world through the horse's eyes, to understanding what motivates him and to making him a partner rather than a servant. This is the philosophical part, the horseman's mindset. When a natural, empathetic mindset is present, traditional methods take on a different flavor. They are applied with more sensitivity. The rider's hands don't yank on that curb bit; they change an angle slightly or squeeze gently, and no one knows except the horse and rider. Riding with contact doesn't mean holding the horse's head immobile; it means just a presence that says "I'm here." Spurring a horse doesn't mean jabbing him until he bleeds; it means touching him lightly, nudging him, stroking him, giving him an opportunity to respond at the most subtle level of communication.

When the horse's point of view is important to the horseman, traditional and natural horsemanship are not so far apart as they first appear.

CLICKER TRAINING

"Clicker training begins with a shift in thinking," states Alexandra Kurland, the guru of clicker training for horses. "Clicker training is a *positive* training tool . . . we don't try to correct unwanted behavior, instead we focus on what we want the horse *to do*."

First widely used in the training of dolphins, clicker training was developed for domestic animals by Karen Pryor and further adapted to horse training by Kurland. The trainer squeezes a small plastic clicker that makes a distinctive chirp-like sound. The sound marks the precise moment the horse did something "good." Each click is followed by a food treat such as a chunk of carrot or bit of grain.

In the beginning, the simplest of behaviors is rewarded, but as training progresses, *units of behavior* of greater duration and complexity can be developed. Clicking and treating mark the end of a unit of behavior.

Interestingly, cues are developed *after* individual behaviors have been learned. They evolve naturally out of the behavior shaping process. Chaining of cues allows longer and more complicated units of behavior to be learned.

Why use the clicker rather than simply saying "yes" or "good"? The clicker sound stimulates the brain in a special way. Pryor, working with German veterinary neurophysiologist and clicker trainer Barbara Schoening, has theorized that the clicker sound is processed by a faster and more primitive part of the nervous system. In an article on her Web site, www.clicker training.com, she writes

> Research in neurophysiology has identified the kinds of stimuli—bright lights, sudden sharp sounds—that reach the amygdala (a structure in the limbic system or oldest part of the brain) first, before reaching the cortex or thinking part of the brain. The click is that kind of stimulus. Other research, on conditioned fear responses in humans, shows that these also are established via the amygdala, and are characterized by a pattern of very rapid learning, often on a single trial, long-term retention, and a big surge of concomitant emotions.
>
> We clicker trainers see similar patterns of very rapid learning, long retention, and emotional surges, albeit positive emotions rather than fear. Barbara and I hypothesize that the clicker is a conditioned "joy" stimulus that is acquired and recognized through those same primitive pathways, which would help explain why it is so very different from, say, a human word, in its effect.

A word uttered by a human being would not be precisely the same each time. Volume, pitch, duration, and emotion, even if varied only slightly, would make it a different sound, requiring the word to be interpreted and correlated to an action. This is a very different—and much slower—process than the near-reflexive action a click can cause. A good compromise when the trainer first wishes to be hands-free is therefore a tongue click rather than a word cue.

Rewarding horses with food is controversial. The main objection is that the horse rapidly becomes obsessed with the food and disrespectful of the trainer. Clicker training avoids this problem by redirecting the horse's attention immediately. "Think of it like filling up your horse's dance card," Kurland advises. "Keep him busy by reinforcing him for what you want, and what you'll get is a well-mannered horse . . . the first step of clicker training teaches the emotional control that is essential in every horse's training." It is

Panda, a miniature horse clicker trained to serve as a guide animal, waits patiently while owner Ann Edie, right, and trainer Alexandra Kurland dine. *(Alexandra Kurland Collection)*

recommended that these early lessons be conducted with the horse inside a stall and the human outside of it, a safety precaution that also sets the horse up for success rather than failure.

Clicker training has been used to solve myriad behavior problems as well as to develop a horse's way of moving, with and without a rider. Although it is quite different, clicker training is remarkably compatible with other approaches. "Clicker training piggybacks beautifully onto other training methods," says Kurland. "It takes what is good in all systems and makes it better by adding a clear 'yes answer' signal and a positive reward . . . we are giving the horse something he *actively* wants to work for."

A fascinating study in the effectiveness of clicker training is Kurland's work with Panda, a black-and-white miniature horse. Panda was trained to serve as a guide animal for a blind friend, schoolteacher and horsewoman Ann Edie, doing all the things, and going all the places that a guide dog would go.

The central challenge in training guide animals is teaching them "intelligent disobedience" at which Panda excelled. She learned to recognize situations—overhead obstacles are a good example—where obeying the human's command to go forward would put the human in danger. In those cases, she learned to disobey the command. Panda also showed the ability to quickly learn complex patterns of behavior, including routes from one place to another in new environments. Kurland believes that the behavior shaping accomplished with Panda is not limited to exceptional equine individuals, but is merely a glimpse of the problem solving and learning potential possessed by all horses that can be brought out with clicker training.

TARGET TRAINING

Clicker training often incorporates an additional element, target training. This has been taken to the highest level by Shawna Karrasch, a former trainer of killer whales, dolphins, and other marine mammals at Sea World of California, under the name "On Target Training."

Target training starts exactly the way clicker training does. Once the horse is responding to the clicker, he is taught to touch his nose to a target. The target can be anything—Karrasch uses a plastic marine float mounted on a dowel stick—and it rapidly becomes familiar and comforting to the horse, which is initially rewarded with a food treat every time he touches it.

According to Shawna, "It can be used to teach the horse many things: lowering his head for clipping, loading on a trailer, free jumping, standing quietly for the veterinarian, farrier, or mounting; and can be successfully applied to work under saddle. Eventually the target is faded out, and the bridge signal indicates recognition of the desired behavior."

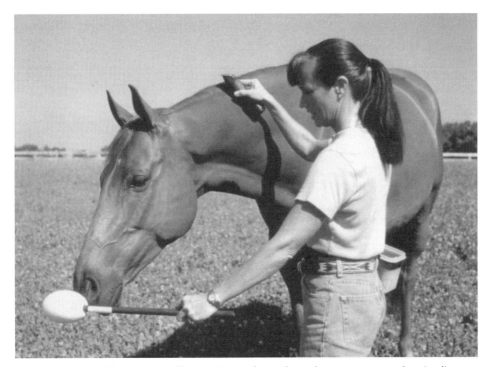

Using a target and food treats, Shawna Karrasch teaches a horse to accept electric clippers.
(Shawna Karrasch Collection)

The bridge signal is another way of rewarding the horse. It can be anything that has come to have a positive association for the horse, from a stroke on the neck to a verbal "good boy."

Clicker and target training are rooted in psychology, especially the behavior modification theories of Burrhus Frederic Skinner (1904–1990), one of the fathers of this branch of science. A key concept is that when behavior is *reinforced*, it is more likely to be repeated. Conversely, behavior that is *punished* is less likely to be repeated.

Let's review the ways that behavior can be encouraged through reinforcement and discouraged through punishment. These are often called the Four Quadrants of Operant Conditioning.

Positive Reinforcement means that *something pleasant is added* to encourage the desired behavior. Example: The horse is clicked and treated when he responds correctly.

Negative Punishment means that *something pleasant is subtracted* to discourage unwanted behavior. Example: The trainer withholds the click and treat.

Positive Punishment means that *something unpleasant is added* to discourage the undesired behavior. Example: Pressure is introduced to get the horse to change his state of motion.

Negative Reinforcement means that *something unpleasant is subtracted* to encourage the desired behavior. Example: Pressure is released when the horse complies.

Operant conditioning also includes the concept of *extinction*, which means that a behavior is weakened and may eventually be eliminated by the absence of any reinforcement.

Both clicker training and target training rely most heavily on positive reinforcement and negative punishment, but in combination with other training methods, all five concepts are utilized.

IMPORTANT: "Punishment" here should not be construed to mean "pain." It is simply Skinner's technical term for an uncomfortable stimulus.

TTEAM™

The Tellington TTouch Equine Awareness Method (TTEAM™) is a way of training, healing, improving athletic performance, and overcoming common resistances in horses. It is the brainchild of Linda Tellington-Jones, a record-setting endurance rider in the 1960s who went on to become an icon in the American horse industry.

TTEAM has three parts:

1. Tellington TTouch™
2. Confidence Course™ (ground exercises)
3. The Joy of Riding

TTouch (pronounced "TEE-touch") is a very specific way of touching a horse that is said to aid in enhancing well-being and health, while also affecting behavior and performance. Tellington-Jones explains, "The intent of TTouch is to release fear at the cellular level and activate the innate healing potential of the body."

The TTouch technique consists of varying, yet specific contact with the skin, muscles, and soft tissue. There are twenty different TTouches, each with its own precise positioning of the hands and fingers. Most have been given animal names to make learning easier. The primary TTouch, the Clouded Leopard, is based on circular motions pushing the skin (rather than moving over it) in approximately one-and-a-quarter revolutions. Other TTouches include the Lying Leopard, the Raccoon, the Bear, the Flick of the Bear's Paw, Noah's March, and Back Lifts.

Like the Eastern arts of acupuncture and acupressure, TTouch is said to cause positive results in unexpected ways. For instance, a special version of TTouch is used on the horse's ears, which are gently massaged from the

Linda Tellington-Jones has created twenty different TTouches for horses. All have a noticeable calming effect. *(Ellen Van Leeuwen)*

base to the tip in a stroking motion. This procedure is recommended by Tellington-Jones when a horse experiences colic (belly pain) or is in shock, as well as for reducing fatigue and stress. A special TTouch for the horse's gums is used when the horse is upset. All have a noticeable calming effect that aids in recovery.

The purpose of TTouch is multi-fold: To improve performance, to connect the function of brain and body, to encourage healing, and to overcome negative behavior patterns. It has been used successfully on many different species of animals, from horses to tigers to boa constrictors, and has been featured on countless television programs worldwide, including America's popular television show "Unsolved Mysteries."

Tellington-Jones's groundwork (Confidence Course) utilizes such obstacles as a labyrinth, ground poles, and plastic, to build a horse's self-control, focus, self-confidence, cooperation, balance, and coordination. A "wand," her variation on the age-old dressage whip, is used to guide the horse through groundwork patterns.

As for the Joy of Riding, Tellington-Jones draws from her experience as a teacher of classical riding, as a competitor, and as an instructor of the Feldenkrais method of human body awareness and self-improvement to create a unique and comprehensive approach to riding that has been respected internationally for decades.

Linda Tellington-Jones is a modern advocate of phrenology, the practice of analyzing the shape of the equine head, including elements of the set and placement of the eyes and ears, and the definition of the profile. She uses these elements to determine the horse's personality, trainability, and behavioral predispositions. Some of these assessments were used by Denton Offutt in the nineteenth century and by Professor Jesse Beery in the twentieth. It was Beery who prompted Tellington-Jones when she was twelve years old to closely observe the shapes of horses' heads and to embark on a lifelong study of equine personalities. In 1965, Tellington-Jones conducted a study of 1,500 horses to evaluate the relationship of the hair swirls (whorls or "cowlicks") on a horse's head to its temperament.

As you might expect, the linking of a horse's physical characteristics to its behavior is not universally accepted. However, it has at least prompted curiosity and a desire to better understand the character of horses. Tellington-Jones's popular book, *Getting in TTouch: Understand and Influence Your Horse's Personality*, on the assessment of equine personality has been translated into seven languages.

Altogether, Linda Tellington-Jones has written eleven books that have been published in twelve languages and has produced eighteen videos of her work. There are more than 600 certified practitioners trained in the Tellington Method in seventeen countries.

ENDO-TAPPING

Good horsemanship, though not natural for humans, is usually logical to us. We can usually understand why it works, why the horse responds as he does. But sometimes, even though experience tells us that something works, we don't understand why. The TTouch is one example. Endo-tapping is another.

Endo-tapping was developed by French-born Jean Phillipe "J. P." Giacomini, a master dressage rider, horsemanship clinician, and breeder of Andalusian and Lusitano horses, who now lives in Lexington, Kentucky. Endo-tapping is a way of relaxing a horse and putting him in a frame of mind that is highly receptive to learning. It is done with an "Endo-stick," a semi-rigid fiberglass stick from 24 to 64 inches in length with a foam rubber or gel-filled rubber ball on the end. The ball is the part that touches the horse.

The technique is to tap the horse with rhythm. The location, duration, and intensity of the tapping vary with what is to be accomplished. The horse may first be annoyed by the tapping—tapping, patting, or slapping is not naturally pleasant for a horse—but he quickly habituates (desensitizes) and becomes oblivious to it.

According to Giacomini, when the tapping is continued well past the point of simple desensitization, something else happens. The tapping so relaxes the horse that its sympathetic nervous system (stress mechanism) yields control to its parasympathetic nervous system (relaxation), allowing the horse to be trained faster and easier, with more permanence.

Why? Does the tapping lull the horse into an altered state of consciousness? Is it

J. P. Giacomini uses an Endo-stick to teach Istoso, a thirteen-year-old Lusitano stallion, the jambette or leg lift, an exercise to help the horse control his balance. *(J. P. Giacomini Collection)*

Texas trick horse trainer Allen Pogue creates positive associations with objects like beanbag chairs and pedestals, what he calls "real estate." *(Allen Pogue Collection)*

similar to what humans experience with hypnotism or meditation, which are often done expressly for the purpose of self-improvement? Does it create, as Giacomini suggests, a change in the "spinal memory" of the horse? Not even Giacomini knows for sure, but the results he obtains suggest that something real is going on.

Trick horse trainer Allen Pogue of Austin, Texas, who was influenced by Giacomini, incorporated the Frenchman's methods in a novel training program of his own. Using Endo-tapping, Pogue instills patience and focus in horses by teaching them to stand on pedestals and sit on bean bags, either alone or with other horses. This training begins right after birth.

MULE TRAINING

Why address mule training in a book on horsemanship? Because the mule, in a sense, is the *extreme* horse.

First, a brief refresher in genetics. The mule is the hybrid offspring of a male donkey and a female horse. (The less common *hinny* is the offspring of a male horse and female donkey.) The mule has an uneven number of chromosomes—thirty-one from the mother and thirty-two from the father—making it, with very rare exceptions, infertile.

The mule inherits physical and behavioral traits from both parents, but not in exactly equal doses. Some mules are very horse-like in appearance; others favor their donkey dads. More importantly, their behavior characteristics also vary. In the past, mules that acted more like horses generally had an easier life and suffered less criticism, while those that exhibited more donkey-like behavior were often misunderstood and handled roughly (hopefully this is changing as people come to understand the mule better).

To understand the mule, you must understand both the horse *and* the donkey.

Remember that the horse evolved on the grassy plains with flight as its primary survival mechanism. When frightened, the horse's instinct is to run first and think later (if at all) from a safe distance. What constitutes a safe distance in the horse's mind depends on what he thinks is chasing him. If a horse can't run away, he will fight, but it is a last resort when he is in a state of fear.

Most types of donkeys evolved in rocky, precipitous terrain where blind flight could be fatal. The donkey thus learned to freeze when frightened and wait to see what happened next. He might end up running away, but it is just as likely that he would stand his ground and even fight when threatened. This characteristic of donkeys has allowed them to serve as guard animals for herds of sheep.

Now consider the mule. The mule has a flight response, but one that is different from that of a horse. A mule may run when frightened, but it won't run blindly. In fact, one of the challenges in training mules for competition is *encouraging* the flight response. Only some mules have enough of it for racing, roping, cutting, or barrel racing.

For other uses where safety is the foremost concern, trainers such as Meredith Hodges teach a mule early on to freeze, like a donkey, when something goes wrong. This is especially desirable for driving mules. An ideal driving animal, horse or mule, is one that will stop and stand quietly when something out of the ordinary happens.

So why call the mule an *extreme* horse? Pat Parelli explained it as well as anyone could in a 1983 *Western Horseman* article by Dr. Robert Miller, co-author of this book. "Mules separate artistic trainers from crude trainers," he said. "They won't tolerate injustice, whereas most horses will."

As we said before, mules *must* be trained the way horses *should* be trained. Horses are forgiving creatures and adapt to fairly incompetent handling by humans. *Mules do not suffer fools.* Push a mule too hard or too fast, and you will find out in no uncertain terms that you have made a mistake. The mule remembers your mistakes. You might even call it holding a grudge.

Because of the influence of the donkey, the mule has a more analytical brain than does a horse. He will not do something we ask him to do unless he believes that it is the safe and right thing to do. You have to give him time to reach that decision. It is much harder with a mule to get that surrender, that submission to our leadership. The mule is not as willing to suppress his own survival instinct just because some human asks him to.

Mules thus represent a greater training challenge than horses. A good horse trainer isn't automatically a good mule trainer. But the reverse is nearly always true: a good mule trainer makes a great horse trainer.

Parelli is a case in point. His skill with horses is due in part to his early work with mules. In 1976, he helped start and was first president of the American Mule Association, which still exists. In 1981, he stunned everyone

Thumper and Pat Parelli proved that mules can compete effectively against horses. *(Pat Parelli Collection)*

Debby Miller and her Hall of Fame mule, Jordass Jean, take home another blue ribbon. *(Robert Miller Collection)*

at the NRCHA (National Reined Cow Horse Association) Snaffle Bit Futurity by entering and nearly winning the event on a mule named Thumper. It resulted not only in a boost to his career but a NRCHA rule change banning mules from future competitions. When Parelli was invited back the next year to give a demonstration on a mule, he performed the same reining pattern without a bridle.

Parelli credits his work with mules as giving him insight into the mind of the equine, the importance of reverse psychology in training, and the value of patience.

Mulemanship has therefore played an important role in the revolution in *horsemanship*.

Mules also played a vital role in the history of the United States, beginning with mule breeder (and first American president) George Washington. Mules could stand the heat and stress of working on Southern plantations. It was oxen and mules, not horses, that pulled the pioneers' wagons westward.

At the beginning of the twentieth century, the United States had 22.5 million equines, 7 million of which were mules. For every two horses, there was one mule. While the automobile dramatically reduced the American horse population, it nearly wiped out the mule. However, with better breeding and better training that begins at the moment of birth, the mule is enjoying an explosion in popularity, and for good reason. Mules live longer than horses. They are stronger, they are hardier, they tolerate heat and thirst better, they are more sure-footed, they are easier keepers, they are more resistant to most equine ailments and unsoundnesses. They have better feet and require less shoeing, they are less excitable and flighty, and they are more versatile.

On the other side of the ledger, mules mature more slowly than horses, they are harder to train, they are less predictable, and of course, they have no breeding potential.

Mules now compete against horses in every conceivable event and against each other at an increasing number of mule-only shows.

There are a number of outstanding mule trainers who work with this equine exclusively. They include Meredith Hodges of Loveland, Colorado; Brad Cameron of Corvallis, Montana; and Steve Edwards of Queen Valley, Arizona, who at this writing, heads the Mule Handling and Management Program at Pierce College in the Los Angeles area.

PART III

Dr. Robert Miller desensitizing a foal moments after birth, as portrayed on the cover of Miller's book, *Imprint Training of the Newborn Foal. (Dwayne Brech)*

CHAPTER 15

FOAL TRAINING

"DO YOU NOT KNOW, THEN, that the beginning in every task is the chief thing, especially for any creature that is young and tender? For it is then that it is best molded and takes the impression that one wishes to stamp upon it."

The words are from *The Republic* by the Greek philosopher Plato, written about 370 B.C., more than 2,300 years ago. Plato's observation has been with us for quite some time, but it wasn't until the twentieth century that we finally began to understand the mechanisms by which young creatures learn.

In every species, there are critical learning times very early in life. When these periods end, a special opportunity to learn certain important things is lost. During these periods, the young creature learns to socialize with other individuals and to recognize its own kind. Mother and offspring form a powerful bond through the process of *imprinting*. Austrian zoologist Konrad Lorenz (1903–1989) first described the natural phenomenon of imprinting in 1935 after observing that geese hatched in an incubator and lacking the presence of a mother would attach to and follow any maternal substitute that they saw moving near them after they hatched. In 1973, Lorenz shared the Nobel Peace Prize for his work.

Among birds and mammals, as we noted earlier, there are two kinds of newborn individuals. Those that are born or hatched in a helpless state, with their senses incompletely developed, are called *altricial* species.

Included are the young of the cat and dog families, of predatory birds (raptors) such as eagles, hawks, and owls, and of humans. Their mothers can protect them right after birth, so their critical learning times are delayed. The wolf cub, for example, is born with its eyes and ears closed, able to do little except nurse for several weeks. Then it emerges from the den and the critical learning begins.

The other kind of newborn young, the *precocial* species, are typically prey animals. Newly hatched chicks, ducklings, geese, turkey, and quail, and newborn lambs, calves, deer, antelope, and horses are precocial. In order to stay alive they must be able to keep up with Mother, even at high speed, shortly after birth. Their senses must be fully functional and they must be able to learn *immediately*.

The newborn foal must be imprinted by its dam and the other members of the band. When a predator threatens wild horses, they run together, and the foals must be able to stay with the group if they are to survive.

The critical learning times in foals thus begin at birth. These are the most powerful learning times in any young creature's life, and they shape and influence its attitudes and responses permanently.

Historically, there have been instances where horse cultures took advantage of this fact. In the Bedouin culture it was said that the foaling mare and the newborn foal were taken right into the owner's tent. The foal began life with exposure to people, as well as to horses and other animals.

There is documented evidence that certain Native American tribes in South America and in North America worked with and trained newborn foals. The method is described in a self-published book by Harold Wadley, *Spirit Blending Foals Before and After Birth: An Old Way Continued*. Wadley was born on the Cherokee reservation in Oklahoma early in the twentieth century and was taught the method by his grandfather.

The man considered to be the father of the current revolution in horsemanship, Tom Dorrance, stated in his book, *True Unity*, "As I got older I found that those young ones learn just as fast, or maybe faster, than the older ones. It's surprising how quick these little ones catch on and how lasting it is."

One of Australia's most respected horsemen, Tom Roberts, wrote in his 1974 book, *Horse Control: The Young Horse*,

> Even in the first week of his life we can start to accustom the
> foal to the handling that will be part of his everyday life later on. As

he grows we can get him used to having a halter on, to being led, and also to having his feet inspected.

These lessons can begin as early as you please and go on whenever the opportunity offers. But the foal must be kept respectful—he must not be permitted to become cheeky or disrespectful.

Professor Robert W. Miller (unrelated to veterinarian Robert M. Miller, co-author) wrote in his 1975 book *Western Horse Behavior & Training*, "If the foal is broke to lead shortly after birth, it can be gentled at that time. Its feet should be handled and it should be brushed all over its body."

Horsemen from various parts of the world and various walks of life observed

Dr. Miller with a newborn foal in Colorado. Note how unconcerned the mare is; she was imprint-trained at birth, too. Imprint training has been done successfully with horses, cattle, zebra, llamas, camels, deer, elephants, a giraffe, and a rhinoceros. *(Debby Miller)*

the same thing: there is tremendous advantage to be had by starting a horse's learning at the earliest possible time.

Veterinarian Miller took the idea furthest and developed a comprehensive training regimen, based on behavioral science and timeless horse-handling principles, that he dubbed *imprint training*. It took several decades to become widely accepted, but it is now practiced around the world.

IMPRINT TRAINING

Robert M. Miller graduated in 1956 and began a veterinary practice career that included all species, including zoo animals, but was primarily equine. He had always been taught, by horsemen and college professors alike, to avoid handling newborn foals. He had no reason to question this traditional advice. At that time, nearly everybody said that excessive contact with a newborn foal could cause the mare to reject it. Too much handling was also believed to make the foal spoiled and disrespectful. Experience with spoiled orphan foals seemed to confirm this concept. Moreover, most people believed that very young foals, like puppies or human infants, were simply too young to learn much.

During the summer of 1959, Dr. Miller observed foals he was forced to handle at birth due to obstetrical emergencies. These foals, when seen again, whether it was the next day, or two, three, or four months later, behaved differently from previously unhandled foals. They seemed less fearful, gentler, and easier to handle. Many of them acted as though they knew him. Being familiar with the work of Lorenz, Miller concluded that, as a result of his contact with these foals at birth, he had imprinted upon them.

The next year he experimented with a foal of his own, a Quarter Horse filly. Rather than minimizing postpartum handling, he maximized it, handling the foal for two hours while the mare bonded with her, licking her or standing nearby. The next day Miller knew that he had made a great discovery. The foal was strikingly friendly, allowed handling of her entire body, and was calm and unafraid. Within a week, the filly was leading, backing, turning, and accepting electric clippers, plastic, ropes, and pressure in the saddle and girth areas. Her feet could be picked up and handled, and veterinary invasion of all body openings was tolerated.

After repeated success with more of his own foals, Miller began recommending the procedure to his clientele and demonstrating it to them. Most indicated no desire to try it, but a few who were willing to experiment had dramatic success. Moreover, as the foals matured, they were ideal patients, cooperative with the farrier, eager to learn, and very responsive to training.

Dr. Miller called the process "imprint training" because it began during the imprinting period right after birth, and took place entirely within the foal's critical learning period, the first week of life.

In 1984, after twenty-five years of recommending imprint training to his clients, Miller made a videotape on general horse behavior (*Influencing the Horse's Mind*) in which imprint training was briefly discussed. This sparked public interest in the topic and led to a second videotape, *Imprint Training of the Foal.*

Knowing that the Thoroughbred industry would be resistant to anything that reduced flightiness in foals, Miller chose for the video newborns from the only three racing Thoroughbred farms in his practice that routinely imprint-trained their babies. These farms had been reluctant to try the process—conventional wisdom in North America at the time was that gentle foals could not race successfully—but they had been pleased with the results.

The second tape was well received by some branches of the horse industry, notably some Quarter Horse breeders and by the Arabian horse industry.

In 1991, *Western Horseman* magazine published Miller's book on the subject, *Imprint Training of the Newborn Foal*. They marketed it effectively and eventually translated it into several languages. In 1995, an updated and expanded videotape, *Early Learning* was released. It demonstrated the procedure on foals of several breeds. An audio tape and double CD of the same title followed in 1998 and 2002, respectively.

Miller left his career practice in 1988 after thirty-two years as a working veterinarian in order to devote the rest of his life to promoting and explaining not only imprint training, but also the revolution in horsemanship that he saw occurring around him.

His books, videotapes, audio programs, and seminars in the United States and abroad popularized imprint training throughout the horse world. As mules became increasingly popular for riding, breeders learned that correct handling at birth could produce an animal that completely negated the contrary image these hybrid animals so commonly have.

The Thoroughbred racing industry learned that well-mannered and unafraid foals race *better* and suffer far fewer injuries. Such illustrious trainers as D. Wayne Lucas endorsed imprint training, saying, "It's common sense!"

Some of the most effective clinicians involved in the revolution in horsemanship became ardent supporters of training baby foals. Pat Parelli adopted the method for all of his foals and introduced novel applications. Parelli encouraged his students to use it, demonstrated its results in spectacular ways, and eventually made a videotape, *A Natural Beginning*, showing his version.

Monty Roberts had all of the foals born on his farm imprint-trained, and devoted a chapter in his book, *From My Hands to Yours*, to the method. Many of his foals became racetrack and show winners. Richard Shrake, Clinton Anderson, and many other influential horsemen have likewise endorsed imprint training to their audiences.

Anything new and nontraditional, however, will elicit controversy. Opposition to imprint training has come from two sources. Although this opposition is rapidly diminishing as the horse industry witnesses the success of the method, it is not likely to go away completely any time soon.

Academic Opposition to Imprint Training

Many academic behaviorists have supported imprint training. Several university studies have supported the efficacy and rationale for training newborn foals. However, other studies that report poor results or even adverse effects have surfaced. Upon further examination, it has been found *in every*

Kay Sharpnack of Hinterland Ranch in Sisters, Oregon, poses in 2002 with her imprint-trained llama. The procedure is known as "mallonizing" in the camelid world. *(Kay Sharpnack Collection)*

case that either the procedure was not performed correctly or the study was not conducted in a scientific manner. Like *all* horse-training methods, foal training must be done correctly.

Some scientists object to the term "imprint" training, feeling that what is occurring is not really imprinting but socialization. This is semantic hair splitting. It is not important what the method is called; what is important is that it works. Moreover, it is certain that foals do imprint on a variety of moving objects, including trees swaying in the wind and such machinery as tractors and wheelbarrows.

Undoubtedly some in academia are annoyed because a horseman lacking their academic credentials in behavioral science came up with something that they hadn't thought of. Dr. Miller, whose education is comparable to that of a physician in general practice rather than to that of a psychologist or psychiatrist, does not claim to have invented anything. Others have taught newborn foals. What Miller did was give the procedure a name, ritualize it, explain why it works, and promote it.

Opposition from Horse Trainers

Some trainers are opposed to imprint training because it is not traditional, because they have been successful with more traditional training methods, or because they have been presented with spoiled colts that were *improperly* trained as foals. Invariably these trainers have not personally attempted the method and have no intention of doing so.

A few trainers are concerned that if owners train their foals, the trainers will lose business later on because they won't be needed. This, of course, is completely fallacious. Good trainers will always be needed, but if the foals undergo proper imprint training at birth, it will greatly facilitate later learning, and significantly reduce the number of injuries suffered by both young horses and the people who handle them.

Another reason why some trainers and clinicians reject imprint training—or any aspect of horse training, for that matter—is just to be different. If ninety-nine people agreed that the sky was blue and one person insisted it was red, whom would you remember? Some people will do almost anything to be noticed.

Lastly, it is likely that some clinicians who oppose imprint training do so because it will spoil their cowboy act at public clinics. It is impressive to see an unbroken, excited, fearful colt transformed into a compliant, obedient, relaxed subject. Starting a calm, unafraid colt that was imprint-trained at birth is not nearly as entertaining a spectacle.

The revolution in horsemanship is about establishing a mutually beneficial relationship with a horse using the simplest and most humane methods available. If all we want is a dramatic show, why not do things the old way? It was very dramatic to see an unbroken bronc roped, snubbed, choked down, held by the ears, a hind leg tied up, blindfolded, hobbled, forcibly saddled, mounted, and then bucked out, whipped, and spurred with every jump until the colt surrendered completely. A lot of useful horses were produced that way. Is that the way we want to do it, by force? Or are we looking for a better, kinder, and more civilized way, one that produces a horse that *wants* to be with us?

If a horse is properly trained from the moment it is born, the result is so much better, for both the horse and the human. That's why the training of newborn foals is an important part of the revolution in horsemanship.

Imprint Training Goes National and Global

Opposition to imprint training had noticeably lessened by the dawn of the twenty-first century, and more and more breeders were adding innovations to the method as they realized that baby foals learn faster and more effectively than older horses do. Advocates around the globe practiced and encouraged others to work with newborn foals.

In Argentina, the ranching family of Malcolm and Gloria Cook and their four sons, all horse trainers, began to influence horsemen in this tradition-bound society to train foals.

In Spain, veterinarian Cecile Clamour and her farrier husband, Maxim, have convinced many horse breeders to give these methods a try. In the same country, Quarter Horse Association president

Imprint training is now popular the world over. This is Spanish writer and breeder Pilar Fabregat with her newborn American Paint Horse foal. *(Robert Miller Collection)*

Pilar Fabregat and her saddle maker husband, Carlos, are enthusiastic foal trainers.

Outside Paris, France, the Parelli Natural Horse-Man-Ship school, La Cense, trains newborn foals.

Harness horse trainer Ole Johanssen in Norway is winning races with his trotting horses trained as foals. He has them driving in harness at one week of age, and they never forget it.

Natural horseman, clinician, charro, and veterinarian Alfonso Aguilar, practices imprint training, as does Thoroughbred trainer, George Cardiel, also in Mexico. George's brother, Mark Cardiel, one of Dr. Miller's earliest converts, is featured in the original videotape on the subject, along with his Malibu Valley Farm's Thoroughbred foals.

On Ireland's famous Kildangen farm, where nearly a thousand racing Thoroughbreds reside, veterinary nurse and broodmare manager Amanda Kelly imprint-trains the foals, although due to the huge numbers of which are born nightly—as many as forty—she does do an abbreviated version. However, every foal is haltered, led about, and handled daily, so that by a week of age most of Dr. Miller's procedures have been done.

Host Don Burke of Australia's popular television show, "Burke's Back-yard," called imprint training "the greatest advance in horse training in the twentieth century, and possibly of all time."

Closer to home, a company called CM Equine Products, of Norco, California, has developed a harness for baby foals to teach them to lead, back up, and stand square. It is called the CM™ Lead and Drive Training System, and it works nicely with imprint training.

When Bill Dorrance first saw the original videotape on imprint training, he telephoned Dr. Miller to introduce himself. "Me and my brother, Tom, always believed in training baby foals, but we never thought about starting them at birth. I think you're on to something!" Bill was horseman enough to understand the implications of early foal training.

Allen Pogue, the Texas trainer who has done so much with Endo-tapping, performs imprint training with his foals. They are remarkably obedient, taught to sit on command or stand patiently on a pedestal. He states, "A few short years ago, the first pioneer in the field of 'imprinting' established a path to follow and most enlightened mare owners have their own versions of the process. It is an opportunity, like few others, to meaningfully experience and guide the awakening of a new life. You see, horses as a species are born 'ready to learn' and there is a logical method to begin the actual training of a horse just a few hours and/or days old."

The racehorse industry, once resistant to intensive foal handling, is rapidly accepting it. There is only one legal stimulant in horse racing, the body's own adrenalin. If the horse goes to the gate excited, its adrenalin is spent before the race begins. Adrenalin is a powerful emergency hormone, giving the individual extra speed, strength, and stamina for a fight-or-flight situation, but it is a short-acting hormone. The horse that goes to the gate calm, relaxed, and free of excitement or fear has a great advantage when the gate opens and it comes out with a surge of adrenalin.

Imprint training may prove to be applicable to any wild precocial species. Dr. Miller receives a steady stream of reports of its successes on species such as white-tailed deer, mule deer, giraffes, elephants, camels, and cattle.

Dr. Miller with a three-day-old zebra. The zebra mare was wild and dangerous, and had to be separated from the foal. The foal, however, was gentle and unafraid. Saddlerock Ranch, Malibu, California. *(Debby Miller)*

Miller teaches the foal to flex its neck while owner Tami Semler desensitizes its feet. *(Debby Miller)*

Desensitizing the foal to plastic. *(Debby Miller)*

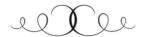

CHAPTER 16

THE HOOF CARE DEBATE

In 360 B.C., XENOPHON wrote in his suggestions for evaluating a horse for purchase,

> . . . the first things which I say you ought to look at are his feet. Just as a house would be good for nothing if it were very handsome above but lacked the proper foundations, so too a war-horse, even if all his other points were fine, would yet be good for nothing if he had bad feet; for he could not use a single one of his fine points.

In 1751 in England, a book was published with a title that expressed the same thought a bit more succinctly: *No Foot, No Horse.* This is the battle cry of the modern horseman, too. Foot problems not only render a horse useless to man, they can also cause him significant pain and a shortened life.

The health of a horse's hoof is affected by genetics, by what he eats, by the environment in which he lives, by the way the hoof is trimmed, by how (and whether) he is shod, and by how the horse is used. In the wild, nature and the horse take care of all of this. In domestication, it falls to man.

Man has struggled with this responsibility for centuries and even today, with the benefits of technology and scientific research, debate over the proper course of action continues. The revolution in horsemanship is not complete where hoof care is concerned, but the ongoing public dialogue among hoof experts is bringing today's owner an understanding of the horse's foot that few in previous generations possessed.

Before trying to understand the equine hoof and the challenge of modern hoof care, let's take a look at the way the hoof evolved.

THE EVOLUTION OF THE EQUINE HOOF

According to the fossil record, the earliest known ancestor of the horse, *Hyracotherium* (formerly known as eohippus, the "dawn horse"), lived in the southern part of North America, with various strains migrating to what is now Europe, 50 to 38 million years ago. It was a lamb-sized quadruped, 10 to 14 inches tall, with four toes on its front feet, three toes on the back, and soft pads at the base of the toes. Living in swamps and forests long before the grassy plains developed, it browsed on leaves and probably had a striped or blotchy coat for camouflage. Its eyes were set close together and it had small ears and small, sharp teeth. *Hyracotherium* bore little resemblance to our modern horse.

As the Earth cooled and dried out, grassy plains developed and the early horse grew larger, longer-legged, and faster in order to escape predators. It became a grazer rather than a browser, and the number of toes decreased to three on each foot.

With *Merychippus*, which lived about 20 million years ago, we see a hint of the modern hoof: the soft pads had disappeared and the middle toe had become prominent, bearing all of the 36-inch animal's weight. The back was longer and flatter, and the skull was heavier.

About 6 million years ago came *Pliohippus*. It was 48 inches tall (twelve hands) and had the general look of the modern horse with a longer muzzle containing larger, longer front teeth for tearing off coarse grasses, and molars with ridges for grinding them. It had a dorsal stripe and may have had stripes on the legs. Most importantly, it now had a single horn-covered toe, or hoof.

Finally came *Equus caballus*, the modern horse, established about a million years ago. Today's horse is thus a single-toed quadruped, although having just one toe to worry about hasn't made matters any simpler.

LAMENESS HAPPENS

The modern horse's hoof (i.e., the foot from the coronary band downward) performs several related functions: It absorbs shock, provides traction, protects the bone structures and tissues inside it, and aids in pumping blood back to the heart.

Nerve endings in the foot signal the brain when something is amiss in the hoof. The horse perceives this as pain and tries to reduce his discomfort by limping or favoring the foot. It may be a temporary condition, perhaps a slight inflammation that will go away on its own, or something incurable, such as arthritis or degeneration of the navicular bone, bursa, or ligaments. Regardless of the severity or permanence of the condition, if a horse limps he is pronounced "lame" and the alarm is sounded.

This is not to imply that lameness is unimportant. In the wild horse, it could be a death sentence if lameness prevented him from escaping a predator, one of nature's ways of removing inferior (or unlucky) individuals from the gene pool. It's called *natural selection*—the species is improved at the expense of lesser individuals.

Lameness is not so bleak for the domestic horse because man is in control of the horse's life. Man is not willing to sacrifice the individual to improve the species, nor is he particularly interested in breeding for optimal feet. Man is more interested in traits such as size, conformation, athletic prowess, color, and temperament rather than what would make the horse best suited for the environment in which he lives. You could say that man exercises *unnatural selection*. It has been this way for centuries.

The horse's hoof was perfectly designed for life on the grassy plains a million years ago. But from the time it was first placed in service to man, the domestic horse has had a very different life. To be useful, the horse had to be kept close at hand, which meant confinement, sometimes for weeks or months on end. This is the fate of many horses today, whether for the sake of necessity or convenience. It is common to find horses kept in 10-by-10-foot stalls for twenty-four hours of each day. Lucky ones may get an hour on the hot walker or in the turnout pen. The horse's hoof is not designed for these living conditions.

The goal of hoof care is to prevent lameness from happening and eliminate it once it occurs. The

Full-time stall confinement is detrimental to a horse's physical and mental health. *(Heidi Nyland)*

debate centers on how to best do so. It is not a simple subject, and the battle lines in this revolution are not clearly drawn.

THE ARGUMENT FOR KEEPING HORSES BAREFOOT

Some people believe that removing shoes, trimming hooves to emulate the feet of wild horses, and keeping the horses in a natural living environment at all times is the path to soundness. German veterinarian Hiltrud Strasser and American farrier Jaime Jackson are the most well known of the bare-footing advocates. Both have written detailed books on the subject, filled with photos and diagrams and compelling argument. Strasser and Jackson have increased awareness among all horsemen of what constitutes a natural lifestyle for a horse. In the process, they have garnered a great deal of support for their views on keeping horses barefoot, especially among horse owners who pursue information via the Internet, although their views are less well received by many farriers and veterinarians.

Strasser and Jackson argue that hoof mechanism, the expansion and contraction of the hoof during the weight-bearing and non-weight-bearing phases of gait, is inhibited by conventional shoeing. With inhibited hoof mechanism, there is less blood-pumping action possible in the hoof, thus circulation in the lower extremities is compromised, healing of injuries is slower, and extra stress is placed on the heart. Less circulation in the hoof means less sensation. Shoeing thus has a numbing effect on the feet, which may mask discomfort that is symptomatic of problems needing medical attention.

Hoof mechanism is analogous to the expanding and widening of our own feet when we put weight on them. You could probably force your foot into a shoe that was a size too small, but once you put weight on it you would feel cramped and uncomfortable. Your foot might even lose sensation. This, according to the Strasser and Jackson school of thought, is exactly what happens when we nail shoes on horses' feet.

An early critic of shoeing was Bracy Clark, F.L.S. (1771–1860), a British equine surgeon who many consider to be one of history's most knowledgeable hoof authorities. His 1829 treatise, *Podophthora: Demonstration of a Pernicious Defect in the Principle of the Common Shoe*, laid out the basic anti-shoeing argument that is still used today. Opponents have claimed that Clark's conclusions were drawn from observation of a single horse and have virtually no scientific merit.

Removing shoes is only the first step in a barefoot regimen. Strasser and Jackson insist that horses must be kept in natural environments, such as large pastures with varied terrain that simulates living in the wild. This allows them to be on the move through much of the day. So much walking, trotting, and running is good for their feet because it causes more hoof mechanism and thereby greater circulation in the lower extremities. Varied terrain also toughens the feet and provides natural abrasion to keep the hooves from growing too long. For Strasser and Jackson, keeping horses in stalls is strictly *verboten,* and their rigidity on this point has caused many conscientious horse owners, who have no choice but to keep their horses in stalls, to turn a deaf ear to the entire barefoot argument.

There is a certain irony in this anti-stall philosophy. Xenophon, whose success with unshod horses is considered exemplary, was pragmatic about the use of stalls:

> Even naturally sound hooves get spoiled in stalls with moist smooth floors. The floors should be sloping, to avoid moisture, and, to prevent smoothness, stones should be sunk close to one another, each about the size of the hoofs. The mere standing on such floors strengthens the feet.

Note that Xenophon did not suggest *doing away* with stalls.

Although they are in general agreement philosophically, Strasser and Jackson do have their differences. For instance, Strasser insists that horses can be conditioned to comfortably handle the roughest terrain and toughest riding use without metal shoes. She points to her own experience in endurance riding with unshod horses as proof. Her only concession is that, in extreme cases, a pair of slip-on rubber hoof boots for the front feet might be needed. After all, her argument goes, the great horse armies of history rode barefoot horses and they would sometimes travel more than 100 miles per day. She does not address the fact that the introduction of horseshoes is often cited as a pivotal development in the history of warfare.

Jackson is less certain of the correct course when riding is involved, for this is very different from the natural life of a horse.

The major difference between Strasser and Jackson, however, is in the trims that each recommends. The Jackson trim is designed to mimic the wild horse's hoof, down to its "Mustang Roll," a rounding off of the toe, which is not significantly different from the shaping of the hoof done by many farriers. The authors are not aware of any reports of horses being injured by the Jackson type of trim.

The Strasser trim is another story. All horses, regardless of hoof conformation, are trimmed to a predetermined set of guidelines. The Strasser trim is characterized by a longer toe and shallower hoof angle relative to the ground (as little as 45 degrees) on the front feet, and a carving out of the sole and bars ostensibly to allow for unimpeded hoof mechanism. This also counters the normal thickening of the sole as it toughens up with use, a significant deviation from the wild horse model. The aggressive trimming of the sole sometimes draws blood, and the Strasser trim can leave horses sorefooted, a condition Strasser claims is normal and temporary on the road to soundness.

That claim is disputed by a number of veterinarians and farriers in Europe and North America, including university clinicians who report horses being seriously and irreversibly injured as a consequence of this type of trimming. "Inadequate sole depth is the most common cause of chronic sole bruising," says Dr. Stephen O'Grady, farrier, veterinarian and 2003 inductee into the International Equine Veterinarian Hall of Fame. "Sole depth can be maintained simply by trimming the hoof wall appropriately and removing very little, if any, sole at each trimming" (*The Horse*, March 2003).

The most common complaint arising from aggressive trimming of the sole is pedal osteitis, an inflammatory reaction on the outer edge of the coffin bone in the front hooves caused by constant concussive trauma and bruising of the sole.

It has been suggested that horse owners are drawn to the Strasser barefoot regimen (and farriers are opposed to it) because it eliminates the cost of shoeing a horse every six weeks. However, if one follows Dr. Strasser's recommendations to the letter, it may be *more* expensive to go barefoot. Trimming is performed at least monthly, sometimes weekly, or even more frequently when problems exist. Strasser-certified hoof care specialists charge for their services. Hoof boots and soaking boots are encouraged.

Then there is the issue of land. To emulate the living conditions and environment of the wild horse, expanses of land are required, much more than most horse owners can afford or would otherwise need. Finally, the complete barefoot regimen requires the owner to be much more proactive and spend more time on his horse's feet. For busy horse owners, time is money.

FOR WANT OF A NAIL

For want of a nail a shoe was lost, for want of a shoe a horse was lost,
for want of a horse a rider was lost, for want of a rider an army was lost,
for want of an army a battle was lost, for want of a battle the war was lost,
for want of the war the kingdom was lost,
and all for the want of a little horseshoe nail.

—Benjamin Franklin

Not all barefoot advocates fall into either the Strasser or Jackson camps. O'Grady, Gene Ovnicek, K. C. LaPierre, Dr. Ric Redden, and Dr. Robert Bowker, among others, have contributed to the development of an ideal barefoot trim without dismissing out of hand the use of nailed-on metal horseshoes.

THE ARGUMENT FOR SHOEING HORSES

The argument for shoeing horses is *not* an argument against barefootedness. Those who advocate the use of horseshoes also agree that horses were meant to go barefoot and should do so, if their living conditions and usage allow it. In fact, periods of barefootedness are often encouraged to counter any ill effects from shoeing. The more domestic horses can live like wild horses, the more appropriate candidates they are for staying barefoot, at least during those periods. The problem is that most domestic horses do not live anything like their wild cousins. They don't eat like them, and they are asked to carry a rider, often one who is overweight and underskilled, to places they would never choose to go on their own and at speeds they would not choose. These are considered extenuating circumstances that make shoeing both necessary and humane.

Just as one cannot lump all barefooted trims together, one cannot lump all methods of shoeing horses together. "Everyday" shoeing varies significantly from performance shoeing and therapeutic shoeing. Shoeing varies for different breeds. And of course, competent shoeing is completely different from incompetent work.

Does shoeing really inhibit hoof mechanism, as Strasser and Jackson claim? Not according to Registered Master Farrier Dave Millwater, a founding member of the Guild of Professional Farriers. "The only part of a healthy hoof wall that can actually flex is in the rear third to half of the foot," Millwater states on his Web site. "That is the part which is attached to a flexible-cartilage internal structure. The front half to two-thirds of the hoof wall is attached to rigid bone. Horseshoes are properly nailed and clipped only to the front (bone-supported) part of the hoof, leaving the rear (cartilage-supported) part of the hoof free to flex."

Eloquent writers on both sides of the shoeing debate appeal to our sense of logic in their arguments. For the conscientious horse owner it is difficult to reach a correct conclusion when both sides are so passionate and convincing. Logicians might point out that both sides pose *valid* arguments in that their conclusions follow logically from their premises, but it is the *soundness* of the arguments that is in question. As any first-year logic student will tell you, a valid argument is not a sound argument unless its premises are true. Each side has its own version of the premises, the *facts* underlying each argument. This is maddening for the horse owner who believes, as any reasonable person would, that the truth has only one version.

EARLY HORSESHOES

Whether shoeing is harmful to horses is one issue where the two sides cannot agree on the "facts." When and why the custom of shoeing started is another.

We do know for certain that early horseshoes took different forms. Ancients used socks made of leather or woven plant fibers, tied around the fetlock, sometimes with a plate of iron, silver, or gold underneath. The Greeks wrapped their horses' feet in bags when traveling through the snow. Greeks and Romans fashioned "hipposandals" from iron secured with leather thongs.

The practice of nailing on metal shoes is believed by some to have begun during the Middle Ages in Europe. Noblemen wanted their horses close at hand, ready on a moment's notice. Horses were thus taken from the natural living environment of the pasture and placed in stalls in the castle complex. This wreaked havoc on their feet: standing in muck and mud in a stall caused a horse's hooves to soften and deform. Metal shoes were devised to address this problem. Shoeing did not become widespread, however, until just a few centuries ago.

That version of the rise of horseshoeing is often recited in the barefoot community. It reinforces the idea that stall confinement causes bad things to happen to a horse's feet. Yet, stall confinement did not begin in the Middle Ages. Xenophon wrote about stalls in 360 B.C. He was quite concerned about the state of a horse's feet and had plenty of opportunity to decry the use of stalls. He didn't.

So stalls didn't cause shoeing. But let's assume that, for whatever reason, nailing on metal shoes did begin in the Middle Ages. Then this practice continued for the better part of the next thousand years with few dissenting voices.

Horsemen of past centuries were not morons. They depended on their horses for life itself. Why would they engage in a practice—shoeing—that was harmful to the horse's health and in the long haul reduced its usability? The answer is that they didn't see shoeing that way.

Millwater continues, "They used horses every day and were very savvy about practical horse care. There were various times and places in history where shortages of iron, horseshoers, and forges made the use of barefoot horses unavoidable. You'd think that if going barefoot was so beneficial to working horses, people would've realized how much better off they were without horseshoes. But instead they took their horses to the smithy before the mortar in the forge had even set up. Do you suppose farmers and freight coach drivers just wanted to be fashionable? Or just maybe they wanted to be able to use their horses hard over rocky roads without them coming up bloody-footed lame."

The historical context for the advent of shoeing is still being debated. It is an important issue because past horsemen had so much more practical

Ancient horse shoes.

experience with horses than most of us have. They may not have had the scientific knowledge that exists today, but what they had was perhaps just as important. They began shoeing horses and persisted in doing it for a reason. That cannot be ignored.

In reality, shoeing probably began at different times, in many places, in many ways, and for many reasons. From this distance across time, we may never learn the whole story. And another complicating factor is that iron was such a valuable commodity in the past that iron horseshoes were often recycled into nails, musket barrels, and other iron goods, leaving less archaeological evidence of their use than one would expect.

KEG SHOES

In the not-so-distant past, horses were routinely shod when excessive travel caused tenderness and lameness. A blacksmith forged iron shoes that were nailed on. In America, farriers learned the trade through formal apprenticeships generally lasting three years, or through a comprehensive course taught by the United States Cavalry division of the U.S. Army.

As the American horse population diminished in the first half of the twentieth century, so too did the supply of master farriers and opportunities for apprenticeship. The United States Cavalry farrier training school closed, and taking its place were private farrier schools offering short courses to

KEG SHOES AND THE CIVIL WAR

According to Fran Jurga, editor of *Hoofcare and Lameness Journal* (www.hoof care.com), mass-produced keg shoes have been around since the 1840s. Originally made of iron and distributed in kegs or barrels—hence the name—keg shoes today are often made of metal alloys. Most of America's horseshoe factories prior to the Civil War were in the Northern states, and that is widely believed to be one reason the Union eventually became so dominant in cavalry campaigns. The South had no factories for making shoes, so Confederate troops had to rely on local blacksmiths to forge shoes for their horses. Union soldiers were ordered to destroy any blacksmith shops they encountered in the South.

prepare students for apprenticeships that were very difficult to find. Thus, when horses started coming back and demand for shoeing increased again, a large number of farrier school graduates began to practice with limited education and experience.

Fortunately, prefabricated keg shoes were available. One didn't have to be a blacksmith or a master farrier to nail them on. Cowboys on cattle ranches and farriers fresh out of school could do it. Keg shoes met the needs of scores of recreational horse owners, but they also changed the level of expertise of the typical farrier, who became little more than a horse shoer, a

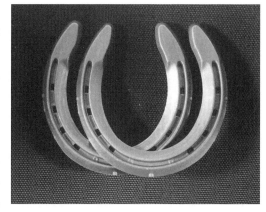

Keg shoes for eventing horses. (*Hoofcare & Lameness Journal*)

mechanic. What was lost was the understanding of equine anatomy and the biomechanics of movement that had made farriery both an art and a science. Some horses suffered as a result, and today the need for standardized farrier education and training, as well as board certification, is well recognized. To this end, the American Farrier's Association now offers a voluntary four-level certification program for members and non-members. Furthermore, *equine podiatry* is emerging as a field of specialization unto itself and may one day fill the gap that currently exists between the farrier and the veterinarian.

What has kept the need for skilled farriers alive is that keg shoes are not appropriate for every horse. Some have special shoeing needs, either because of the way they are used or because of problems with their feet. Performance disciplines such as reining, gaited horse showing, and racing, for example, require specialty shoes and experts in their application.

Likewise, hoof health problems are often addressed through specialty shoeing procedures. Corrective shoes provide extra support, usually for the frog and bars, and sometimes alter the hoof's angle of engagement with the ground. The two most important hoof problems for which therapeutic shoeing is recommended are chronic laminitis and navicular syndrome.

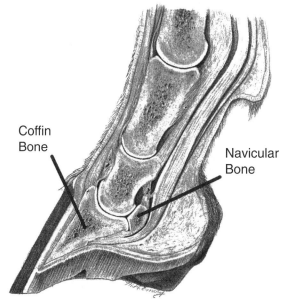

Coffin Bone

Navicular Bone

A lateral cutaway view of the horse's foot shows the coffin bone and the navicular bone. (*Hoofcare & Lameness Journal*)

The carbohydrate (sugar) level in grass varies with season, stage of growth, and time of day. Overeating when levels are high can lead to laminitis. *(Heidi Nyland)*

LAMINITIS

The largest bone inside a horse's hoof has many names: the coffin bone, the pedal bone, the distal phalanx, the third phalanx, PIII, and P-3. We'll call it the coffin bone, a colorful allusion to its lying buried inside the hoof capsule.

Laminitis, an inflammation of the fragile network of tissue connecting the coffin bone to the hoof wall, is often caused by what the horse eats. One of its aliases, "spring pony disease," reminds us of a situation in which it is likely to occur: when horses are turned out after a winter on hay to graze unrestricted on fresh, succulent, irresistible, sugar-rich—and deadly—spring grass. Overconsumption of such grass may cause a metabolic upset that manifests itself in laminitis. It may also interfere with normal digestive tract function, leading to colic, but that's another unfortunate story.

Similarly, laminitis may occur from overindulgence in grain, such as when a horse gains access to the feed room. It may happen also as a reaction to certain drugs or secondary to certain illnesses. In some cases, laminitis can be caused or at least worsened by obesity.

Laminitis in its most severe form is frequently called *founder*, a lay term for chronic laminitis. Just as a ship founders when it sinks, chronic laminitis is associated with rotation and/or sinking of the coffin bone, sometimes to the point of perforating the sole, due to failure within the Velcro-like laminae. Laminitis is a very painful condition from which some horses do not recover.

Not all cases of laminitis are related to the horse's eating or obesity. *Road founder* is the result of excessive concussion on the horse's feet.

Treatment for Laminitis

Laminitis is most often treated with drugs and therapeutic shoeing. Traditionally, various shoeing methods have been used. One method was to apply a conventional shoe backwards, a technique still used sometimes today. In recent decades, more radical methods have been developed, including the use of heartbar shoes.

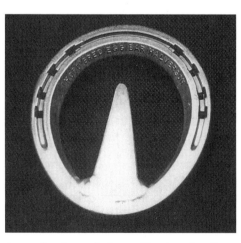
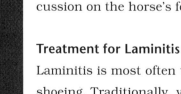

An eggbar (round) shoe with a heartbar feature to support the frog. *(Hoofcare & Lameness Journal)*

Other treatments include surgical procedures, such as tenotomy, and rebuilding the hoof with plastic materials. Good management will prevent most cases of laminitis.

NAVICULAR SYNDROME

Navicular syndrome is another matter entirely. It is an enigmatic condition that is not entirely understood, partially because the central player, the navicular bone, like the much larger coffin bone, is buried deeply inside the horse's hoof. It is surrounded by and interacts in complex ways with multiple anatomical structures in the heel.

Navicular syndrome is often called "navicular disease" or just "navicular."

Dr. David Ramey, author of *Concise Guide to Navicular Syndrome in the Horse*, defines navicular syndrome to be "a chronic, incurable condition associated with deterioration of the navicular bone." Some veterinarians have a broader definition and include tendon or ligament problems that result in heel pain to be part of the syndrome.

What causes navicular syndrome? There are numerous theories, but none has been proven. Certain factors seem to predispose a horse to the condition. It is most likely to affect athletic horses in the prime of life, between seven and fourteen years of age, although it has been diagnosed in horses as young as two. There may also be a genetic predisposition. Studies are beginning to suggest that the shape and condition of the navicular bone are hereditary. Unfortunately, successful show horses that develop the symptoms of navicular syndrome are often retired from the show circuit to become broodmares and possibly pass the predisposition on to future generations. Even with a predisposition to navicular syndrome, however, a horse may not develop the condition.

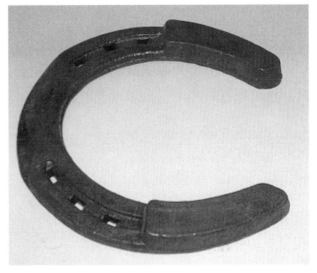

Other factors that may contribute to the development of navicular syndrome include conformation, nutrition, use, and management. These become more relevant when the genetic predisposition is present.

Because it is so difficult to diagnose and the prognosis for recovery is so bleak, some

A modern navicular shoe. Note the elevated heel section and abrupt step-up. *(TFT Horseshoes)*

veterinarians will not consider a case of heel pain to be navicular syndrome until at least three months of therapy have failed to produce an improvement.

The Navicular Shoe

Although a horse never recovers from navicular syndrome, shoeing can provide relief from discomfort and even make the horse ridable again. Shoeing solutions may take the form of wedge pads under the shoes, or special egg-bar shoes.

Most interesting, however, are those shoes that have changed where breakover occurs. When a horse shoe is flat, the toe alone is in touch with the ground when the heel rises off of it. The toe is thus defined to be the point of breakover.

The so-called Tennessee Navicular Shoe, originally introduced to the public by co-author Miller in 1989, moves the point of breakover to the middle of the shoe, approximately below the navicular bone and accomplishes this by an elevated heel section with an abrupt step-up. Several companies now offer their own versions of the original design.

Dr. Ric Redden's Full Rocker shoe, with its continuously curving ground surface (much like the rails on a rocking chair), accomplishes the same thing but with an added benefit of allowing the horse to self-adjust its own precise point of breakover. According to Redden, rocker shoes have been in use for more than 400 years and are "so old they are new again."

Horses with navicular syndrome have been kept serviceably sound for many years and some have even competed in performance events while wearing navicular shoes.

NATURAL BALANCE AND EDSS

Another important development is the Equine Digit Support System (EDSS) by farrier Gene Ovnicek, creator of the Natural Balance trimming and shoeing methods. The system offers adjustable lameness treatment for navicular syndrome, laminitis, and other hoof problems.

The system starts with the EDSS Sole Support Impression Material, which is used to create a flexible rubber-like mold of the bottom of the horse's hoof. Its purpose is to act like dirt compaction, distributing pressure evenly across the sole. For laminitic horses, part of the mold may be trimmed away from the painful area. For treating navicular syndrome, contracted heels, and quarter cracks, complete loading of the sole is required.

The EDSS Pad, a semi-transparent urethane pad, goes over the mold and is held in place by nailing on the EDSS Shoe, a modified Natural Balance shoe. The pad is designed to allow easy attachment of a frog insert to give additional support to the frog if needed. The final components are hoof rails. If needed, these attach to the rear two-thirds of the shoe and come in three different wedge-shaped thicknesses.

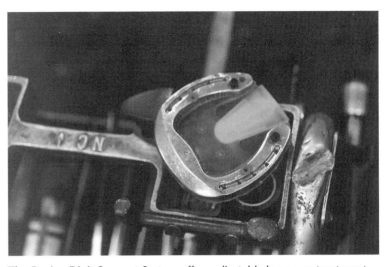

The Equine Digit Support System offers adjustable lameness treatment. *(Gene Ovnicek)*

The Natural Balance principle, upon which this therapeutic shoeing system is based, was introduced in 1995 by Ovnicek as a result of wild horse studies conducted in 1986 and 1987.

Ovnicek discovered that self-maintaining feet, whether on wild or domestic horses, showed the following characteristics:

1. The hoof wall was worn to the level of the sole and the sole was thus a weight-bearing structure.
2. The area of the foot around the frog and bars was packed with dirt, which seemed to serve a supportive function.

Gene Ovnicek takes an imprint of the foot of a wild horse. From studying many such impressions, he developed his Natural Balance principles for trimming and shoeing. *(Gene Ovnicek)*

3.   The apex (front edge) of the frog was much closer to the toe than expected; it was also enlarged and heavily callused.

4.   There were four primary points of contact with the ground for each hoof, one on each side of the heel and one on each side of the toe; if the hoof were a clock face, these points would be at about 10:00 and 2:00 for the toe, and 7:30 and 4:30 for the heel.

5.   Relative to the widest part of the hoof, the heel points of contact were twice as far away as the toe points of contact.

Ovnicek also concluded that the heel landed first, slightly ahead of the rest of the foot. He determined that the point of breakover occurred not at the end of the toe, as previously thought, but a bit farther back at the points of contact he identified. The positioning and buildup of the frog, on the other hand, suggested to him that it served to support the apex of the coffin bone. Using all of this information, Ovnicek developed his Natural Balance theories for trimming and shoeing horses. Because of the key roles that the frog, bars, and sole play in supporting the internal structures of the hoof, they are exfoliated only, and never carved out in the manner of the Strasser trim.

ALTERNATIVES TO NAILED-ON METAL SHOES

Man-made protection for a horse's feet is sometimes necessary. Everyone agrees on that point. The hoof boot is one solution that both sides of the debate have embraced, although with different purposes in mind.

Riders with shod horses often carry a single Easy Boot™ to serve as a "spare tire" in case a shoe comes loose. It can make the difference between leading a horse home and riding him.

Riders with barefoot horses may use Old Mac® hoof boots, Horsneakers, or the equivalent on the front feet when riding on rough terrain. Extremely rough conditions might prompt them to put boots on all four feet.

As a practical matter, hoof boots of any type require some maintenance. If you take the horse through water or deep sand, the boots need to be removed and emptied periodically. You must also be careful of chafing the horse's skin, especially at the coronary band.

Glue-on shoes are also a solution on which both sides could seemingly agree.

Three decades before this book was written, Dr. Victor Tierstein, a California veterinarian, was experimenting with plastic horseshoes that were glued to the horse's feet. The adhesives used were inadequate, and most of the shoes detached prematurely.

"I know," he said, "that if the proper technology could be developed, the glued-on shoe will eventually re-place the nailed-on shoe."

The technology may finally be here. Among the numerous glue-on shoes that have hit the market in re-cent years is one developed by Rob Sigafoos, C.J.F., chief of farrier ser-vices at the University of Pennsylva-nia's New Bolton Center. He calls it the "Sigafoos Series I" and it is manufac-tured by Sound Horse Technologies in Unionville, Pennsylvania.

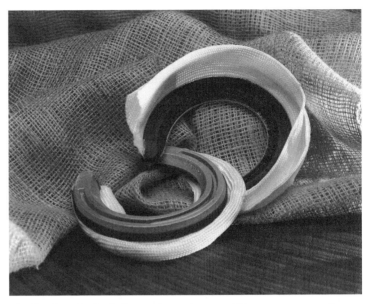

The Sigafoos Series I glue-on horseshoe could be more secure than a nailed-on shoe. *(Sound Horse Technologies)*

Ten years in development, the product consists of a lightweight alu-minum horseshoe with a 1/4-inch urethane rimpad for shock absorption and a fabric cuff which extends more than halfway up the hoof wall. When saturated with the company's own acrylic polymer adhesive, the cuff report-edly bonds with the hoof wall to create a tensile strength of 1,800 pounds, twice that of nailed-on shoes. It is claimed that the shoe will not come off until the farrier chooses to take it off. Originally intended for sore-footed horses, Series I has been expanded to include race and sport shoes. Bar shoes and custom therapeutic shoes are part of the Series II system.

CONCLUSION

Do horseshoes kill horses, as some of the more outspoken barefooters have claimed? Is it malpractice to recommend the Strasser trim to horse owners, as some veterinarians have suggested? Is there a happy medium between full-time turnout in megapastures, and full-time confinement in a stall? Can we balance good horsemanship with good stewardship of the land? Is bare-footed soundness worth the additional cost in time, money, and discomfort to the horse? If shoeing a horse makes him comfortable and usable today, will the benefit be lost by shortening his useful life? What about the quality of his life in the meantime? Does a horse's long-term welfare always out-weigh a human's needs?

There are many questions, some practical and some philosophical, which we must answer for ourselves in deciding how to care for our horse's feet.

For what it is worth, the authors have three simple guidelines for how we care for our own horses and mules:

1. Shoe only when necessary.
2. Shoe or trim at regular intervals.
3. Provide barefoot vacations as frequently and for as long as possible.

THE LEGEND OF ST. DUNSTAN, 925–988 A.D.
(Courtesy of the International Museum of the Horse)

Why do many people place a horseshoe over their door to ward off evil? In the Middle Ages, there lived a blacksmith named Dunstan. One day the Devil came to Dunstan's forge to have his cloven hooves shod. Dunstan agreed to make the Devil's shoes, but instead he lashed the Devil to the anvil and furiously beat him with his hammer. The Devil begged for mercy. Dunstan made the Devil promise never to visit a door where a horseshoe hung. The Devil quickly agreed; and since then, blacksmiths and others have placed a horseshoe over their doors. The horseshoe must be placed with the toe down so that it can catch goodness from heaven. And what of the noble Dunstan? He did not remain a simple blacksmith, but became the Archbishop of Canterbury and was made a saint after his death.

CHAPTER 17

THE REVOLUTION
IN EQUINE HEALTH CARE

DURING THE DECADES THAT FOLLOWED World War I, the automobile changed the lifestyle and culture of the industrial nations more than any invention before or since. Although the automobile was not invented in the United States, its production, improvement, and availability were greater here than anywhere else in the world. The internal-combustion engine changed life on the farm as profoundly as it did in the cities. Draft power on the farm had always required great numbers of horses and mules. In a nation that required more than 20 million domestic horses at the dawn of the twentieth century, only one-tenth of that number were left by mid-century. Tractors had largely replaced horsepower in agriculture.

In the cities the change was even more noticeable. Where streets once teemed with horses and wagons, cars and trucks were now everywhere.

The veterinary profession came into existence during the era of the Roman Empire. The *veterinarius* was the auto mechanic of ancient times. Right into the twentieth century the profession existed, prospered, and was vital mainly because of the horse.

It was, ironically, the invention of the pneumatic tire by Scottish veterinarian John Boyd Dunlop (1840–1921) that signaled the apparent demise of the profession. The pneumatic tire greatly expanded the speed, adaptability, and versatility of the gasoline-powered vehicle. Many thought that the veterinary profession would no longer be needed. A lot of veterinarians retired from their profession to make a living in other endeavors. Others switched to food animal practice, or small animal practice, a decision that was often difficult because the horse had been regarded as a pillar of society, and the doctors who had them as patients were esteemed. Many veterinarians in the past would not consider treating other species.

Many great veterinary schools closed during those years, including the one at Harvard University as well as the Kansas City Veterinary College, which had larger classes than any of today's schools. Forty-seven years were to pass before a new textbook on equine medicine was to be published.

In 1956, the last class was graduated from an American veterinary school in which the primary animal studied in a yearlong anatomy course was the horse. Today, it's the dog.

However, the equine population in the United States would more than triple in the next few decades, soaring to more than 7 million, with an average value far exceeding the average value at the turn of the century. Racing, horse shows, pleasure riding, and other equine sports grew as the economy and the standard of living grew, and horses worth thousands, tens of thousands, and even hundreds of thousands of dollars became commonplace.

With the reviving population of horses, and their escalating economic value, came a resurgence of interest in equine veterinary medicine. The exploding technology in human medicine and in other areas of veterinary medicine spun off into equine medicine.

The first challenge facing the equine practitioner is to prevent disease. The second is to diagnose disease, and the third is to treat disease. The revolution in equine healthcare has been manifested in all three.

The gains made in equine medicine and surgery include every aspect of medical science, but a number of them may be termed "revolutionary" because they have so profoundly affected the health, the welfare, and the life span of the horse. The strides we will cite also occurred in other species, including our own, but the order of importance is not necessarily the same.

PARASITES

At the top of the list, in terms of health benefits to the most horses, would have to be vermifuges, chemicals that kill internal parasites.

All species are parasitized, but since domestication usually dictates that the horse resides in an enclosure contaminated with manure, and manure contains countless parasite eggs and larvae, domestic horses are subject to serious infestations of worms and other internal parasites. Regular removal of manure helps but cannot eliminate the problem. (Interestingly, wild horses are parasitized as well, but not to the same extent because they generally do not graze where manure is deposited.)

Keep in mind that parasites of all species do not want to kill their hosts. If they do, they will also die. Parasites, in their marvelously complex life cycles, simply want to reside in and live off of their hosts. However, excessive parasite loads can kill horses. Migrating roundworms (ascarids) cause pneumonia in foals. Bloodworms (strongyles) damage blood vessels, cause colics that can be fatal, and lead to the development of weak spots called aneurysms in arteries. These aneurysms can rupture quickly, causing the horse to bleed to death internally. Such deaths were common until the introduction of newer and better dewormers in the latter years of the twentieth century. Ruptured aneurysms often killed young horses, and many mature horses died long before their time for the same reason or because of colic due to parasites such as ascarids, strongyles, or bots. Pinworms caused itching and caused horses to rub their tails until all the hair was gone at the top of the tail. Other parasites caused skin diseases, robbed the horse nutritionally, and caused eye disease.

Around the midpoint of the twentieth century, only two drugs were available to treat these parasites in horses: phenothiazine and carbon disulfide. Both were quite toxic and had to be used with skill and caution. Carbon disulfide could only be administered by passing a tube through a nostril down into the stomach, a daily chore for veterinarians practicing in the 1950s.

Today we have a host of parasiticidal drugs, easily administered in gel, paste, granule, or liquid forms. They are far more effective and much safer than what we had in the past. The life span of horses has been increased significantly because of the availability of these drugs, and the general health of horses and especially of foals has been greatly improved.

DENTISTRY

Equine teeth are very different from our own. Technically, they are called *hypsodont* or tall crown teeth. They are almost fully formed, 3.5 to 5 inches long and embedded deeply in the jaw when the horse is born. Throughout his life, the horse's teeth erupt at about 1/8 inch per year. The teeth must be worn down at approximately the same rate to avoid problems. In the wild, most horses get enough abrasion through their diets to produce this kind of wear. However, modern feeding practices have altered natural abrasion on the teeth. That, and the fact that some horses have malocclusion causing irregular wear, necessitate the routine dental procedure known as "floating" or rasping down the teeth. If properly cared for, a horse's teeth will last more than thirty years. Few horses actually live this long, and dental problems in their geriatric years is a contributing reason.

Equine dentistry is much more refined now than in the past. Motorized tools similar to those common in human dentistry are used, in addition to traditional rasps and files. New connections are being discovered between a horse's dental health and his overall physical condition, especially when the tempero mandibular joint (TMJ) is involved.

Today equine dentistry is a significant part of many equine practices. Additionally, the certified equine dentist is a respected professional with specialized training in dentistry, but no veterinary degree. The dentist often receives much of his business in the form of referrals from equine veterinarians, who must be present to supervise or administer drugs needed in accordance with state laws.

SURGERY

The latter part of the twentieth century saw another great milestone in equine medicine: improved anesthetics and better technology in their administration. Veterinarians before the 1970s knew how to perform most of the complex orthopedic, gastrointestinal, and other surgical procedures that have now become routine and commonplace. What they didn't have was safe, controllable, predictable methods of anesthesia. The change may properly be called revolutionary.

Surgically, the most revolutionary advance was laparoscopic abdominal surgery. Operating on a horse's visceral organs no longer necessarily requires opening up its abdomen. Many orthopedic procedures are also now done arthroscopically. The laparoscope, which is inserted through a small incision, provides a remarkable internal view of the horse displayed on a video monitor to guide the surgeon through his work. Surgical tools can similarly be inserted through another small incision. The risk of infection and recovery time for such surgeries is dramatically reduced.

HOSPITALS

Horse hospitals have gone through dramatic changes, too. In the past, they were found mostly at veterinary schools and many of them left a great deal to be desired. Horses were lost, not from lack of knowledge about how to save them, but from lack of facilities and equipment.

Today, virtually all North American equine veterinary schools have sophisticated equine hospitals. Especially in more populated areas, private equine surgical and medical centers proliferate to meet the demand for state-of-the-art care. Even specialized rehabilitation centers are popping up.

Cutting-edge technologies and techniques in such facilities can dramatically speed the healing of equine patients.

DRUGS

It wasn't until the 1960s that the first tranquilizers for horses became generally available, and in the following decades other tranquilizers, hypnotic, disassociative, and behavior-altering medications were developed. These drugs are immensely valuable in controlling the reactions of large, physically powerful, highly reactive and flighty animals. Today's veterinary students are overwhelmingly female, and these drugs have made their jobs easier by greatly reducing the physical aspect of horse practice.

Prior to the 1960s, we had antibiotics such as penicillin, corticosteroids ("cortisones"), and NSAIDs (non-steroidal antiinflammatory drugs) such as aspirin and phenylbutazone ("bute"). Since then, each of these pharmaceutical categories has been greatly expanded. The same applies to hormones. A few of them existed prior to 1960, but there are many more now and they are especially useful in reproductive medicine.

Of all the great medical discoveries ever made, certainly vaccination has saved more human lives than any other. Former scourges such as smallpox, diphtheria, poliomyelitis, measles, and yellow fever have either been eradicated or at least minimized due to vaccination. Horses have similarly benefited by immunizing procedures. Prior to 1960, vaccines were available for strangles, tetanus, and sleeping sickness (Eastern and Western encephalomyelitis), but today these vaccines are vastly improved, more effective, and freer of side effects.

In addition, new vaccines have been developed for old diseases such as influenza, rabies, and rhinopneumonitis, which causes both respiratory disease and abortions in mares. We also have vaccines now for diseases that we did not have in North America until recently, such as Venezuelan encephalomyelitis and West Nile Virus.

DIAGNOSTIC PROCEDURES

Years ago, in addition to the horse's history, the symptoms, and physical examination, there were a variety of tests that could be run, and we had X-ray, so valuable for understanding the changes in bone, joints, and soft tissues that cause lameness in horses. Lameness in most animals and in humans is a problem, of course, but in horses it usually means the end of their useful performance career, so radiology was important in equine medicine as soon as it became available. Today, however, myriad other techniques are available, including magnetic resonance imaging (MRI), CT scans, thermography, endoscopy, ultrasonography, and an amazing variety of laboratory tests.

According to Dr. Jack Snyder, professor and equine surgeon at the University of California at Davis veterinary school, Synthetic Aperture Radar (SAR) may someday be capable of detecting enteroliths, which are stones that form in the intestinal tracts of horses, especially those on diets containing a high percentage of alfalfa. These stones, an ever-increasing cause of colic, cannot always be detected with X-ray equipment because of the size of the equine abdomen.

SPECIALIZATION

Half a century ago, there were no formal board-certified specialties in veterinary medicine, except for pathology. Every veterinary school graduate was, in effect, a general practitioner, although many developed skills in particular areas of practice.

How different the situation is today, with formally trained specialists in almost every branch of veterinary medicine that exists in human medicine, including neurologists, endocrinologists, dermatologists, radiologists, internal medicine specialists, surgeons, ophthalmologists, and cardiologists. As in human medicine, there are even super-specialists.

With this specialization comes more research into new medicines and surgical procedures to help sick and injured horses.

AAEP

The American Association of Equine Practitioners (AAEP) was formed in 1954 with a membership of eleven veterinarians engaged in Thoroughbred practice. Today the AAEP, headquartered in Lexington, Kentucky, boasts an international membership of more than 6,500 veterinarians and veterinary students from fifty-seven countries. The organization is a vital source of continuing education to all veterinarians who have equine patients.

In his installation speech, 2003 AAEP president Dr. Larry Bramlage expressed well the peculiar role of the horse in modern society at large and how the AAEP seeks to serve: "In our increasingly urban society a love of the spirit of the horse has largely replaced familiarity with the individual. Horse-manship has been replaced by an abstract reverence for the horse that borders on passion, but is rooted more in the cinema than the corral. It is our goal to temper this enthusiasm with understanding, but without damp-ening it, and to assure it is channeled to the benefit of the horse, not its detriment."

CHAPTER 18

EQUINE NUTRITION

Zoo veterinarians have learned that in order to provide a proper diet for their patients, they must first assess the diet that nature intended for each animal. If it is not possible to duplicate that natural diet, the nutritional equivalent may then be substituted. What all animals need is not food, but *nutrients*.

A common example is dog food. Wild dogs exist on a diet of fresh game, carrion, and a wide variety of foods of plant origin, such as fruits, nuts, and berries. Yet, the pet food industry has been able to develop nutritious dog foods in various forms, and dogs thrive upon them. Indeed, our dogs eat better-balanced diets than we do.

Humans are another good example. We evolved to subsist on fish and game, plus roots, seeds, fruits, nuts, and other plant materials. Yet we seem to do just fine on the modern civilized diet, with our diseases due mainly to excess rather than deficiency. In different parts of the world, humans do well on radically different diets, which may include pizza, rice, blubber, potatoes, and grubs.

The horse was originally a small, swamp-dwelling consumer of leaves and succulent plants, but it evolved as its habitat dried out to become a grazer. Modern horses thrived on the prairies of North America long before the first humans migrated into their habitat. Grassland-dwelling creatures, their natural diet was the mare's milk until the colt was sometimes two years of age, and then grass. The grass was green part of the year and dry at other times. Seasonally, the seeds of the grass (what we call "grain") would be eaten, and sometimes bark or small bushes would be consumed for added fiber. Essentially that was all the horse needed: a variety of grasses in an endless prairie over which it could migrate.

A century ago horses were fed much as nature intended. They ate grass in the form of pasture or grass in the form of hay, which is simply cut and dried grass. Horses worked hard, and grain, especially oats, was offered as an additional caloric source.

Then technology came on the scene. First, hay was baled. Some horsemen were afraid to feed baled hay because "it wasn't natural." Eventually hay was compressed into cubes (tiny bales) and processed into pellets in the latter days of the twentieth century.

Crops other than grass were dried into hay. Legumes like clover and alfalfa were found to be nourishing, effective, and very palatable to horses. In fact, alfalfa is more palatable to most horses than is grass, their "natural" diet. However, palatability is not necessarily a measure of efficacy. Sugar is very palatable to horses, dogs, and humans, but not an ideal food for any of those species and, in quantity, is harmful. As mentioned earlier, excessive alfalfa consumption has been linked to the development of enteroliths and obstruction colics in horses.

Although grass is the species' natural diet, the horse has adapted in other parts of the world to amazingly diverse diets including frozen fish. Again, animals require *nutrients* rather than food. However, this fact does not recognize the preferences of species. Although horses have been shown to subsist upon a diet of powder containing all of the vitamins, minerals, proteins, fats, and carbohydrates they require, they are not *happy*. They need, psychologically, to chew and to graze.

In recent years, a revolution has occurred in the feeding of horses. Extruded composite feeds, chopped feeds, meals, sweetened concentrate mixtures, silage, pelleted feeds in all sized pellets, plus an amazing variety of supplements in block form, liquid, powders, granules, pastes, and cookies are now available.

"Complete" feeds have been designed by equine nutritionists working on expansive research farms. Neat and convenient packaged complete feeds are now available for horses at every stage of life, from junior feeds designed to stimulate growth, to high-energy performance feeds for working horses, to senior feeds designed to be highly digestible and easy to chew.

We have also learned how our feeding practices can hurt a horse. Feed with excessive carbohydrates causes a predisposition to laminitis, azoturia ("tying up"), and hyperexcitability. Where extra calories are indicated, adding fat to the diet is preferable. For instance, a cup or two of corn oil daily, poured over the regular feed, is better for the horse than extra grain.

Some concentrated feeds have been too rich and powerful for the growing horse's own good. Young show horses that have been overfed to achieve size and competitive advantage have suffered growth-related problems with their bones. Too-rapid growth is now known to be too much of a good thing.

As Cherry Hill puts it in *Horsekeeping on a Small Acreage*, "The horse's digestive system is adapted to a high amount of bulk and a low amount of concentrate. High-quality hay should be the mainstay of your horse's diet. Do not feed too much grain."

COLIC

Overwhelmingly, the greatest threat to a horse's health from our feeding practices is colic.

By definition, colic is belly pain, a symptom of something wrong inside the horse's gastrointestinal tract. However, through usage, the word has come to mean both the symptom and the cause. We will follow that convention.

Colic, the number-one killer of horses, can be the result of an impaction, excessive gas, a torsion ("twisted gut"), dehydration, or anything else that prevents normal movement of excrement through the horse's bowel. Because the horse cannot regurgitate to rid his body of matter he should not have eaten, it is crucial to his health that he eats things his body can handle and that will move smoothly from one end to the other.

Left to his own in the wild, the horse has the ability to travel great distances to get what he needs. In domestication, he is completely dependent upon us. He must eat what we put in front of him in order to survive. Although horses in nature graze intermittently all day long, in our busy urbanized society, twice-a-day feeding is the norm. We know now that smaller, more frequent meals are better for the horse. In fact, studies at the University of California at Davis veterinary school concluded that three or more feedings per day reduces the chance of colic. Accordingly, automatic feeders have been developed that dispense feed—grain, pellets, or hay flakes—at user-selectable intervals. By feeding horses more often, ravenous hunger and overeating are avoided.

We know that changes to a horse's diet should be made *gradually* over seven to ten days. Although one of the reasons for the horse's success in domestication is its ability to adapt to different diets, that adaptation takes time. The microflora that live within the digestive tract of the horse are adapted to the horse's regular ration. A sudden change of diet often means that the microflora cannot metabolize the newly introduced feed. This is a common cause of several kinds of colic.

Supplementation of nutrients has been both a boon and a bane for horses. If done correctly, supplements aid in making the horse more robust and vital. If done improperly or indiscriminately, especially when the owner is unduly influenced by a manufacturer's advertising, nutritional balance can be upset. Well-meaning owners of non-working horses sometimes micro-manage their horses' nutrition when it just isn't necessary.

Dehydration predisposes a horse to a number of health problems, the most serious being, again, colic. Horses do best when watered generously at regular intervals and given plenty of time to drink. Horses don't need free-choice water, however. Given free choice, some horses drink to excess (called polydipsia nervosa, a common vice in horses confined to stalls). Others become "sippers" that can't tolerate hard work and thirst.

Having a ready supply of water at all times, even during freezing conditions, is another relatively recent innovation.

OVEREATING

A negative aspect to the revolution in equine nutrition became a significant problem in the late twentieth century and worsens each decade. It is a form of malnutrition that plagues the American culture, and it's not limited to horses. Dogs, cats, and their owners are also affected. In our children it has become a critical problem.

We are talking about overeating.

At the dawn of the twenty-first century, Americans have become the fattest people in all human history. More than 65 percent of our adult population is overweight. More alarming, a third of our children are overweight. Many are, frankly, obese, a rare situation two generations earlier. We eat too much. Our portions are too large and grow ever larger. With every fast-food order, we are asked, "Would you like to supersize that order, sir?" Our meals are already supersized, and we snack constantly between them.

Never before in history have the poorest people in a society suffered most from obesity, a sad tribute to the success of our nation. We are the most efficient producers of low-cost food in the world. Not only do we eat too much, but we also eat the wrong kinds of food. Our sugar consumption is prodigious and escalates every year. We consume too much fat and especially the wrong kinds of fats.

Although controlling our own diets is a matter of education and self-discipline, what about our animals? Must we overfeed our pets and our horses? Overweight horses are predisposed to arthritis, foot problems, and a variety of other pathologies. Recent advances in the science of nutrition have brought us knowledge that enables us to avoid nutritional diseases due to deficiency and to imbalance of essential nutrients. But what do we do about *excess*?

We overfeed our horses partly because show standards favor sleek, fat individuals, but also because of misguided love. Like us, animals love to eat. Horses, especially, will eat anytime, and it makes *us* feel good to see them happily munching away.

We need to discipline ourselves to resist the temptation to overfeed, whether the food goes in our mouths or our horses' mouths. We must strive in nutrition to achieve that state of condition that is neither too thin nor too overweight. Moreover, the horse, being an athlete, should *look* like one. It's called "being in shape."

CHAPTER 19

ALTERNATIVE THERAPIES

THE CONCEPT OF ALTERNATIVE THERAPIES is so controversial within the healing arts that it tends to push practitioners into one of two extreme camps: those who flatly oppose them because most have never been proven by the recognized scientific process, and those who accept them because they *want* to believe.

This is unfortunate but understandable. Some so-called alternative therapies fly in the face of reason, and those of us who worship at the altar of science expect legitimate modalities to stand up to logical and scientific scrutiny. Many alternative therapies don't.

Does that mean they don't work? No. And therein lies the rub.

Anecdotal evidence, the experiences of real people in the real world, supports the efficacy of certain alternative therapies that cannot be proven scientifically valid. When all else has failed, alternative therapies offer hope, which for some people is simply irresistible.

Among equine veterinarians, alternative therapies receive a mixed reception, perhaps for the simplest of reasons: the term is too broad. It includes therapies as respected and popular as acupuncture, but places them side by side with others that have virtually no credibility in the medical community, such as crystals or aromatherapy.

What further complicates matters is that some alternative therapies have actually risen in stature as time has gone by. For instance, prior to 1990 the application of chiropractic to large animals like the horse was a medical community joke in America. Yet, by then, in Australia, equine chiropractors were busy. Today they thrive here in America. The original concept of chiropractic—that disease originates from subluxations of the spine—jars the minds of modern medical doctors. But chiropractic "adjustments" *do* help many human patients, and the authors have witnessed horses in pain respond to such treatment.

Could it be that we don't know what we don't know? Intellectual honesty dictates a hearty "yes!"

Few equine practitioners today abandon proven traditional medicine in favor of alternative therapies, yet more and more are willing to use the two in combination. In this role alternative therapies are more properly considered "complementary" therapies and the resulting mix "integrative medicine."

THE POWER OF BELIEVING

Perhaps the most difficult thing to accept about alternative therapies is that they reportedly work better if you believe in them. This is a particularly tough pill for Western thinkers to swallow. In matters of science, we are accustomed to withholding belief in something until it has been proven to be true. The importance of a positive attitude in healing is well understood, but we also expect medicine to work its wonders independently of what we think it will do. In the world of alternative therapies, the mind–body connection is so strong that faith in the outcome is practically a prerequisite for success.

In treating horses, it doesn't much matter what we think, but our desires to achieve certain results may color our perceptions of what has actually happened. It's important to remember that most health problems in humans and animals disappear on their own. *Any* therapy administered during the illness or injury will therefore seem responsible for the patient's improvement.

But enough generalizing. Let's look at some specific alternative or complementary therapies in use today.

ACUPUNCTURE AND MOXIBUSTION

The most widely used and successful alternative therapies are acupuncture and some other techniques that are part of "traditional Chinese medicine" (TCM).

In an acupuncture treatment, extremely thin needles are inserted into the horse's skin at locations known as acupuncture points. The number of needles, depth of penetration, placement on the body, and time in place vary with the goal of the treatment. The horse feels very little discomfort.

The acupuncture points lie along meridian lines, which are defined to be lines of energy throughout the body. Inserting needles is said to stimulate the body's energy and cause an increase or return of the energy flow in the corresponding body part. This increases circulation and stimulates nerves, helping the area to return to normal functioning.

To supercharge an acupuncture session, the needles can be rigged to emit almost imperceptible electrical impulses. Moxibustion, the burning of the herb mugwort in a special holder near the acupuncture points, adds the element of heat with the purpose of further stimulating the circulation.

Acupuncture is used to provide relief from pain in a variety of conditions.

ACUPRESSURE

Similar to the Japanese technique of Shiatsu, acupressure is acupuncture without the needles. The fingers are used to exert firm pressure at specific points on the horse's body. It is said to produce positive results related to the immune, lymph, and circulatory systems, while decreasing heart rate, reducing pain, calming nerves, and promoting a feeling of contentment.

Acupressure reportedly produces results similar to but not as dramatic as those produced by acupuncture. It is often suggested for use by the horse owner between acupuncture sessions.

HOMEOPATHY

Homeopathy is based on the "law of similars" or the principle that "like cures like." It was developed in the early nineteenth century by German physician Samuel Hahnemann, who believed that a substance that causes certain symptoms in a healthy person could be used to cure those same symptoms in a sick person.

Often the substance used in a homeopathic remedy would be toxic to the patient were it not diluted so heavily. The dilution is normally in the ratio of a few parts per million. Multiple dilutions normally occur, with vigorous shaking ("succussing") of the mixture between dilutions.

It is claimed that the potency of a particular homeopathic solution depends on how many times it has been diluted and succussed. However, the solution is supposed to become *more* potent at each stage rather than less, a very difficult aspect of homeopathy for the average person to accept. Chemically, there is nothing of the original substance left in the solution, but it has been suggested that every substance leaves behind "footprints," or in the jargon of quantum physics, "energy fields," which may someday fully explain potentization.

Prescribing of homeopathics is best left to a veterinarian. They are sometimes used for reduction of stress, inflammation, and internal organ problems, and treatment of problems with specific body areas like the skin and hooves. Although homeopathy is largely unaccepted by medical science, it remains popular with some practitioners.

CHIROPRACTIC

Chiropractic is the manipulation of joints, particularly of the spine, to elicit a therapeutic response. The original concept of chiropractic, that disease is caused by subluxations (partial dislocations) of the spine, is outdated. However, the principle that spinal dysfunction causes pain and dysfunction elsewhere is accepted.

Manipulation of body parts can help certain orthopedic conditions, and horses have responded to such manipulation by chiropractors.

Chiropractic adjustments are usually done with manual manipulation—tugging, pulling, and pressing on the horse in different ways—with the goal of treating soft tissue injuries or articular (flexibility) dysfunction. Sometimes chiropractors use mallets made of rubber and wielded manually or use a newer spring-loaded variety that can exert precise amounts of pressure.

According to the American Association of Equine Practitioners, as reported in the *Los Angeles Times* May 25, 2004, more than 60 percent of equine veterinarians have referred horses to equine chiropractors.

HERBS

Medicinal herbs were once widely used and even today many pharmaceutical drugs are still made from compounds of herbs or synthetic copies of them. However, the whole plant is never used. Researchers identify and isolate the active or principal components only, discarding the rest of the plant, and turn the components into refined concentrates that tend to be more potent, faster acting, and of shorter duration.

Herbal medicine goes back to the whole green plant, believing that the complex mix of chemicals in the entire plant contributes to the positive benefits, benefits that may come on more slowly but have more lasting effect and are generally better for the patient.

Herbs used for treating horses include yucca, Pau D'Arco, garlic, psyllium, kelp, goldenseal, dandelion, and aloe vera. Chinese herbal formulas are also available for horses. Herbs are available for coughs, immune system stimulation, stomach ulcers, chronic colic problems, respiratory disease, digestive disorders, and irritability in mares. Some herbs, such as valerian root, are claimed to have a calming effect.

Using the wrong herb or combination of herbs can cause harm, so consulting a veterinarian or a licensed, formally trained herbal specialist is recommended.

LASERS

The laser is a new technological twist to alternative therapies. Waves of light are used to treat conditions ranging from eye problems to muscle and tendon injuries to wounds. Depending on the problem being treated, the light may be directed at the area or at acupuncture points.

Different light therapy products deliver the technology in different ways. Some systems use clusters of LEDs (light emitting diodes) on pads that can be secured to the treatment area. The LEDs are programmed to fire in a prescribed way to create the desired effect.

Other laser devices are more like flashlights, putting out a single beam of light that is triggered manually.

Light therapy may be particularly valuable in stimulating healing when a horse cannot tolerate certain medications. New uses are being found for it all the time.

MAGNETIC THERAPY

Presently there are more than 5,000 different magnetic field therapy products on the market around the world. It is a healing method that has been used for centuries. It is easy to use and easy to understand, even though it remains quite controversial to the medical community. Most claims have not yet been proven scientifically.

The theory is that by placing magnets near a particular body part, a magnetic field is created there. The iron in the blood is energized by the magnetic field, and circulation is thus increased, along with oxygen utilization and cell function. Increasing circulation is a common way that alternative therapies are said to aid the body in healing itself.

Magnetic therapy is used for treatment of fractures, wounds, degenerative leg diseases, circulatory deficiencies, strained ligaments, and joint problems. Magnets come in wraps that can be applied to the hocks or shins. Turnout blankets are available with magnets located in strategic places. Tiny magnets can even be glued to horses' hooves to stimulate hoof growth, again by increasing circulation.

MASSAGE THERAPY

Nearly everyone has experienced the positive benefits of massage. Applied to horses, it can mean anything from a gentle, relaxing rub given by the owner to deep tissue work done by a professional.

Deep tissue massage can reduce muscle soreness, improve performance, and speed recovery from injuries. Physical strength and knowledge of the horse's muscle and skeletal structure are definite assets in doing the work. Interestingly, sight is not necessary. New Zealand equine massage therapist Ray Morris, who is blind, often advises his students to close their eyes if they are having trouble in massaging a horse. The sense of touch seems to be sharpened when clutter from other senses is reduced.

Not all massage professionals have the same degree of training or experience, and certification has not been standardized. If you need one, it is best to seek a referral from a veterinarian.

Light massage can be performed by the owner anytime, however, and has the additional benefits of both teaching the horse to tolerate handling of his body and increasing the depth of the horse–human bond.

EXTRACORPOREAL SHOCK WAVE THERAPY

Since the early 1980s, extracorporeal shock wave therapy (ESWT) has been used successfully in the treatment of kidney stones and gallstones in humans. Acoustic shock waves administered from outside the body break down stones into dust that can be passed easily out of the body. ESWT has also been used for human orthopedic problems such as heel spurs, tendonitis, and non-healing fractures.

Since 1998, the technology has been applied to the treatment of equine ligament, soft tissue, and bone injuries that have not been healed by conventional methods. The goal is not to pulverize bone, but to promote healing by enhancing blood flow and cellular metabolism, and to stimulate ligament and bone growth. In the process, pain is reduced and rehabilitation time is decreased.

Acoustical shock waves used for medical purposes are like a series of tiny explosions that displace the mass surrounding them. The way in which shock wave therapy works is not completely understood at this time, but ESWT has had a positive effect in about 80 percent of the cases in which it was tried at University of California at Davis, according to Dr. Jack Snyder.

At present, soft tissue injuries typically require three 2,000-shock treatments. Each treatment takes about 30 minutes. Treatment of orthopedic conditions such as stress fractures is usually completed in a single session.

Two types of acoustical pressure wave systems are now on the market: *extracorporeal shock wave therapy* produces a high-energy focused shock wave that can be directed to a specific spot on a horse's body. *Radial pressure wave therapy* generates a lower, unfocused pressure wave. Clinical studies report that both approaches produce therapeutic (healing) and analgesic (pain-reducing) results. Further research will determine which approach works best with which types of injuries and may shed further light on the exact mechanism of action.

NUTRACEUTICALS

Nutraceuticals are food supplements that purport to enhance the function and structure of a horse's body. They are made from substances that occur in nature, often in the horse's body or his natural diet. Some of the better-known nutraceuticals include the following.

MSM (methyl sulfonyl methane), derived most often from kelp, is an important source of sulphur and is recommended for arthritic horses and performance horses. It is also said to help in scar formation and may be useful in treating ulcers in the digestive tract.

Chondroitin is derived from cow and pig tracheal cartilage and from sea cucumbers. It is used to help horses repair the cartilage in their joints. It is also believed to neutralize destructive enzymes in joints.

Glucosamine is another aid in the repair of joint cartilage. It is usually obtained from the shells of crustaceans. Glucosamine products often contain ascorbic acid (vitamin C) and manganese to aid in absorption. As with chondroitin, glucosamine is available in powder or liquid form, and recently as an injectable.

Shark cartilage is controversial and its uses are still being studied. Combating arthritis and cancer tumors are possible applications. Shark cartilage is claimed to prevent angiogenesis, the formation of new blood vessels, in abnormal tissues only. This would reduce inflammation and arrest, or possibly reverse, tumor growth. However, it may also slow healing of wounds and interfere with conception. Studies have been conducted on humans and dogs, but not horses.

Colloidal silver is a mineral supplement made up of electromagnetically charged particles of silver suspended in deionized water. Its proponents claim it is effective against bacteria, viruses, and fungi but there are known problems with its use. Silver stays in the body and can cause a permanent blue-gray discoloration of the skin if used to excess. Colloidal silver is another therapy of last resort, usually for stubborn infections that don't respond to antibiotics.

Coenzyme Q10, also known as ubiquinone, occurs naturally in the body and helps transport and break down fat into usable energy. Nutritional deficiencies and the normal aging process can cause a shortage, which affects all tissues but especially the heart. Coenzyme Q10 has been proven useful in treating heart disease in other animals, but at present it is prohibitively expensive in horse-sized doses. Research is ongoing to determine if coenzyme Q10 can help horses maintain peak performance with less damage to their bodies.

Nutraceuticals are not considered drugs, so they are not subject to federal regulation. Thus, manufacturers may make any claims they wish in their advertising. Unfortunately, some of these claims are fraudulent. Buyers must beware. When choosing nutraceuticals, the horse owner should consider the reputation and the experience of the company producing the product.

As pointed out earlier, most alternative therapies have not been proven effective by science. Yet anecdotal evidence—reports by their users—supports them. It's important to be clear about what this means.

Being scientifically *unproven* is not the same as being proven *wrong*. It just means that the testing has not been done, it did not yield conclusive results, or the matter does not lend itself to testing in the conventional way. Likewise, popular opinion isn't a measure of truth. At one time, a lot of people believed that the Earth was flat, but that belief did not make it so.

Western scientific thinking is oriented very much to cause and effect and the use of the scientific method to establish truth. Many alternative therapies reflect Eastern thinking, which does not operate from the same basic ground rules; hence it is possible that they may never be proven "true" to the satisfaction of Western thinkers.

Alternative therapies exist in this no-man's-land, this gray area, an alternate reality that is more comfortable for some people to explore than for others. Some venture into it because they feel conventional medicine is too quick to medicate or cut. Some turn to alternatives when they are out of all other options. Some just like to explore other avenues of knowledge and belief.

The first rule in all of health care is to do no harm. We have seen that most alternative therapies, when used correctly under the supervision of a veterinarian, are not likely to harm the patient. This in itself is a very positive thing. Whether they represent the best use of available resources is a matter for each individual to decide.

The mysteries of life unfold at their own pace. There is much that we still don't know. Fortunately, we have some pretty good tools for dealing with this uncertainty: open-mindedness and skepticism, the give and take of the intellectual process. Without skepticism, we become gullible; without open-mindedness, we become arrogant. Balanced against one another, they help us make some sense of the world around us.

CHAPTER 20

THE REAL IMPORTANCE
OF THE REVOLUTION

NO ONE BECOMES INVOLVED with horses to make himself a better human being or to find greater meaning in life or to make the world a better place, but sometimes that's exactly what happens.

In the beginning, you play with horses because it's fun, a pleasant diversion. Then you find that it feels good in a deeper and more lasting way than many other recreational pastimes. You may love riding motorcycles,

Horses are a source of pleasure and relaxation for millions of people. *(Photos by Coco)*

but your Harley doesn't nicker at you in the morning. There is something very special about horses that makes you want to do better with and for them.

But just wanting to do better isn't enough, because this is something very different and very unnatural for us humans. It takes time and effort to learn to communicate effectively with a horse. You must be willing to go back to school, to learn and to change the way you behave. You have to set your ego on the shelf and leave it there while you reinvent yourself as a horseman and as a human being.

This new person observes, remembers, and compares. He listens more and talks less. He takes responsibility rather than assigning blame. He controls his emotions. He becomes aware of his body language. He tries to improve himself. He commits himself to acting justly. He cultivates patience. He forgives. He lives in the moment rather than stewing over the past or waiting for the future. And of course, he places the wants and needs of another living creature ahead of his own.

He does it all, at least in the beginning, because it will make him a better horseman.

It isn't easy. We cannot wave a magic wand or drink a magic potion and change the nature of our species any more than a leopard can change its spots. It takes work and lots of it. It takes willpower and persistence, focus and thought. In an age of mindless entertainment and instant gratification of our every physical and emotional craving, those don't always come easy. But if we persist, the payoff makes it all worthwhile.

TAKING IT TO THE STREET

The revolution in horsemanship has given us the motivation and means for meaningful self-improvement, and the world outside of the horse industry has taken notice. Major corporations, for example, are finding that they can inspire a different and better form of leadership, build stronger, more effective teams, and foster a more enjoyable workplace by incorporating the principles of the revolution in horsemanship.

Some of these corporations are going to Monty Roberts for help. Roberts has crafted a message of trust-based management, using Join-Up® as a metaphor, and has delivered it to companies such as American Express, Johnson & Johnson, and Dean Witter. Educators, psychologists, children with autism, at-risk teens, victims and victimizers have also benefited from Roberts's work.

Clinician Frank Bell offers an all-day, hands-on horsemanship course for corporate employees and clients as a means of developing concentration and focus to better prepare them for the challenges of the workplace. Interestingly, it was the work of legendary sales trainer Dale Carnegie (*How to Win Friends and Influence People*) that taught Bell the importance of making a good first impression and inspired his seven-step Safety System for preparing a horse to be ridden. Now he is using horsemanship to help people reach their full potential, bringing him full circle.

Frank Bell teaches people how to make a good first impression with horses and humans. *(Frank Bell Collection)*

Canadian clinician Chris Irwin teaches Equine Assisted Personal Development. EAPD is an innovative form of "experiential" therapy for people with a broad range of needs, from troubled teens and families in crisis to corporate teams seeking empowerment. Working with the horse is the experience from which the insights flow. Irwin sees the task before the human as learning to communicate and lead in terms the horse, or another person for that matter, understands. He calls it "becoming the better horse." He explains, "If we trainers, coaches and therapists can facilitate people in learning how to become 'better horses,' we are assisting them in developing and balancing essential life skills such as awareness, focus, patience, empathy, assertiveness, boundaries, consistency, clarity, compassion, calm, courage, and multi-tasking."

The horse is truly a vehicle for not only transporting but also elevating the human species, for taking us closer to that elusive goal of realizing human potential.

THE HORSE AS THERAPY

That potential is different for each of us. Some are born with every advantage. They have healthy bodies and minds, healthy home environments in which to grow, and go through life without many real setbacks. For such people, the possibilities are practically endless.

Other people are burdened with tremendous disadvantages from birth, spiral out of control through poor life choices, or suffer debilitating injuries. What the horse can mean for them is perhaps even more astounding.

For example, two decades ago, one of the authors met an intelligent and articulate young woman—we'll call her Terri—who had very little function

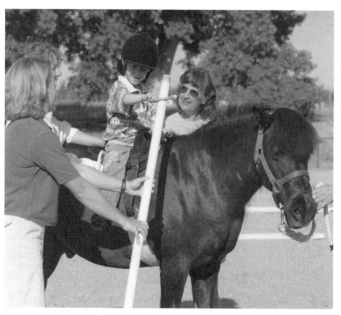

Therapeutic riding has proven beneficial in a wide variety of situations. *(L. Hanselmann/NARHA)*

below her neck. A rare neurological disease had robbed her of control of most of her body. Although she had partial use of one hand, she was, for all intents and purposes, a quadriplegic.

Terri was the founder of an Oregon therapeutic riding organization. She loved horses and refused to let her condition stand in the way of her own riding. With perseverance, Terri acquired a special saddle with extra back support and a harness system to hold her in place. She found a gentle horse that would take care of her. And she started riding, first in an arena, then outside.

Over time, Terri's rides became more adventurous, and she eventually was taking solo trail rides into the Cascade Wilderness. When asked why she would do something that was risky for any rider but unthinkable for someone with her condition, her answer was filled with emotion. "How can I make you understand what it means to me," she said, "a completely dependent person, to ride alone on a forest trail, to hear the sound of a distant waterfall, and then to find it by myself? Alone. Just my horse and me and the waterfall."

At five months of age, Bridget McGrath was diagnosed with infantile spasms, a seizure disorder. The condition was stabilized with medication, and a program of physical therapy was started in the hope that she would someday be able to walk. By the age of two, still unable to stand, Bridget seemed to stop trying. Equine-Assisted Therapy at the Somerset Hills Handicapped Riding Center in New Jersey made the difference.

Within six months, Bridget could sit straight up in the saddle, with the help of volunteers, and grab a Hula-Hoop while trotting. Then speech therapy began. At three, she spoke her first words, and today at age seven she runs to the stables calling her horse's name.

The value of horses and riding for disabled individuals has been recognized for centuries. The ancient Greeks used horseback rides to cheer the spirits of those considered untreatable or incurable. An 1875 study in Paris concluded that riding could lead to improvements in posture, balance, joint movement, muscle control, and morale. Today we understand why. When riding, the human's pelvis moves back and forth similar to the way it does when crawling or walking. Riding helps develop the muscles needed for walking. Riding provides physical therapy and motivation that is unmatched in preparing a disabled child to someday walk.

The horse has also been helpful in breaking through the mysterious veil of autism. Children who have been completely uncommunicative with the world around them for years have responded to the experience of being placed on the back of a gentle therapy horse.

Worldwide organized therapeutic riding got its start after Denmark's Liz Hartel won a silver medal for dressage in the 1952 Helsinki Olympics. Although afflicted with polio, Hartel had rehabilitated herself from wheelchair to horseback and gone on to riding excellence.

The horse has proven to be powerful therapy for body and mind. *(L. Hanselmann/NARHA)*

AUTISM AND HORSES

Autism is a condition that affects the normal development of the brain in the areas of social interaction and communication skills. Sensory input of all types—sounds, sights, touches—is magnified to the point of being overwhelming and painful, so the individual often shuts down as a means of self-preservation. Dr. Temple Grandin, an assistant professor of livestock handling and behavior at Colorado State University, is a "high-functioning" autistic who has provided significant insight into this condition. According to Grandin, severe autistics do not think in language, but in pictures and categories, similar to the way a horse thinks. This, coupled with hypersensitivity to sensory input, which an autistic human also shares with the horse, may explain why he may connect with a horse in ways he can't connect with other humans. Whatever the reason, therapeutic riding has repeatedly provided breakthroughs in this area.

By 1969, an organization known as the North American Riding for the Handicapped Association, or NARHA, had been formed. There is no more respected and beloved organization in America's horse industry today than NARHA and its hundreds of local chapters. Corporations, clinicians, and the general public support them generously.

It would not be fair to claim that the revolution in horsemanship is responsible for the rise of modern therapeutic riding. The two have developed on parallel tracks over the past three decades, yet they are highly compatible and complementary pursuits. The primary difference is one of emphasis. With therapeutic riding, improving the human is the end goal. With natural horsemanship, developing a partnership between horse and human is the end goal, and improving the human is a *means* of reaching that goal.

Horsemanship and rehabilitation intersect most dramatically in the mustang-gentling programs implemented by numerous prisons in America. The Comstock Wild Horse Program mentioned earlier is one example. The Hutchinson Correctional Facility Wild Horse Program in Hutchinson, Kansas, is another. This program's motto, "Saving horses—changing men," says it all. To participate in this program of gentling and preparing wild horses for auction, an inmate must put pride and ego aside and learn to control his emotions and his behavior. He must work toward a long-term goal and delay his gratification.

An inmate connects with a horse at the Hutchinson Correctional Facility, whose motto is "Saving horses—changing men." *(Hutchinson Correctional Facility)*

For an inmate, the horse may represent the first totally honest relationship in his life. The horse does not lie. There is no ulterior motive in the horse's behavior. To be successful, the inmate must be observant, look for the smallest change, and reward it. He must prepare in advance, think ahead, and he must provide rest and reward. Most of all he must develop empathy, the ability to see the world through another individual's eyes, an ability many in the correctional system have never developed. As the inmate learns how to develop the trust of a wild horse, he also comes to trust that there is a better path for his own life.

The revolution in horsemanship is a revolution in relationships—between horses and people and the world in which they live.

TIME

Impatience is a very common human trait today. In our busy lives, we are accustomed to looking for fast-acting medications, timesaving products, and quick-start solutions. There is an insidious, unspoken assumption in most of what we do that *this moment* is not worth savoring, that we should rush through it to get to some more worthy moment that we can and should savor. The problem for many of us is that we never get to those truly worthwhile moments.

Life is what happens to us while we are waiting for it to begin.

The horse responds best to us when we slow down and live in the moment with senses and minds fully engaged. How long something takes means nothing to a horse. Teachers of horsemanship today often suggest that we leave our wristwatches at home when we work with our horses, and we are reminded with an expression worthy of baseball great Yogi Berra, to "take the time it takes and it will take less time."

Precious few of us can ever completely dismiss the element of time from our lives, but we can certainly reduce our fixation on it. In doing so, maybe we stop rushing quite so much. Maybe we think about what we are doing right now instead of what we need to do next. Perhaps we find joy in the living of life instead of just getting to the finish line. Maybe we learn how to enjoy the journey. If so, we have the horse to thank for that.

WHY THE REVOLUTION?

So there you have it: a revolution in horsemanship.

This revolution has certainly made it easier and safer and more enjoyable for humans to interact with horses for recreational purposes. In our busy, stressful lives, that would be enough to make it a significant historical event. But we've seen that there is something much more profound going on. More than just the quality of our recreation, this revolution has improved the quality of our lives.

It has shown us that the human being—every human being—has so much further he can go in his growth. It has challenged us to try harder, to think more clearly, and to be more fully realized human beings, more of what was clearly intended for this species.

But why the horse?

The horse is the antithesis of the human being. It is the ultimate prey to our ultimate predator. There could be no more incompatible pairing of species on the planet, and yet, we have found that, when given the chance, the horse completes us. It is the day to our night, the hot to our cold, the light to our dark. In terms our Eastern brethren understand better than we do, the horse is the yin to our yang.

Perhaps this is the reason why this revolution occurred: to hand us a powerful tool for developing the rest of our humanity, the part that wasn't genetically endowed, the part that, in fact, goes against our genetically endowed, predatorial instincts. The part we have to work to obtain and is therefore most valuable to us.

Who among us would not agree that the world would be a better place if our leadership was benevolent, our purposes clear, our intentions honor-

When given a chance, the horse completes us. *(Stephan Miechel)*

able, our behavior consistent, and our relationships empathetic? This has been the message of countless religious and social leaders throughout history, and now it comes to us again carried by an equine messenger, a former beast of burden that is otherwise irrelevant to modern life. It would not be the first time that important truths were delivered by an inauspicious messenger.

The horse was on its way to becoming an historical curiosity, something we read about in history books or saw only in zoos. But it came back in a wholly different way than ever before. Maybe it came back to save us.

We all know that there is something different and special about horses. But perhaps it is really that there is something different and special about us when we're with them. We recognize in the horse a means to reach our highest calling as humans. Perhaps that is the real importance of this revolution in horsemanship.

AFTERWORD

It is a sign of the magnitude of this revolution in horsemanship that many worthy participants—clinicians, trainers, riders, writers, and others—have not been mentioned by name in these few pages.

Some of you are known to us. Others are not. Some seek the limelight while others prefer to avoid it. Some will make future contributions that we cannot even imagine. All of you have both our admiration and our gratitude, for you are taking this better way to the people, bringing out the best in horses and humans alike, and making the world a little better for all of us.

APPENDIX:
TEACHERS OF HORSEMANSHIP

Name	Telephone	Web site
Alfonso Aguilar	005–443–303–5101	
Craig Alexander	505–876–4909	
Clinton Anderson	888–287–7432	www.clintonanderson.net
Doug Babcock	785–675–3080	www.dougbabcock.com
Mike Beck	831–484–2810	www.mikebeck.com
Frank Bell	800–871–7635	www.horsewhisperer.com
Eitan Beth-Halachmy	530–346–2715	www.cowboydressage.com
Ted Blocker	503–631–2380	www.blockerranch.com
Buck Brannaman		www.brannaman.com
Mike Bridges	530–344–1133	www.mikebridges.net
Peggy Brown	419–865–8308	www.anatomyinmotion.com
Lester Buckley	808–325–5567	
Brad Cameron	406–961–1381	www.muletrainer.com
Craig Cameron	800–274–0077	www.craigcameron.com
Peter Campbell	800–349–7078	www.willingpartners.com
Chris Cox	940–327–8113	www.chris-cox.com
Peggy Cummings	800–310–2192	www.peggycummings.com
Leslie Desmond		www.lesliedesmond.com
Paul Dietz	623–742–7285	www.pauldietzhorsemanship.com
Steve Edwards	602–401–9703	www.muleranch.com
Greg Eliel	509–968–4234	www.gregeliel.com
Matt Gable	704–663–4851	www.gablehorsemanship.com
J. P. Giacomini	281–934–1736	www.equus.net
Jayne Glenn	+61 3 5777 3831	www.wranglerjayne.com
Julie Goodnight	719–530–0531	www.juliegoodnight.com
Karen Parelli Hagen	209–785–7066	www.naturalhoofprints.com
Van Hargis	903–383–2160	www.vanhargis.com

This information is provided for the convenience of our readers only.
Nothing may be inferred from the inclusion or omission of any individual.

Kenny Harlow	434–983–2221	www.kennyharlow.com
Clay Harper	719–942–4429	www.clayharperinc.com
Susan Harris	607–753–7357	www.anatomyinmotion.com
Cherry Hill		www.horsekeeping.com
Meredith Hodges	970–663–0066	www.luckythreeranch.com
Wil Howe	800–987–7875	www.wilhowe.com
Ray Hunt	208–587–4192	www.rayhunt.com
Mel Hyland	403–362–8220	
Chris Irwin	877–394–6773	www.chrisirwin.com
Bob Jeffreys	845–692–7478	www.bobjeffreys.com
Shawna Karrasch	800–638–2090	www.on-target-training.com
Alexandra Kurland		www.theclickercenter.com
Rick Lamb	877–843–4677	www.ricklamb.com
Willis Lamm		www.kbrhorse.net
John Lyons	970–285–9797	www.johnlyons.com
Josh Lyons	970–285–9797	www.joshlyonstraining.com
Marty Marten	303–665–5281	www.martymarten.com
Dr. Jim McCall	870–554–2450	www.the-old-place.com
Buster McLaury		users.elknet.net/circlewind
Ken McNabb	307–645–3149	www.kenmcnabb.com
Dr. Robert Miller		www.robertmmiller.com
Terry Myers	740–666–1162	www.tmtrainingcenter.com
Bryan Neubert	530–233–3582	www.bryanneubert.com
Lynn Palm	800–503–2824	www.lynnpalm.com
Pat Parelli	800–642–3335	www.parelli.com
Linda Parelli	800–642–3335	www.parelli.com
Curt Pate		www.curtpate.com
GaWaNi Pony Boy		www.ponyboy.com
Sam Powell	615–826–2826	www.asksampowell.com
Mark Rashid	866–577–9944	www.markrashid.com
Dennis Reis	800–732–8220	www.reisranch.com
Michael Richardson	254–796–4001	www.michaelbrichardson.com
Monty Roberts	888–826–6689	www.montyroberts.com
Steve Rother	503–970–4002	www.horseteacher.com
Dave Seay	540–582–5815	www.seayhorse.com
Karen Scholl	888–238–3447	www.karenscholl.com
Richard Shrake	541–593–1868	www.richardshrake.com
Steve Sikora	480–232–3261	www.ssequinetraining.com
Bill Smith	307–864–5671	
Lee Smith	480–633–2618	www.leesmithdiamonds.com
Dan Sumerel	800–477–2516	www.sumereltraining.com
Sally Swift	215–438–1286	www.centeredriding.org
Linda Tellington-Jones	800–854–8326	www.lindatellingtonjones.com

Jerry Tindell	760–948–1172	www.jerrytindell.com
Terry Tryon	812–877–6190	www.leanintranch.com
Don West	800–821–3607	www.donwest.net
Harry Whitney	800–267–4729	www.harrywhitney.com
Charles Wilhelm	510–886–9000	www.cwtraining.com
Richard Winters	805–640–0956	www.wintersranch.com
Patrick Wyse	406–266–3311	www.horsewyse.com

BIBLIOGRAPHY AND
SUGGESTED READING

Anderson, Clinton. *Clinton Anderson's Downunder Horsemanship: Establishing Respect and Control for English and Western Riders.* Trafalgar Square Publishing, North Pomfret, VT: 2004.

Arrigon, James R. *Mental Equitation.* Alpine Publications, Loveland, CO: 1999.

Beery, Jesse. *A Practical System of Colt Training.* The Parmenter Printing Co., Lima, OH: 1896.

———. *Prof. Beery's Illustrated Course in Horse Training* (eight booklets). The Jesse Beery Company, Pleasant Hill, OH: 1908.

———. *Prof. Beery's Saddle-Horse Instructions* (five booklets). The Jesse Beery Company, Pleasant Hill, OH: 1909.

Belasik, Paul. *Dressage for the 21st Century.* Trafalgar Square Publishing, North Pomfret, VT: 2001.

Benedik, Linda, and Veronica Wirth. *Yoga for Equestrians.* Trafalgar Square Publishing, North Pomfret, VT: 2000.

Bennett, Deb, Ph.D. *Conquerors: The Roots of New World Horsemanship.* Amigo Publications, Solvang, CA: 1998.

Blazer, Don. *Horses Don't Care About Women's Lib.* Joyce Press, Inc., San Diego, CA: 1978.

———. *Nine Secrets of Perfect Horsemanship.* Success Is Easy, Cave Creek, AZ: 1998.

Bowker, Nancy. *John Rarey: Horse Tamer.* J. A. Allen & Company, Ltd., London, England: 1996.

Brannaman, Buck. *Groundwork: The First Impression.* Rancho Deluxe Design, Marina Del Rey, CA: 1997.

———. *The Faraway Horses.* The Lyons Press, Guilford, CT: 2001.

Brennan, Mary L., D.V.M. *Complete Holistic Care and Healing for Horses: The Owner's Veterinary Guide to Alternative Methods and Remedies.* Trafalgar Square Publishing, North Pomfret, VT: 2001.

Brown, Sara Lowe. *Rarey, the Horse's Master and Friend.* F. J. Heer and Company, Columbus, OH: 1916.

———. *The Horse Cruiser and the Rarey Method of Training Horses.* F. J. Heer and Company, Columbus, OH: 1925.

Cameron, Craig, and Kathy Swan. *Ride Smart: Improve Your Horsemanship Skills on the Ground and in the Saddle.* Western Horseman, Colorado Springs, CO: 2004.

Carnegie, Dale. *How to Win Friends and Influence People.* Simon and Schuster, New York, NY: 1936.

Cavendish, William. *A General System of Horsemanship.* 1658.

———. *A New Method and Extraordinary Invention to Dress Horses and Work Them According to Nature.* 1667.

Connell, Ed. *The Hackamore Reinsman.* The Longhorn Press, Cisco, TX: 1952.

———. *Reinsman of the West: Bridles & Bits.* Lennoche Publishers, Bakersfield, CA: 1964.

Cumming, Peggy. *Connected Riding.* Primedia Enthusiast Publications, Inc., Gaithersburg, MD: 1999.

de Kunffy, Charles. *The Ethics and Passions of Dressage.* Half Halt Press, Incorporated, Middletown, MD: 1993.

Dorrance, Bill, and Leslie Desmond. *True Horsemanship Through Feel.* Diamond Lu Productions, Novato, CA: 1999.

Dorrance, Tom. *True Unity: Willing Communication Between Horse and Human.* Give-It-A-Go Enterprises, Bruneau, ID: 1987.

Duarte I, Dom. *Livro de Ensynanca de Bem Cavalgar toda a Sela.* 1434.

Edwards, Elwyn Harley, ed. *Encyclopedia of the Horse.* Crescent Books, Avenel, NJ: 1994.

Evans, Nicholas. *The Horse Whisperer.* Delacorte Press, New York, NY: 1995.

Evans, J. Warren. *Horses, a Guide to Selection, Care and Enjoyment.* W. H. Freeman and Company, New York, NY: 1989.

Foreman, Monte, and Patrick Wyse. *Monte Foreman's Horse-Training Science.* University of Oklahoma Press, Norman, OK: 1983.

Galvayne, Sydney. *Horse Dentition: Showing How to Tell Exactly the Age of a Horse up to Thirty Years.* Thomas Murray, Glasgow, Scotland: 1885, 1950.

———. *The Horse: its Taming, Training and General Management: with Anecdotes &c. Relating to Horses and Horsemen.* Thomas Murray, Glasgow, Scotland: 1888.

———. *War Horses Present and Future, or, Remount Life in South Africa.* London, England: 1902.

———. *The Twentieth Century Book of the Horse.* Robert Atkinson Limited, London, England: 1905.

Grisone, Federico. *Textbook on Riding.* 1555.

de la Guérinière, François Robichon. *École de Cavalerie.* 1729.

Haworth, Josephine. *The Horsemasters: The Secret of Understanding Horses.* Methuen, London, England: 1983.

Hayes, Alice. *The Horsewoman: A Practical Guide to Side-Saddle Riding.* W. Thacker & Company, London, England: 1893.

Hayes, M. Horace, F.R.C.V.S. *Veterinary Notes for Horse Owners.* Thacker, Spink & Company, Calcutta, India: 1877.

———. *Riding on the Flat and Cross Country.* W. Thacker & Company, London, England: 1881.

———. *Illustrated Horse Training.* W. Thacker & Company, London, England: 1889, 1896.

———. *Points of the Horse.* W. Thacker & Company, London, England: 1893.

———. *Training and Horse Management in India.* Thacker, Spink & Company, Calcutta, India: 1893.

———. *Among Men and Horses.* T. Fisher Unwin, London, England: 1894.

———. *Stable Management and Exercise.* Hurst & Blackett, Ltd., London, England: 1900.

———. *Riding and Hunting.* Hurst & Blackett, Ltd., London, England: 1901.

Henderson, Carolyn, ed. *The New Book of Saddlery & Tack.* Howell Book House, New York, NY: 1998.

Hill, Cherry. *Becoming an Effective Rider.* Storey Communications, Inc., Pownal, VT: 1991.

———. *Making Not Breaking.* Breakthrough Publications, Inc., Ossining, NY: 1992.

———. *Horsekeeping on a Small Acreage.* 2nd ed. Storey Publishing, North Adams, MA: 2005.

Hill, Cherry, and Klimesh Richard, C.J.F. *Maximum Hoof Power.* Howell Book House, New York, NY: 1994.

Holmes, Tom. *The New Total Rider.* Half Halt Press, Boonsboro, MD: 2001.

Hunt, Ray. *Think Harmony with Horses.* Give-It-A-Go Enterprises, Bruneau, ID: 1978.

Irwin, Chris. *Horses Don't Lie.* Great Plains Publications, Ltd., Winnipeg, Manitoba, Canada: 1998.

Jackson, Jaime. *The Natural Horse.* Star Ridge Publishing, Harrison, AR: 1992.

———. *Horse Owners Guide to Natural Hoof Care.* Star Ridge Publishing, Harrison, AR: 1999.

Jahiel, Jessica, Ph.D. *Riding for the Rest of Us.* Howell Book House, New York, NY: 1996.

———. *The Horseback Almanac.* Lowell House, Los Angeles, CA: 1998.

———. *The Complete Idiot's Guide to Horseback Riding.* Alpha Books, Indianapolis, IN: 2000.

———. *The Horse Behavior Problem Solver.* Storey Publishing, North Adams, MA: 2004.

Jeffery, Kell B. *A New Deal for Horses.* Australia.

Johnson, Dusty. *Saddle Savvy, a Guide to the Western Saddle.* Saddleman Press, Loveland, CO: 1998.

Jones, Dave. *Practical Western Training.* University of Oklahoma Press, Norman, OK: 1968.

Jurga, Fran. *Understanding the Equine Foot.* The Blood-Horse, Inc., Lexington, KY: 1998.

Karrasch, Shawna and Vinton. *You Can Train Your Horse to Do Anything.* Trafalgar Square Publishing, North Pomfret, VT: 2000.

Kevil, Mike. *Starting Colts.* Western Horseman, Inc., Colorado Springs, CO: 1992.

Kirk, Des. *Horse Breaking Made Easy with Des Kirk.* Des Kirk, Australia: 1977.

———. *The Gentle Art of Horse Breaking.* Phyllis Kirk, Australia.

Kurland, Alexandra. *Clicker Training for Your Horse.* Sunshine Books, Inc., Waltham, MA: 1998.

———. *The Click that Teaches.* The Clicker Center, LLC, Delmar, NY: 2003.

Loch, Sylvia. *The Classical Rider.* Trafalgar Square Publishing, North Pomfret, VT: 1997.

Lyons, John. *The Making of a Perfect Horse: Communicating with Cues, Part I.* Belvoir Publications, Inc., Greenwich, CT: 1998.

———. *The Making of a Perfect Horse: Communicating with Cues, Part II.* Belvoir Publications, Inc., Greenwich, CT: 1999.

———. *Bringing Up Baby.* Primedia Enthusiast Publications, Gaithersburg, MD: 2002.

Lyons, John, and Sinclair Browning. *Lyons on Horses.* Doubleday, New York, NY: 1991.

MacLeay, Jennifer M., D.V.M., Ph.D. *Smart Horse: Training Your Horse with the Science of Natural Horsemanship.* J & J Press, Fort Collins, CO: 2000.

Magner, Dennis. *The Classic Encyclopedia of the Horse.* Warren, Johnson & Company, Buffalo, NY: 1875.

———. *The New System of Educating Horses.* Lovell Printing and Publishing Company, Rouses Point, NY: 1876.

———. *The Art of Taming and Educating the Horse.* Review and Herald Publishing, Battle Creek, MI: 1884.

———. *Magner's Standard Horse and Stock Book.* Werner Company, Chicago, IL: 1897.

———. *Magner's Horse Book and Veterinary Handbook.* 1906.

———. *The Standard Horse Book.* Saalfield Publishing, Akron, OH: 1913.

Marlewski-Probert, Bonnie. *Debugging Your Horse.* K & B Products, Red Bluff, CA: 1996.

Marten, Marty. *Problem Solving.* Western Horseman, Inc., Colorado Springs, CO: 1998.

McBane, Susan, and Helen Douglas-Cooper. *Horse Facts.* Barnes & Noble Books, New York, NY: 1991.

McCall, James, Ph.D. *Influencing Horse Behavior.* Alpine Press, Inc., Loveland, CO: 1988.

————. *The Stallion: A Breeding Guide for Owners and Handlers.* Howell Book House, New York, NY: 1995.

McCall, James, Ph.D., and Lynda McCall. *Horses Behavin' Badly: Training Solutions for Problem Behaviors.* Half Halt Press, Boonsboro, MD: 1997.

Miller, Robert M., D.V.M. *Health Problems of the Horse.* Western Horseman, Inc., Colorado Springs, CO: 1967, 1998.

————. *Imprint Training of the Newborn Foal.* Western Horseman, Inc., Colorado Springs, CO: 1991.

————. *Understanding the Ancient Secrets of the Horse's Mind.* Russell Meerdink Company, Neenah, WI: 1999.

Miller, Robert W. *Western Horse Behavior & Training.* Doubleday Publishing, New York, NY: 1974.

Murray, Ty. *Roughstock.* EquiMedia Corporation, Austin, TX: 2001.

Offutt, Denton. *Best and Cheapest Book on the Management of Horses, Mules, &c.* Wm. Greer, Washington, D.C.: 1843.

————. *A Method of Gentling Horses, their Selection, and Curing their Diseases.* 1846.

————. *A New and Complete System of Teaching the Horse on Phrenological Principles.* 1848.

————. *The Educated Horse.* Washington, D.C.: 1854.

Ortega, Luis B. *California Stock Horse.* News Publishing Company, Sacramento, CA: 1949.

Parelli, Pat. *Natural Horsemanship.* Western Horseman, Inc., Colorado Springs, CO: 1993.

Pluvinel, Antoine de la Baume. *Le Manege Royal par Antoine de Pluvinel.* 1623.

Pony Boy, GaWaNi. *Horse Follow Closely.* BowTie Press, Irvine, CA: 1998.

Powell, Sam. *Almost a Whisper.* Alpine Publications, Loveland, CO: 1999.

Pratt, O. S. *The Horse Educator: A Practical System of Educating Horses and Dogs to Perform Different Tricks.* Craig, Finley & Rowley, Philadelphia, PA: 1870.

————. *The Horse's Friend: The Only Practical Method of Educating the Horse and Eradicating Vicious Habits.* Professor O. S. Pratt, Buffalo, NY: 1876.

Price, Steven D. *Essential Riding.* The Lyons Press, New York, NY: 2000.

————. *The Illustrated Horseman's Dictionary.* The Lyons Press, New York, NY: 2000.

Ramey, David W., D.V.M. *Concise Guide to Navicular Syndrome in the Horse.* Howell Book House, New York, NY: 1997, 2002.

Rarey, John S. *The Modern Art of Taming Wild Horses.* Ohio State Journal Company, Columbus, OH: 1856.

————. *Rarey's Art of Taming Horses.* Additional chapters by Samuel Sidney. Routledge, Warnes and Routledge, London, England: 1858.

Rashid, Mark. *Considering the Horse.* Johnson Books, Boulder, CO: 1993.

————. *A Good Horse Is Never a Bad Color.* Johnson Books, Boulder, CO: 1996.

————. *Horses Never Lie.* Johnson Books, Boulder, Colorado: 2000.

————. *Life Lessons from a Ranch Horse.* Johnson Books, Boulder, CO: 2003.

Richardson, Clive. *The Horse Breakers.* J. A. Allen & Company, Ltd., London, England: 1998.

Roberts, Monty. *The Man Who Listens to Horses.* Random House, New York, NY: 1996.

————. *Shy Boy: The Horse That Came in from the Wild.* HarperCollins Publishers, New York, NY: 1999.

————. *Horse Sense for People: Using the Gentle Wisdom of Join-Up to Enrich Our Relationships at Home and at Work.* Viking Press, New York, NY: 2001.

————. *From My Hands to Yours.* Monty and Pat Roberts, Inc., Solvang, CA: 2003.

Roberts, Tom. *Horse Control and the Bit.* Claire Tilbrook Brothers, Australia: 1971.

————. *Horse Control: The Young Horse.* T. A. and P. R. Roberts, South Australia: 1973.

————. *Horse Control: The Rider.* T. A. and P. R. Roberts, South Australia: 1973.

————. *Horse Control Reminiscenses.* T. A. and P. R. Roberts, Richmond, South Australia: 1984.

Rojas, Arnold R. *These Were the Vaqueros.* Arnold R. Rojas, CA: 1974.

Saunders, Tom B., IV. *The Texas Cowboy: Cowboys of the Lone Star State.* Stoecklein Publishing, Ketchum, ID: 1997.

Schinke, Robert J. and Beverly. *Focused Riding.* Compass Equestrian Limited, London, England: 1997.

Self, Margaret Cabell. *Horsemastership: Methods of Training the Horse and Rider.* A. S. Barnes and Company, Inc., New York, NY: 1952.

Shrake, Richard. *Resistance Free™ Riding.* Breakthrough Publications, Tarrytown, NY: 1993.

————. *Resistance Free™ Training.* Trafalgar Square Publishing, North Pomfret, VT: 2000.

Shrake, Richard, with Pat Close. *Western Horsemanship.* Western Horseman, Inc., Colorado Springs, CO: 1987.

Strasser, Hiltrud, D.V.M. *A Lifetime of Soundness.* Sabine Kells: 1998.

————. *Shoeing: A Necessary Evil?* Sabine Kells: 2000.

Sumerel, Dan. *Finding the Magic.* Warwick House Publishers, Lynchburg, VA: 2000.

Swift, Sally. *Centered Riding.* St. Martin's/Marek, New York, NY: 1985.

Tellington-Jones, Linda. *A TTouch of Magic for . . . Horses: The A–Z Book of Unique Training and Health Care Techniques.* Thane Marketing International, La Quinta, CA: 1994.

———. *Improve Your Horse's Well-Being.* Kenilworth Press, Addington: 1999.

———. *TTouch and TTeam Training for Your Horse: A Step-by-Step Picture Guide.* Trafalgar Square Publishing, North Pomfret, VT: 1999.

Tellington-Jones, Linda, and Ursula Bruns. *An Introduction to the Tellington-Jones Equine Awareness Method.* Breakthrough Publications, Millwood, NY: 1988.

Tellington-Jones, Linda, and Robyn Hood. *The Tellington TTouch for Horses.* 1994.

Tellington-Jones, Linda, and Sybil Taylor. *Tellington TTouch: A Breakthrough Technique to Train and Care for Your Favorite Animal.* Viking Press: 1992.

———. *Getting in TTouch: Understand and Influence Your Horse's Personality.* Trafalgar Square Publishing, North Pomfret, VT: 1995.

———. *The Tellington TTouch: A Revolutionary and Natural Method to Train and Care for Your Favorite Animal.* Penguin Group (USA) Inc., New York, NY: 1995.

Tellington-Jones, Linda, with Andrea Pabel, and Hilmar Pabel. *Let's Ride! With Linda Tellington-Jones: Fun and Teamwork with Your Horse or Pony.* Trafalgar Square Publishing, North Pomfret, VT: 1997.

Twelveponies, Mary. *Everyday Training: Backyard Dressage.* Breakthrough Publications, Millwood, NY: 1983.

Wadley, Harold. *Spirit Blending Foals Before and After Birth: An Old Way Continued.* Harold Wadley (self published).

Watson, Mary Gordon, Russell Lyon, and Sue Montgomery. *Horse, the Complete Guide.* Barnes & Noble Books, New York, NY: 1999.

White Jr., Lynn. *Medieval Technology and Social Change.* 1962.

Wilton, James Douglas. *Breaking of the Saddle Horse by Training.* Australia.

———. *The Horse and His Education.* Australia: 1972.

Wright, Maurice. *The Jeffery Method of Horse Handling.* R. M. Williams Pty, Ltd., Prospect, South Australia: 1973.

———. *The Thinking Horseman.* Maurice C. D. Wright, Dyamberin, Armidale, New South Wales, Australia: 1983.

Young, John Richard. *The Schooling of the Western Horse.* University of Oklahoma Press, Norman, OK: 1954

Xenophon (translated by Morgan, Morris H.). *The Art of Horsemanship.* J. A. Allen & Company, Ltd., London, England: 1962.

GLOSSARY

airs   Certain advanced movements in classical horsemanship, such as the piaffe, passage, Spanish walk, and the airs above the ground.

airs above the ground   The movements in which two or more of the horse's feet leave the ground, such as the levade, capriole, and courbette. These so-called high school movements (from the French *haute école*) are said to have come from the requirement during the late Middle Ages that a mounted warrior's horse act as both an offensive weapon and a shield. A rearing horse could disable an opponent or his steed while also stopping a sword or spear thrust directed at the rider.

alpha   The first letter of the Greek alphabet. In studies of behavior, it is used to denote the most dominant individual in a group of animals.

American Paint Horse   The American breed having patches of white and another color above its knee and also having at least one parent registered with the American Paint Horse Association, the Jockey Club (Thoroughbreds) or the American Quarter Horse Association. A solid colored horse may be registered as a Breeding Stock Paint if both parents are registered American Paint Horses.

Appaloosa   The American breed most often seen with a spotted "blanket" over its rump (although leopard Appaloosas have spots all over their bodies). Appaloosas also have striped hooves, a white sclera around the pupil of the eye and mottling of the skin around the eyes, nose, and genital area. Appaloosas are often found doing ranch work, competing in Western horse shows, and as jumpers and pleasure mounts.

ascarid   A parasitic roundworm that, when ingested as eggs during grazing, causes diarrhea, colic, and other internal problems. In the larval stage, ascarids can migrate through the lungs, causing verminous pneumonia. Problems with ascarids can be both prevented and treated with medication.

bars   (1) The section of gumline, containing no teeth, that lies between the incisors and molars in a horse's mouth. The bit is carried in this space; (2) An inward continuation of the hoof wall on the bottom of a horse's hoof. The bars form an inverted V, inside of which lies the frog.

bonding   Developing an emotional connection with another creature, most often through touching in a friendly and soothing way.

bosal   A loop of braided rawhide that is the part of a hackamore that applies pressure to a horse's nose and chin.

bots   The parasitic larvae of the gasterophilus fly. Bots appear as tiny yellow dots on a horse's lips and front legs and are ingested into the stomach, where they can cause colic and weight loss. A deworming program reduces the chance of a horse's being afflicted, as does shaving any eggs found on the horse's hair. Removing manure, in which the larvae and flies live, is another preventive treatment.

bradoon   The snaffle bit of a double bridle.

breakover   (1) The point on the bottom of a horse's foot that remains in contact with the ground at the moment the heel begins to rise off the ground; (2) The moment this occurs.

brumby   The wild horse of Australia.

bulldogging   The rodeo sport in which a rider on a horse chases a steer, dives from the horse onto the steer's back, and wrestles the steer to the ground by the horns. Also known as steer wrestling.

cantle   The elevated rear part of a saddle.

cavesson   A noseband designed to keep a horse's mouth closed. Most often seen as part of an English bridle, but may also be a separate piece of tack.

chestnuts   Vestigial toes seen as hard knoblike growths on the insides of a horse's legs (also called nighteyes). Because chestnuts are as distinctive as human fingerprints, they are used as a mark of identification by breed registries and racing commissions.

coffin bone   The third phalanx bone in a horse's foot. It is also known as the distal phalanx, P3, and the pedal bone.

collection   A state of self-carriage in which the horse has a more compact frame, with his back elevated, his poll flexed, and his hindquarters more underneath him. Although horses can be trained to do this on a loose rein, collection is usually obtained by urging the horse forward with the rider's legs while simultaneously holding the bit immobile through the reins.

curb bit   A bit with shanks, a solid mouthpiece, and usually a port or spade rising in the middle of the mouthpiece. The shanks act as levers and apply pressure to the bars and roof of the mouth in accordance with the rider's use of the reins. Because the mouthpiece is not jointed, a curb bit can be operated with reins held in one hand. See also snaffle bit.

cutting   A judged Western riding sport that derived from the practical need to separate or cut a cow from a herd. The horse and rider enter the herd and slowly get between one cow and the rest of the herd. Once the individual cow is selected, the clock starts and the rider can no longer guide the horse. The horse blocks the cow's attempts to return to the herd by mirroring its every movement. The cutting ends when the cow gets past the horse, it is evident that the cow cannot return to the herd, or time expires.

dally   To wrap a lariat rope around the saddle horn after a steer or calf has been roped. The word comes from the Spanish phrase *de la vuelta*, to make a turn (of the rope). The sport of team roping uses the dally method, while calf roping has the end of the lariat rope tied "hard and fast" to the saddle horn.

dam   A horse's female parent.

disengaging hindquarters   When a horse moves his hindquarters laterally (sideways) by stepping over one hind foot with the other. Also known as untracking. Because this movement puts the horse momentarily out of balance and unable to run, rear, or kick, it is taught to a horse early in the training. Done at the trainer's request, it is also a submissive act and requires the horse to think about where his feet are instead of misbehaving.

doubling horse   When a rider bends the horse's head and neck around to one side, usually for the purpose of regaining control or creating a submissive attitude. Doubling causes a horse to disengage its hindquarters. Also known as the one-rein stop and the emergency hand brake stop.

dressage   A French word meaning training. In horsemanship, it is an approach to schooling based on progressive, well-defined stages of training, and riding tests that horse and rider must pass before moving to the next level. Dressage is probably the oldest form of horsemanship practiced today. It is sometimes called classical horsemanship and is thought of by the public as one of the English riding disciplines, although its roots are more French than English.

drive line   An imaginary vertical line on a horse's body, approximately where a rider's legs would hang. Pressure applied behind the drive line makes the horse want to go forward. Pressure in front of the drive line makes the horse want to slow down, stop, or back. Pressure in front of the drive line on one side and behind on the other makes the horse want to pivot on his fore or hindquarters.

emergency hand brake stop   See doubling horse.

enteroliths   Stones that form in the intestinal tract of horses, especially those on diets containing a high percentage of alfalfa. May also be caused by mineralization of a foreign body.

floating   Filing or rasping the sharp edges of a horse's teeth to keep them from cutting the inside of his mouth. A horse's teeth erupt or grow throughout his life. Domestic horses do not get enough abrasion through their diets to offset this. Thus, periodic floating is necessary for the horse's comfort, nutrition, and responsiveness when wearing a bit.

forehand   The front legs and shoulders of a horse. Also called forequarters or front end.

frog   The soft triangular-shaped mass of tissue between the bars and the heel on the bottom of a horse's foot.

gelding   A male horse that has been castrated. Geldings are considered more even-tempered and easier to manage than stallions or mares, and are therefore more appropriate for beginning riders. Stallions not of breeding quality should be gelded shortly after birth. If castrated young, a gelding typically grows taller, with a more graceful body, than the heavier, more muscled stallion.

gentling   The process of teaching a horse to trust and respect humans by eliminating disrespectful or fear-based behaviors. In the past it has been called taming and breaking, although the latter implies breaking a horse's spirit, which is no longer seen as necessary in preparing a horse for riding or driving.

green   Having little or no experience. Injuries often result from pairing a green horse with a green rider—hence the saying, "green on green equals black and blue."

greenhide   Australian term for untanned leather, what Americans call rawhide.

gymkhana   Mounted games, such as pole bending and musical chairs, that were originally a popular training exercise for British cavalrymen stationed in India. Gymkhana is from a Hindu word meaning "ball-house." Today, the games are played mostly by youngsters in Pony Club, 4H, and similar organizations.

hackamore   A bitless bridle that controls the horse by means of pressure from the bosal on the animal's nose. From the Spanish *jaquima*, the hackamore was used by *vaqueros* and became the centerpiece of the California system of preparing a bridle horse.

headstall   The Western bridle excluding the bit.

heifer   A young cow, especially one that has not yet given birth to a calf.

hobble   A restraining strap attached to a horse's leg or legs for the purpose of controlling his movement.

hooking on   A term, popularized by Ray Hunt, for what happens when a horse decides he would rather be with a human than away from the human. See Join-Up.

isolation chute   An enclosure with slatted or solid sides that is just large enough for a horse to fit inside, but small enough to prevent kicking, bucking, or striking with the forefeet. Sometimes used for veterinary procedures or for gentling wild horses through total control of their movement.

join-up   A term, popularized by Monty Roberts, for the moment a horse decides he would rather be with a human than away from the human. See hooking on.

keg shoes   Mass produced metal horse shoes, so-named because they were often shipped in barrels.

laminitis   Inflammation of the laminae, a fragile network of Velcro-like tissue that connects the coffin bone to the hoof wall inside a horse's hoof. Severe, chronic laminitis can lead to rotation or sinking of the coffin bone, a condition commonly called founder.

lateral flexion   The act of bending to the side. Although the typical horse can bend nearly in half to get at a fly, it is not inclined to do so at a human's request, probably because the position is not conducive to flight. Lateral flexion exercises reinforce the rider's leadership role, teach the horse to yield to pressure, and make the horse more physically supple and lighter to handle. A horse that flexes well laterally is more easily taught vertical flexion, i.e., tucking the head to put the face in a vertical plane.

latigo   The leather strap that fastens the cinch on a Western saddle.

laying a horse down   A gentling method used by many trainers through history, particularly in the nineteenth century. Usually involved applying a one-leg hobble to inhibit the horse's movement, then placing him off-balance until he chose to lie down. Once down, the horse was rubbed and comforted. When the hobble was removed and the horse was urged back to his feet, he was much more submissive and trainable. Also known as casting or throwing a horse.

long lining   The training procedure in which the handler walks behind the horse and guides the animal with driving reins. Although used to teach a horse to be driven in harness, long lining is also used to school young horses before they are ridden. Also known as ground driving if done with a driving horse or long reining if done with a saddle horse.

longe   To cause a horse to make a circle around its handler at the end of a rope attached to its halter. The length of the rope varies with the purpose of the longeing. Shorter ropes (twelve to fifteen feet) are used in gentling a horse and preparing him to be ridden. Longer ropes (up to thirty-five feet) are for exercising the horse, working on his self-carriage, or the rider's technique. To free longe is to cause the horse to circle the handler in a round pen with no rope attached. Also spelled lunge.

lunge   American spelling of the French word longe.

martingale   A strap attached from the girth and running between the horse's forelegs to either the cavesson (standing martingale) or the reins (running martingale). A martingale is used to restrict a horse's head movement and thus increase the rider's control.

mustang   The wild horse native to the Western United States. Descended from escaped or stolen Spanish horses brought to North America during the colonial era, the present-day mustang is a small (approximately fifteen hands) and rugged animal that continues to roam the West's remaining rangeland in herds. From the Spanish word *mesteño*.

navicular syndrome   A chronic, incurable condition associated with deterioration of the navicular bone.

one-rein stop   See doubling horse.

opposition reflex   See positive thigmotaxis.

pastern   The portion of a horse's lower leg between the fetlock and the foot.

pillars   A training tool, believed to have been invented by the French horseman Antoine de la Baume Pluvinel (1556–1620), which was used to teach a horse the leaping movements known as airs above the ground. With or without a rider, the horse was tied to one immovable pillar, or between two such pillars, and urged into attempting these difficult and dangerous airborne maneuvers.

poll   The highest portion of a horse's head, between its ears.

pommel   The elevated front part of an English or Western saddle.

positive thigmotaxis The natural tendency of horses (and other organisms) to move into or against a source of pressure. Also known as opposition reflex. Through training, horses overcome this and learn to yield to pressure.

pressure point In saddle fit, a place on the horse's back where pressure from the saddle and rider are focused rather than dispersed evenly over a wide area. Evidence of pressure points can be found by observing the sweat pattern under the saddle and pad after a workout. Sweat should evenly cover the entire area. Dry spots indicate pressure points where blood flow to sweat glands was inhibited. The goal of saddle fit is to eliminate pressure points.

Quarter Horse The most populous breed of horses in the world, noted for its even temperament, agility, and quick bursts of speed. The breed originated in the colonial era in America after a Thoroughbred named Janus was bred to native mares that were probably of Spanish descent. The American Quarter Horse Association was started in 1940 and promotes the use of this versatile breed in racing, Western and English horse showing, driving, ranching, and recreational riding.

quirt A short riding crop with a wrist loop on one end and a rawhide lash on the other. The quirt is used to urge a horse forward.

reata Spanish for a braided rawhide rope. Also spelled riata.

reining The Western riding sport in which a horse is judged on his ability to execute a pre-arranged pattern of such maneuvers as run-downs, sliding stops, rollbacks, large and small circles, and spins. Each ride begins with seventy points; full or half points are added or deducted for the way in which the horse performs each movement. The scores of three judges are added to give the final score.

riata See reata.

roached mane A mane that has been trimmed so short that the hairs stand up. It is done for appearance, ease of care, and to keep the mane out of the way of the rider. In some places, partial roaching of the mane indicates the stage of training of the horse.

romal (1) A type of rein in which the straps coming from the bit join into one rein at the point where the rider holds them; (2) The Western style of riding in which the rider uses such a rein.

rough string In cattle outfits of the past, a string of difficult horses—buckers, biters, bolters, and kickers—separated from the rest of the remuda (herd of saddle horses). The rough string was assigned to one cowboy, who earned extra pay for riding them.

sacking out Desensitizing a horse to the feel of various objects and materials. Feed sacks were and still are often used for this purpose. The method is to rhythmically rub the horse all over his body with the sack, stopping or moving to a new area only when the horse is standing still and is completely relaxed. Sacking out is meant to cause the horse concern but not panic. Relaxing is the sign that he has desensitized to the stimulus.

saddle bronc   A bucking horse used for saddle bronc competition in rodeo.

saddle tree   The framework of a saddle, usually made of wood, consisting of the bars, pommel, and cantle. The saddle tree is seldom visible in a finished saddle; the bottom is covered with sheepskin and the top with leather. Trees come in many different shapes and sizes.

shank   The two pieces of a curb or leverage bit that attach to a rein on one end and the mouthpiece on the other. The length of the shanks determine the amount of leverage afforded by the bit.

shoulder-in   A schooling movement, credited to Guérinière, in which the horse moves forward with its forequarters bent toward the inside of the arena. When done properly, the inside hind foot and the outside forefoot travel on the same track.

sidepull   A schooling halter with rings on the side for attaching a line or reins.

snaffle bit   A bit with a straight or jointed mouthpiece, no port, and rings at each end of the mouthpiece for attaching reins and headstall. The snaffle operates on direct pressure from each rein rather than leveraged pressure as in a curb bit. Snaffles are used with driving horses, in training young saddle horses, and increasingly, with finished saddle horses. Traditionally, snaffles have been considered mild bits and curbs harsher bits. In truth, the rider's hands determine that.

spade bit   A type of ornate curb bit favored for finished bridle horses by the *vaqueros* of California. A spoon or spade-shaped piece rises from the solid mouthpiece where the port would normally be, allowing the rider to apply pressure higher in the roof of the horse's mouth. The mouthpiece attaches to the shanks either by a hinge or a solid weld. Although it appears brutal, the spade bit in the hands of an experienced rider is no harsher than any other bit.

spinning   In reining, a maneuver in which the horse makes one or more 360 degree turns while pivoting around an inside hind foot.

stakes winner   A horse that has won a stakes race. A stakes race is one for higher-caliber horses in which the owners of entered horses post a nominating and starting fee, which is added to the purse.

starting a horse   Training a horse to be ridden or driven. In some circles, the term breaking is still used, even if there is no intention of breaking the horse's spirit.

strongyle   A bloodworm that causes anemia and intestinal tissue damage, including aneurysms that can rupture and kill the horse prematurely. A deworming program is both the best prevention and cure.

subjection   An old term for teaching a horse to submit to a human's leadership.

surcingle   A strap that encircles a horse's barrel. The surcingle can be used to hold a blanket in place or give extra security to a racing saddle by serving as an overgirth. In the nineteenth century, leather surcingles with rings attached were often used in the taming of vicious horses. Today, they are useful in preparing a horse to accept a saddle and in ground driving (long lining).

swells In a Western saddle, the lateral extensions of the pommel that aid in keeping the rider in the saddle and give a roper something to lean against while making his throw. "Beartrap" saddles of the past had extreme swells that extended over the rider's legs and held him in the saddle. Slick fork saddles, such as those built on the Wade tree, have no swells at all, and riders often add bucking rolls to give them greater security when riding difficult horses. Most Western saddles have moderate swells.

thoatlatch (1) The portion of the horse's body between the neck and the lower jaw bone; (2) The bridle strap that buckles under a horse's throat. Its purpose is to prevent the bridle from slipping over the animal's head.

Thoroughbred The breed closely associated with flat and steeplechase racing because of its superlative speed at distances greater than a quarter mile. All Thoroughbreds can trace their ancestries back to one or more of the three foundation sires: the Byerly Turk, Darley Arab, and Godolphin Barb. The Thoroughbred has excelled as a show hunter and jumper, foxhunter, and dressage mount, and has contributed to such breeds as the Standardbred, Saddlebred, American Quarter Horse, and European Warmbloods.

throwing horse See laying a horse down.

tie-down Western term for a standing martingale.

untracking horse See disengaging hindquarters.

using horse A Western term for a horse that can do something useful; a working horse.

vaquero Spanish for "cow man"

war bridle A crude bitless bridle fashioned from a single length of rope. A war bridle usually consists of a single loop which passes behind the horse's ears and through his mouth, sometimes under the upper lip. Alternatively, it my pass over his nose. Although associated with Native Americans, the war bridle has a more diverse history. Sometimes it was used as a training tool and other times it served simply as an improvised halter.

withers The highest part of the horse's back, where it meets the base of the neck. A horse's height is measured from the withers to the ground. Well-defined withers are desirable for holding a saddle in place. Horses with flat, poorly-defined withers are said to be "mutton-withered."

ABOUT THE AUTHORS

ROBERT M. MILLER, D.V.M.

Dr. Robert M. Miller is an internationally acclaimed equine behaviorist, author, and horseman. His work with the early learning capabilities of newborn foals, embodied in a regimen known as imprint training, is one of history's most profound advancements in horsemanship.

Dr. Robert M. Miller and Rick Lamb. *(Tevis Photographic)*

Dr. Miller earned his doctorate in veterinary medicine from Colorado State University in 1956 and later founded what is now Conejo Valley Veterinary Hospital in Thousand Oaks, California. Since his retirement from veterinary practice in 1988, he has traveled the world promoting and lecturing on imprint training and the broader revolution in horsemanship in which he has played such an important role. His expertise is sought from breeding farms in Kentucky to college campuses in Europe.

A prolific writer and cartoonist, Dr. Miller has authored five books on horse care and training, nine books of veterinary cartoons, fifty scientific papers, and countless magazine articles. He and his wife, Debby, live in California, where they ride and breed horses and mules.

RICK LAMB

Rick Lamb is host of two nationally syndicated radio programs, *The Horse Show with Rick Lamb* and *The Horse Show Minute*. Since 1997 he has conducted more than 1,000 interviews with trainers, instructors, clinicians, competitors, veterinarians, and other horse experts. A master interviewer and an engaging host, Mr. Lamb has won six national awards, and his programs have made him one of the most popular and respected educators in America's burgeoning horse industry.

Mr. Lamb received a B.S. degree in Mathematics and Philosophy from Wichita State University in 1973. Four years later he started Lambchops Studios, now one of the Southwest's top audio production facilities and home base of *The Horse Show*.

Mr. Lamb has written more than 700 radio commentaries, hundreds of broadcast commercials, six magazine articles, and one book. A professional musician since the age of fourteen, he still performs when time allows. He resides in Arizona with his wife, Diana. They raise and train their own horses.

INDEX